D1518706

# The FIRST WORLD WAR

## on CIGARETTE and TRADE CARDS

### AN ILLUSTRATED AND DESCRIPTIVE HISTORY

CYRIL MAZANSKY

Schiffer Publishing Ltd®

4880 Lower Valley Road • Atglen, PA 19310

**Published by Schiffer Publishing, Ltd.**
4880 Lower Valley Road
Atglen, PA 19310
Phone: (610) 593-1777; Fax: (610) 593-2002
E-mail: Info@schifferbooks.com

For our complete selection of fine books on this and related subjects,
please visit our website at **www.schifferbooks.com.**
You may also write for a free catalog.

This book may be purchased from the publisher.
Please try your bookstore first.

We are always looking for people to write books on new and related
subjects. If you have an idea for a book, please contact us at
**proposals@schifferbooks.com.**

Schiffer Publishing's titles are available at special discounts for
bulk purchases for sales promotions or premiums. Special editions,
including personalized covers, corporate imprints, and excerpts can
be created in large quantities for special needs. For more information,
contact the publisher.

**OTHER SCHIFFER BOOKS ON RELATED SUBJECTS:**

*Paper Empires: 100 Years of German Paper Soldiers* by Rafael de Francisco
López. ISBN 978-0-7643-4740-5

*Brushes with War: Paintings and Drawings by the Troops of World War I: The
WWHAM Collection of Original Art* by Joel R. Parkinson.
ISBN 978-0-7643-4634-7

*World War I Posters* by Gary A. Borkan. ISBN 0-7643-1516-1

Type set in CaslonOpnface BT/Adobe Caslon Pro

ISBN: 978-0-7643-4759-7
Printed in China

To my wife Harriet

the eternal source of my happiness

Good-bye ! I'm just off to the War!

# CONTENTS

# ACKNOWLEDGMENTS

The origins of this book can be traced back over thirty years to when I first began my collection of cigarette and trade cards. The thematic subject matter I have pursued in this collection may be broadly titled as: "*A Cigarette and Trade Card Collection of the Social, Civil, Regal, Political, and Armed Forces History of Great Britain and the British Empire; Its Allies and Adversaries; and Other Related International Aspects.*" It began with only an interest in the strict military aspects, but then over time grew to encompass these broader and interrelated subjects.

Having the mindset of one who has to be organized, as this collection matured over a prolonged period of time I created a rather detailed classification system. One of the major categories is Warfare, of which the First World War is a significant part. The creation of this classification then further helped me to focus my collecting activities. Most of these cards were acquired through several well-recognized British card auction houses. A number were also purchased through the dealers, some of whom were also the auctioneers. I also have been a member of the major card-collecting society in the world, the Cartophilic Society of Great Britain.

Over the decades I developed relationships with the heads of the auction houses and the card dealers. They were always helpful in providing advice and assistance, as well as clarification to my many queries as I sought both individual cards (known as type cards) as well as sets, to fill the gaps in my collection. To this end I want to thank Ian Laker, Yalcin Berktay and Frank Doggett of the London Cigarette Card Company. Not only did their auction lists contain many cards needed to build up my collection, but their extensive collection of cards for sale helped me fill many gaps. Martin Murray who until his retirement owned Murray Cards (International) Ltd. was another such individual who helped me acquire my collection. Many of the cards used in this book were obtained from his excellent auctions that somehow always featured many of the sets or individual cards, a number of which are today rare and hard to come by, that I needed for my collection. A number of the First World War cards are from this source. William Hoad, now retired, also provided a number of cards via his auctions. His specialty seemed for me to be with individual cards needed to fill the gaps in my collection.

Over the years there have been members of the Cartophilic Society of Great Britain who have been a significant resource. Particularly John Devaney, the previous editor of the society magazine, Gordon Howsden, its current editor, and Martin Murray of the research department have been most helpful.

It has been a pleasure working with all members of the Schiffer Publishing team. From my perspective some appeared to play only a small part. Others were entirely invisible. Yet my brief interactions with the former and the impact of those with whom I had no direct interaction, are all positively manifest in this book. Two individuals of this team, however, stand out for their contributions, their support, advice and their patience. I have worked closely with them. First is Ian Robertson, who over a nearly eighteen-month period patiently and graciously tolerated all the changes I was constantly making to each so-called "final version." Finally, when his part was complete Sandra Korinchak, the Senior Editor, played her critical and most helpful part in carefully editing and correcting a variety of technical errors. Her many suggestions as well have only enhanced the quality of the book. I am deeply indebted to these two individuals for being at my side throughout this project.

Finally my eternal gratitude goes to my dearest wife Harriet. Throughout our decades of a wonderful marriage, not only has she had to put up with my "craziness," but more importantly, she has always shown a keen interest in my pursuits and encouraged me in them. She has always had a particularly soft spot for my cartophilic collection.

# INTRODUCTION

This book is about the Great War, the war that has classically been described as the "war to end all wars," a term first used by H. G. Wells in August 1914, but also later mentioned by Lloyd George and President Wilson. It became known as World War I or the First World War only after the next and even more devastating Second World War that began just over twenty years following the end of the Great War.

In an article written in the *Journal* of the World War One Historical Association in 2012 on the thoughts and meaning of the First World War, the author, Michael S. Neiberg, ponders on how long it will take to assess this war. As the centennial of its onset is now being commemorated, although hundreds, and probably even thousands of historical and other related books have already been written on this subject, more will certainly follow. Each one will likely provide some fresh information and another perspective. According to Neiberg this war, however, is particularly difficult to assess. It did not have a compelling narrative. It might have been just a part of the Second Thirty Year War ending in 1945, or perhaps an even much longer war, ending with the collapse of Communism in 1989. He furthermore points out that the memory of the War has to be politically and socially acceptable, even if it is not so historically. Thus the memory of the War carries significantly different meanings for the Canadians, the Australians, the British, the Europeans, and obviously the Americans. Encapsulating these vastly different meanings only adds to the complexity of the War narrative.

Historical books are essentially retrospective studies of a period in history written years, decades or even centuries after the event. This particular book approaches this war from a unique perspective, one that has not been previously published. It opens a window on aspects of the war not usually found in general history books of this period. One aspect of this uniqueness is derived from the fact that the information presented (both written and pictorial) is from the many cigarette and trade card sets produced mainly just before and during the war, with a minority issued after the war. Another important aspect is that the narrative parts of the cards, in the form of the descriptions, usually on the reverse side, are similar to an "oral history" provided by the participants. Its content and style of narrative reflect the feelings of the population at that time, even if not necessarily always historically correct. It is thus predominantly a contemporaneous historical work with the information documented as the war was unfolding. Most of the card sets were issued during the first two years of the war, but with increasing material shortages as well as increasing governmental oversight and censorship where necessary, only a few sets were issued during the latter part of the war.

As has been pointed out, this war carried different significance to its various participants. This aspect can be gleaned from the information on the cards that covered all the Allies, and to some extent the Central Powers as well. These cards not only covered the major Allies, particularly the British, French and Russians, but also the lesser ones, and to a large extent the Colonial Allies. Many cards are devoted to the important role of these Colonial Allies—Indians, Australians and New Zealanders (ANZACS), Canadians and South Africans. For example, in the many cards illustrating and describing the Gallipoli Campaign there is appropriate emphasis on the heroic role of the Australians and New Zealanders. Equally as much (although not described in detail in this work), the German issued sets provide their perspective on the War.

Since the majority of these cards are contemporaneous in nature, in that they were published during the war, they can now be analyzed in a retrospective historical perspective in an attempt to gain insight into the British society and its view of the War. Although that is not the purpose of this book, perhaps in the future a historian may undertake such a project. A striking feature that is common to a number of the cards is the strongly patriotic and perhaps even jingoistic aspect of both the images on the fronts of the cards and the descriptions found mostly on the reverse sides of the cards. The language used in the descriptions may also be related in part to the literary style and the turn-of-century phraseology. They also aim at boosting the morale of the viewer by glorifying the role of the Allied soldiers and describing the enemy in a derogatory manner. Since some of the cards were merely illustrations of what was both government-produced material as well as in the newsprint media, the card issuers were following what was the expected public impression of the war. This approach lends itself at times to both exaggeration and hyperbole. Even though by the mid and latter part of the twentieth century the "myth" of this attitude was accepted, the contemporaneous nature of these cards provides significant insight into public attitudes at the time these events occurred.

A brief history of the development and use of cigarette and trade cards is provided. Since this book is about the war as viewed through the lens of these cards, they have been used as the major reference source material. This reference material is derived from cigarette and trade cards of predominantly

British manufacturers. Therefore, the historical narrative is essentially the war as viewed from the Allied perspective and particularly that of the British. There are, however, a number of cards in these sets that illustrate and describe the Central Powers leaders, as well as their military conflicts with the Allies.

Based on the images on the front of the cards and (as found on most sets) the descriptions on the reverse sides, a unique but comprehensive educational and thought-provoking perspective of this war is brought to the reader. Since these cards were originally meant mainly as a marketing tool, and then during the war as a strongly patriotic contribution, the information, although mostly accurate, was unlikely to have been subject to rigorous academic scrutiny prior to its publication on the cards. Although uncommon, there is the potential for several inaccuracies. What is probably more likely in the descriptive language of the cards, is an exaggeration of praise for the British "Tommy" and the deeds of the Allies, while at the same time, there is an excessive demonization of the enemy. This aspect may be perceived as a limitation by strict historians. Yet it is this very aspect that provides critical social and psychological insight into the society at that time. Furthermore these cards do, nevertheless, provide a wealth of critical information in many and varied ways. These are some of the aspects that make this book a unique contribution to the literature of that period.

When they were issued, the aim of the card set producers was not to provide a chronological, detailed history of the war, but rather to emphasize aspects of it. Despite the potential limitations of such an approach, by the sheer depth and breadth of subject matter covered, almost every aspect of the war was included, oftentimes in some detail. It was the aim of the author to piece together these various components into a comprehensive overview of the war. Since a clear and chronologically detailed history of the war cannot be provided by these cards alone, Chapter 2 in the book provides a brief history of the war from the political, military, naval and air perspectives. There is nothing original in this descriptive history. It is purely factual, drawn from several standard sources. Yet it, along with Chapter 3's timeline, provides helpful supplemental background information to the reader to better appreciate the content and the context of these cards. The aim has been to link the cards presented in the descriptive chapters to this brief historical overview.

The illustrations on the fronts of these cards came from portraits and photographs of the personalities, photographs and illustrations taken from the battlefront and on the home front, and from works of art in public places. War artists and card illustrators were also important contributors to the illustrations. Since this was still the early days of photography, the battlefront photographs are limited. Most battle scene images are therefore by war artists and illustrators.

The subject matter of the chapters clearly indicates how complete was the coverage of that war by these various card issuers. Major emphasis is placed on the leaders of the countries—both regal and political, as well as the leaders who actually planned and fought the war on land, at sea, and, as the war progressed, more and more in the air. This was the first modern, technologically-based and industrialized war. This technology led on the one hand to gaining far more sophisticated and critical information about the enemy to better plan the various battles. But, on the other hand, and tragically to a far greater extent, this technology was directed at the manufacture of devastating firepower, with its horrific toll on human life. This was also the war where the mechanized vehicle took over as the major form of transportation. All these aspects are amply illustrated and described on these cards.

Formal recognition of the bravery of the individual soldier on the battlefield has always been standard military practice. Many card sets have been issued over the decades illustrating and describing almost every conceivable medal and award, both British and international, that has been awarded to servicemen. These various awards were all given to the participants in this war as well. However, the card companies chose not to repeat this information on the war-related card sets, but rather, chose the highest award, the Victoria Cross (V.C.). In covering several hundred such awards, they illustrated and described the awardees and some of the battle scenes where their acts of tremendous bravery and heroism took place, resulting in their receiving this great honor. For an award that is truly difficult to earn, the large number of V.C.s that were awarded during the war is testimony to the tremendous selfless acts shown by the common soldier. In a similar manner, the many card sets on all aspects of the actual fighting during the war and on the battlefront portray many hundreds of such individual scenes. It is through these vignettes of individual soldiers and individual war scenes that a very good understanding not only of the progress, but also of the devastating aspects of the war, can be appreciated in a larger context.

The war was not only fought on the battlefront. It was also fought on the home front, not only in the news media, predominantly the written word with accompanying illustrations, but also by the civilians in different ways. A large effort had to be made by the non-combatant civilian workforce to not only supply the war effort, but also to keep the local economy and home life functional. To a large extent this responsibility fell to the women since so many of the traditionally male-dominated workforce were fighting on the battlefield. This tremendous workforce reallocation resulted in dramatic and permanent social changes. These are all well-documented on the appropriate card sets. One of the powerful propaganda media tools used was that of posters that were both patriotic and morale-building. Mocking the enemy in the more sophisticated newsprint media also played a prominent role in the propaganda war. Cards with examples of these subject matters are surveyed in some depth in this book.

There is a brief overview of a few German issued card sets. Although the language is German, the illustrations are universal. What strikes the viewer immediately is the similarity of subject matter and themes in these sets, compared with the British-produced sets.

Most of the card sets utilized in this book consist of between twenty-five and fifty cards per set. It is not feasible to describe and illustrate all these cards. Only a minority have been used from all the sets. The goal was, through the careful selection of cards in each set, to use a sufficient number that would provide a comprehensive overview of each topic discussed.

Spelling is based on American English. However, card titles and quotations from the card descriptions use the British spelling.

Finally, although each individual card used in the narrative is identified in the text, a comprehensive listing of all the sets utilized in this book is provided at the end for the potential collector of these cards, or for one who may do research on them.

CHAPTER 1

# The HISTORY of CARD COLLECTING

## THE ORIGINS

The term "cigarette cards" is a loosely used term to describe all cards used for advertising. For collectors and hobbyists the term used is *cartophily*. This is a word derived from the Greek meaning love of cards. However, from a more practical point of view cartophily covers as well illustrated silk or cloth pieces and even metal and plastic items. Other paper items may also fall into this category of collecting. In a strict sense it should be considered any two dimensional item. However, from a practical perspective over the one and a half centuries that these have been around as a distinct item, cartophily has become synonymous with a card, even though silk items and to a lesser extent metal items have been a part of the hobby of cartophily. The silk items are often supported with a cardboard stiffening back.

Tobacco was first introduced into England in the sixteenth century by Sir Walter Raleigh (Figs. 1a, 1b, 1c, 1d). However, it was not until after the Crimean War (1854–1856), when the returning soldiers (Figs. 2a, 2b, 2c, 2d, 2e, 2f, 2g) brought the habit of cigarette smoking back to England, that it became more popular. At about the same time the Second Industrial Revolution or Technological Revolution was beginning. Tradesmen and businessmen were developing marketing skills. It was at this time that tradesmen's cards, coinciding with developments in printing and engraving, became a more sophisticated advertising tool. Initial advertising cards were not as artistic as they later became but were rather factual. The earliest trade card produced may have been in France in the 1840s.

The cigarette card per se began as a stiffener for the paper packets in which cigarettes were sold in the latter part of the nineteenth century. It was mainly in North America, and especially in the already-developed tobacco belt of Virginia, that cigarette salesmen and marketing of cigarettes had become a well-established business practice. This was driven by twenty-six tobacco companies. Originally the stiffener had some simple form of advertising, but this rapidly evolved to developing a series of cards having a particularly interesting subject. Until fairly recently, the earliest cigarette card that was thought to have been produced was that of the Marquis of Lorne, first referenced in a publication of 1879. Subsequently there was found, in the large Burdick cigarette card collection in the Metropolitan Museum

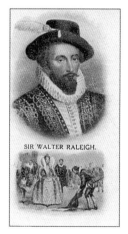

**Fig. 1a. Sir Walter Raleigh** (J.A. Pattreiouex, Builders of the Empire, 1929, No. 10)

**Fig. 1b. Raleigh, reverse side** (J.A. Pattreiouex, Builders of the Empire, 1929, No. 10)

**Fig. 1c. Sir Walter Raleigh** (J Milhoff & Co. Ltd., Men of Genius, 1924, No. 21)

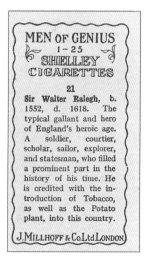

**Fig. 1d. Raleigh, reverse side** (J Milhoff & Co. Ltd., Men of Genius, 1924, No. 21)

**Fig. 2a. Crimean War Soldiers**
(John Player, Regimental Uniforms, 1914, No. 3)

**Fig. 2b. Crimean War Soldiers, reverse side**
(John Player, Regimental Uniforms, 1914, No. 3)

**Fig. 2c. Crimean War Soldiers**
(John Player, Regimental Uniforms, 1914, No. 12)

**Fig. 2d. Crimean War Soldiers**
(John Player, Regimental Uniforms, 1914, No. 18)

**Fig. 2e. Crimean War Soldiers**
(John Player, Regimental Uniforms, 1914, No. 23)

of Art in New York, an illustrated card issued by the cigar firm R.C. Brown. It showed a man with a top hat and inscribed "1877" and "Happy New Year," which meant that the card might have been produced in 1876. Creating a series of cards seems to have originated with an American journalist, Edward Bok, who in the late 1870s thought added value could be gained by illustrating the card, and then on the previously blank back, provide a descriptive text. Improvements in printing and the addition of color lithography provided further enhancements to the cigarette cards. This then attracted skilled artists and also more scholarly content to the descriptive backs. In 1880 Halls's Actresses and Presidential Candidates appeared. In the United Kingdom, 1885/1886 is probably the time of the earliest appearance of a British card set. However, it was distributed by an American cigarette company—Allen and Ginter. By this time, America no longer was dominating the card set business, as it was shifting to the United Kingdom. Non-insert counter cards were issued by the firms Hignett and Ogden. Wills was most likely the first British firm to issue an insert card. In 1895 their set of Ships (Figs. 3a, 3b) and in 1896 of Cricketers, followed in 1901 with several other sets, firmly established the trend. Other British firms soon followed with their own sets.

The late nineteenth century was still the era when people were far less literate, and illustrative forms of leisurely print had not yet developed. Newspapers did not contain illustrations until after World War One. Most individuals did not read newspapers in the late nineteenth century. The illustrated cards thus brought some form of entertainment into what were otherwise drab existences with little leisure time. Against such a background card collecting began at about this time. When it finally reached its full maturity in the first third of the twentieth century, the card subject matter could be divided into a large number of broad categories. These covered various types of leaders, military aspects, sports and other pastimes, stage, screen and radio personalities, land,

**Fig. 2f. Crimean War Soldiers**
(John Player, Regimental Uniforms, 1914, No. 46)

**Fig. 2g. Crimean War Soldiers**
(John Player, Regimental Uniforms, 1914, No. 49)

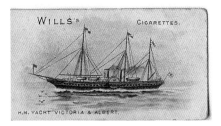

**Fig. 3a. Ships**
(Wills, Ships, 1895)

**Fig. 3b. Ships, reverse side**
(Wills, Ships, 1895)

sea and air transportation, nature and various novelties.

What made and still makes card collecting so fascinating a hobby? There are several reasons. There is the simple beauty of the artistry of the cards. Since these cards were produced specifically for marketing and collecting, and since they had the name of the cigarette company imprinted on them, it was in the self-interest of the issuer to produce a high quality and informative card set. The purchaser had to be motivated to acquire the rest of the set by continuing to buy the same cigarette brand. With the shortage of spare time in the late nineteenth century and in the frenetic existence of current times, admiring, studying and cataloguing these cards provides a quiet respite. What started off as the classical image of a young child pestering the adult smoker to part with the card in the cigarette packet, is now mainly the pursuit of adults. The other fascination with cards is the knowledge that can be gained from studying them. Although the information on some cards may be inaccurate, overwhelmingly the documentation on the reverse side of the card is authentic and with the enormous number of card sets, the cumulative information is encyclopedic. Today, despite the tendency to underplay the importance of the monetary value of the cards, many of the older and rarer sets have become very costly to purchase. The financial value of any substantial collection can no longer be ignored. With the maturing of the hobby, card collecting clubs and societies, as well as dealers in these, became common. There is the added benefit of the social fraternizing that then occurs as a result of this hobby.

How these cards were produced is a whole separate topic in its own right. Suffice it to say that the methods included the letterpress process, lithography, the photogravure process and direct photographic prints. A number of the earlier cards were actually printed by German printing firms. The artists who illustrated these cards and the writers who prepared the informative material were many in number, some achieving significant fame.

## THE EARLY PERIOD OF MASS PRODUCTION OF CARDS AND THE TOBACCO WAR

By the beginning of the twentieth century the tobacco industry in Britain was extremely competitive. This led these companies to produce many high quality sets to promote customer loyalty and increase sales. Player produced in 1898 the valuable set England's Military Heroes (Figs. 4a, 4b). Lambert and Butler had a beautiful set of Actresses. Cope produced its well-known Golfers series. What truly stimulated the explosive growth of cigarette cards was the Anglo-Boer War of 1899 to 1902. For example, Gallaher issued the South African Series in 1901 (Fig. 5). This coincided with a rapid growth of smoking during the Edwardian era and received a major boost from the war itself. Many military-based sets were printed during and just after this war. In the regal sphere it was the coronation of Edward VII, as Wills illustrated it in its 1902 Coronation Series set (Figs. 6a, 6b), that stimulated the production of a variety of royalty-related sets.

In the late nineteenth century James Duke was the most powerful American tobacco company owner. He absorbed or drove out of business nearly two hundred fifty firms. He then formed the large conglomerate, the American Tobacco Company (A.T.C.). Also in the late 1890s he started exporting his business products. Duke started making a foray into the British market. In 1901 he bought the Liverpool-based tobacco company of Ogdens Limited, paying over five million dollars. This stimulated the British to wake up and react to Duke. There was a coalition of thirteen British firms formed called the Imperial Tobacco Company Ltd. (I.T.C.). The largest and most influential firm in this coalition was W.D. and H.O. Wills. Other important tobacco firms, all of whom produced many famous card sets, were Stephen Mitchell and Son, Lambert and Butler, John Player & Sons, Hignett Bros., Franklyn Davey and Co., Wm. Clark and Son, Edward Ringer and Bigg, Richmond Cavendish Co., Adkin and Sons, and D. and J. MacDonald. Other firms like J. and F. Bell, T. Brankston and

Co., W.A. and A.C. Churchman, W.T. Davies and Sons, W. and F. Faulkner, W. Williams and Co. also worked together.

This was the beginning of what has since famously come to be known in the cartophilic world as the Tobacco War, fought mainly between 1901 and 1902. James Duke was at the head of the American onslaught and Sir William Wills led the British defense. However, the real winner and beneficiary in this war was the public. One of the major weapons used in this war was the cigarette card. The war stimulated a vibrant community of card collectors and although the number of card sets issued in this two-year period was somewhat limited, after the formation of the I.T.C. the number of issues increased and there was also a greater distribution of them.

In 1902 an agreement was struck between Duke and Williams. Duke sold back Ogdens to the I.T.C. at a great profit. Duke agreed to restrict the sales of the American Tobacco Co. to America, while Williams restricted the sales of the I.T.C. to the United Kingdom. This still left the world market and Duke had his eye on this. He had already penetrated the Asian market. The British did not roll over and leave that to him, and after further negotiations the two business leaders agreed to the formation of the British-American Tobacco Company (B.A.T.) to handle world trade. This company also handled the card issues.

## THE POST TOBACCO WAR PERIOD

After the brief but intense Tobacco War there followed a vibrant period of card issues until the First World War. More serious and interesting subjects then replaced the early topics of Actresses and Beauties. Among a number of topics were ones on nature, geography, more military aspects and travel. In addition to the larger firms and those in the I.T.C. fold, there were also many small independent firms that issued very interesting sets. Some only produced a few sets. There was one firm that remained independent and that was originally founded in 1740. It was James Taddy and Co. It was successful until the

**Fig. 4a. England's Military Heroes**
(John Player, England's Military Heroes, 1898)

**Fig. 4b. England's Military Heroes, reverse side**
(John Player, England's Military Heroes, 1898)

**Fig. 5. South African Series**
(Gallaher, South African Series, 1901)

early twentieth century but had to close down in 1920. In the early years of the twentieth century it produced some of the most beautiful sets on a wide variety of subjects. Today many of these are rare and all of them are valuable. They produced many sets with military themes and its six issues of Victoria Cross recipients are particularly impressive and beautifully done. A number of these were from the Anglo-Boer War (Fig. 7). This era was most fruitful for collectors of the time as well as for current collectors. The subject matter brought to ordinary people not only a wealth of information beautifully illustrated, but also exposed them to many interesting aspects of the lives of the powerful and influential. Their pastimes in the fields of entertainment and sports were also covered.

**Fig. 6a. Edward VII**
(Wills, Coronation Series, 1902)

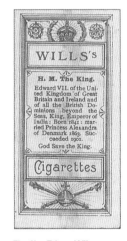

**Fig. 6b. Edward VII, reverse side**
(Wills, Coronation Series, 1902)

## THE OUTBREAK OF WORLD WAR I

The onset of this war changed significantly the types of card subject matter. This war resulted in an outpouring of cards by the tobacco companies, due to the dual incentives of patriotism and financial reward as a result of great public interest. The issues from this period covered almost all aspects of this major conflagration. Military subjects formed a major component of the issues. Since this war saw the first real effects of the technological advances in destructive equipment manufacture and the resulting devastation that these wrought, these arms and the war scenes where they had their impact were amply illustrated on cards. The military leaders of the Allies were also extensively illustrated and described on many different sets. A variety of patriotic sets was also issued. Humor always coexists with tragedy and card sets illustrating these were also issued. Essentially all of these sets had a propaganda aspect to them emphasizing the honor and bravery of the Allies and particularly the British Armed Forces, while other sets mocked the enemy. Since most of these cards had accurate descriptions and illustrations as well as having a wide circulation, they were

**Fig. 7. Louis Botha**
(Taddy, Boer War Leaders, 1901)

15

subject to censorship. Unfortunately, as a result of raw material shortages, by 1917 most card issues ceased and did not start up to any significant degree until 1922.

## BETWEEN THE FIRST AND SECOND WORLD WARS

This period has often been referred to as the golden age of cigarette cards. The reissuing of card sets took its first tentative steps in the early nineteen twenties, but then rapidly gained steam. The larger firms were soon producing many sets. Players, Churchman, Wills, Ogden, Godfrey Phillips and Gallaher all were active in the issuing of cards. Many other smaller firms also produced fine sets, although some were restricted in their numbers. Abdulla, Mitchell and Drapkin also produced sets. One firm, Carreras, which had issued very little prior to 1914, became a prolific issuer in this period. Ardath was another tobacco company that also became active. However, there were also casualties in this period and a number of smaller firms went out of business. One of the most notable "tragedies" from a cartophilic perspective was the firm of Taddy.

Another important change that took place in this period was the production of larger card sizes. This coincided with the tobacco firms packaging more cigarettes in larger boxes rather than the smaller packets. The firm of Wix, under its brand of Kensitas, issued mainly large-sized card sets. Another introduction of the 1930s was the manufacture of special albums to store these sets. These were usually for cards that were made with adhesive backs. Fortunately for collectors, many of these sets did not end up in these albums.

The topics that were covered in these sets included all forms of sports, of which football (soccer) was the most popular, but current events in Britain and the colonies and a number of royalty related issues were others, but only a relatively few military sets were issued in this period. The railways, particularly with the centenary of its invention in 1925, were also amply illustrated on card sets. Once again, what these card subjects showed was the strong connection they had with society in all its forms. In this way they differed significantly from that of other types of collectibles, for example philately.

The onset of the Second World War in 1939 once again saw the cessation of card production, but on this occasion with an almost immediate halt as a result of rapid government intervention to conserve valuable raw materials.

## THE MODERN ERA

Following the Second World War and for several years thereafter, the persistence of shortages and rationing prevented the reintroduction of cards. However, even when supplies became more readily available, the tobacco companies did not get back into the degree of card production that had occurred prior to the war. The variety of topics selected became very limited and not all firms issued sets. Government restrictions on tobacco advertising further limited the incentive to issue cards. The post-war period through to the present still shows a vibrant card production, but with one difference. The field is now almost entirely dominated by the trade issues. In every issue of the Cartophilic Society of Great Britain magazine there are a number of new card issues listed and described.

## TRADE CARDS

The discussion so far has concentrated almost exclusively on the production of cards by tobacco companies. Another important source for the production of card sets was in the non-tobacco business world. These cards are referred to as trade cards. Perhaps the most prolific and oldest producer is the European based Leibig Company, which has been producing cards since 1872. Most of these have non-English descriptions. English language cards are rare. One of the earliest English manufacturers of cards was Huntley and Palmer, the biscuit makers, which first produced a set in 1885. Other major card issuers were Kardomah, Lever Bros., Rowntrees of York, Typhoo Tea, D. C. Thomson Ltd., and Amalgamated Press. The chocolate firms of Cadbury and J. S. Fry and Sons (Figs. 8a, 8b) also produced a number of now-famous sets. The subject matter of all of these companies was similar to that of the tobacco companies. However, Brooke Bond among all the trade companies must stand out as the most prolific issuer of card sets. So extensive have they been that there is a dedicated catalog to its issues.

This brief review of the history of cards clearly demonstrates, through the myriad of topics covered in the many thousands of sets issued, that they are truly representative of the social, political, scientific and military influences of an ever-changing society. It is from this enormous output that a comprehensive collection of World War One related card sets has been assembled by the author and from these a small sample of cards have been used in this book.

Fig. 8a. Wellington
(J.S. Fry & Sons, Days of Wellington, 1906)

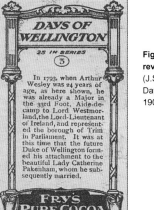

Fig. 8b. Wellington, reverse side
(J.S. Fry & Sons, Days of Wellington, 1906)

# CHAPTER 2

# A BRIEF OVERVIEW of the WAR

In order to appreciate the historical and educational value of the large variety of World War One cards it is helpful first to provide a brief overview of the war.

Since the cartophilic images and descriptions of the War are overwhelmingly contemporaneous in nature, the most appropriate place to begin this brief overview would be with the events from late June 1914. However, because there are several cigarette card sets that were published in the early twentieth century of the Russo-Japanese War of 1904, brief mention will be made of this war since it had such a direct impact on forging the final alliances leading into the First World War.

Following this there are descriptions of the various battles on land, at sea and in the air, for each of the four years of the war. The countries that fought these battles, the rulers of these countries, their political leaders and the men who organized and led the battles are mentioned. All of these are subsequently described based on the illustrations and reverse descriptions on the many cards.

Specific chapters are dedicated to these various aspects of the war as illustrated and described in the many sets issued. This permits a good cross-reference between the standardized history and the one provided by these card sets.

## 1914

### BACKGROUND

Christopher Clark in his work on how Europe inexorably went to war in 1914 describes how a number of the European countries, and to some extent Great Britain, were connected by a series of alliances from the mid-nineteenth century to the early twentieth century. In several situations the same country had different liaisons or alliances with several different countries. This occurred because of conflicting interests of these countries, most notably in the Balkans and to a lesser extent in the Adriatic. However, the net result of these was, according to him, a polarization of Europe. This became a crucial precondition for the outbreak of war in 1914. Thus there was the Triple Alliance between Germany, Austria and Italy. There was the Reinsurance Treaty between Germany and Russia. Britain was somewhat tied into Europe through the Mediterranean Agreement with Italy and Austria. In the last decade of the nineteenth century a Franco-Russian Alliance was created. This link with the Alliance increased via the Entente Cordiale with France in 1904. In 1907 there was the Anglo-Russian Convention where the Anglo-Russian Entente was signed, ending decades of a power struggle between the two countries. The Franco-Russian Alliance and the Anglo-Russian Entente then later became the Triple Entente among Great Britain, France and Russia

To understand the end of British neutrality in European affairs and the final Anglo-French-Russian Alliance it is necessary to step back to the creation of the German Empire in 1871. The British Leader of the Conservative Party, Benjamin Disraeli, commented on this event. According to Clark, Disraeli's concern was that with the defeat of France and the abrogation of the 1856 Treaty of Paris that prohibited Russian military intervention in the Mediterranean, Russia would move ahead with a process of expansionist militarization in opposition to the British. This aspect, not Germany, therefore dominated British foreign policy. Its expansion into Asia and China specifically strongly impacted the British, who had a greater trade potential there than in Africa. However, Russia's expansion also brought it into conflict with Japan. Britain responded to this threat by developing closer relations with Japan and France. Meanwhile the growing forces of both Japan and Russia in China finally resulted in the Russo-Japanese War of 1904–1905 where Russia suffered a significant defeat. The British saw great opportunity in this outcome and the then new Foreign Secretary, Edward Grey, worked to bring Russia back into the European fold. As mentioned above, in 1907 Russia and Britain signed a treaty resolving their differences in several other Asian countries. Thus the Russo-Japanese War may be seen as the significant event of the early twentieth century that created the final arrangements that culminated in the structural alliances of the First World War.

## IMMEDIATE CAUSES OF WAR

It was the assassination of the Archduke Franz Ferdinand of Austria on June 28, 1914, in Sarajevo that became the immediate cause of the First World War. It was widely believed that a secret radical Serbian organization, the Black Hand, was behind the assassination. This event brought to a head the tensions between Serbia and the Austro-Hungarian Empire which had been brewing ever since the latter had absorbed Bosnia, and which had been ratified by the Treaty of Berlin in 1909. This treaty also permanently damaged relations between Russia and Austria-Hungary. The Austrians and Germans wanted to use the assassination as an excuse for a localized Balkan conflict to restore the damages suffered in the Balkan wars. To cover their intention to destroy Serbia, they delivered an ultimatum to Serbia that had such punitive clauses they were sure it would be rejected. To everyone's surprise Serbia accepted the ultimatum within the time limit. However, with Germany encouraging Austria to declare war on Serbia, Vienna did not accept the Serbian response and declared war on July 28.

At the onset of the war Britain, Europe and their colonial empires were divided into two large political alliances. The Allies or the Triple Entente consisted mainly of Britain, France and Russia. The Central Powers consisted mainly of Germany and the Austro-Hungarian Empire.

On July 29, the day after declaring war, Austria invaded Serbia. Russia then immediately mobilized. Germany followed up by declaring war on Russia on August 1. The German plan of attack was based on the Schlieffen Plan, developed in the early part of the twentieth century. It was aimed at ensuring a swift victory over France. This plan required German forces to rapidly advance through the three neutral countries of Luxembourg, Belgium and Holland. Thus Germany invaded Luxembourg on the 2nd. On the 3rd Germany declared war on France and on the 4th invaded Belgium. The Schlieffen Plan was also erroneously built on the premise that Britain would not fulfill its treaty obligations to Belgium. However, the invasion of Belgium prompted the immediate declaration of war by Britain against Germany.

Italy joined the Allies later in the war, while other smaller countries such as Serbia, Montenegro, and Greece also joined the Allies. Turkey sided with the Central Powers. Further afield worldwide, the colonial countries allied themselves with their colonial masters. Japan, and ultimately the United States of America, joined the Allied countries.

The nature of the naval warfare of the First World War was on the one hand an attempt by the large fleets of the Allied Powers to blockade the sea routes of the Central Powers. In turn the goal of the Central Powers was to break this blockade as well as to effect a blockade of Britain and France with the use of submarines and other vessels. When the war began both Britain and Germany had significant navies. Britain's survival had always depended on a powerful navy supporting its vital seaborne trade. Germany in turn had aimed to build a navy strong and large enough to free its overseas trade and colonial empire from British naval goodwill. This resulted in an arms race that had begun a number of years before the war. This race was no better highlighted than by the famous dreadnought battleship rivalry of the early twentieth century.

## 1914 LAND BATTLES

After invading Belgium the Germans rushed to Liege where they were expecting only minimal resistance. However, the forts surrounding the city delayed their advance by three days. In mid- to late August the Belgian city of Louvain, located between Liege and Brussels, was attacked by the Germans. This led a short while later to the massive destruction of the city. Its famous library was also destroyed.

Once Germany invaded Belgium, Britain rushed to send an expeditionary force (the British Expeditionary Force or BEF) to that country via France. This plan was based on the Haldane Reforms of 1906–1907. The BEF under Sir John French positioned itself to the left of the French about twelve miles from Mons. With the Germans rushing towards Paris, the first battle of the war between Britain and Germany began with the Battle of Mons. It was a subsidiary action to the larger Battle of the Frontiers, which consisted of a series of early battles on the eastern border of France and southern Belgium. On August 29 the first Battle of St. Quentin or Battle of Guise took place with the French Fifth Army attacking. The Commander of I Corps, Louis Franchet d'Esperarey, forced the Germans to fall back. The German advance on Paris was halted at the River Marne at the First Battle of the Marne. Some historians consider the Battle of Mons to have been a part of the Marne Battle. Immediately after this battle there was the First Battle of the Aisne. It was an offensive action by the Allied forces against the German First and Second Armies. It began on September 13 in a dense fog when most of the BEF crossed the River Aisne. The French Fifth Army crossed nearby. When the fog cleared the British were caught in a blast of gunfire. The Germans counter-attacked and demonstrated what became a hallmark for much of the war: that they had the demonstrable superiority in defensive warfare. The following day Sir John French ordered the BEF to entrench. Thus began the stalemate that would essentially lock the enemies into a relatively narrow strip over the next four years.

Meanwhile with the Belgians providing strategic support to their British and French allies, the Belgian army was forced to retreat into the city of Antwerp. The Germans ultimately laid siege to the city in late September. On October 1 the Belgians informed their allies that they would have to evacuate the city in a few days. The British government allowed the First Lord of the Admiralty, Winston Churchill, to go over to Antwerp to determine if assistance could be provided. However, despite the help of a British brigade, the Germans broke through the Belgian defenses and the Belgian army evacuated the city. One million refugees followed.

The First Battle of Ypres (First Battle of Flanders), in October and November of 1914, was fought to gain control of the West Belgian town of Ypres. Each side viewed the battle for this strategic town in western Belgium as one for control of critical territory. For the Germans it was to outflank the enemy. For the French it was to prevent this outflanking. For the British it was to secure the English Channel ports of Boulogne-sur-mer and Calais for the maintenance of the British supply lines. It was the culminating battle of the Race to the Sea. Like the Marne, this battle was a victory for the Allies. The First Battle of Ypres was broken into several parts: the Battles of Yser, Armentieres, Messines, Langemarck, Gheluvelt and Nonne Boschen. In the Battle of Yser, the Germans could not defeat the Belgians and failed to take the Yser Canal. This allowed the Allies to retain that corner of Belgium.

In the early battles for the Race to the Sea, the Germans occupied the commune of Bray-sur-Somme. Following the Race to the Sea the Germans managed to hold onto most of Belgium, except for the small area on the northwest tip of the country adjacent to France that included Ypres. From Ypres to the sea was held by the Belgians and the opposing armies faced each other from Nieuport near the coast to Bethune in the south. The Allies then began to entrench themselves along this front.

On the Eastern front the Russian attempt to advance into East Prussia led to their defeat. Furthermore, the Germans conquered some Russian territory. A pivotal battle in this period was that of the German victory at the Battle Tannenberg under Paul von Hindenburg. On the Southwestern Front the Russian Army under the command of General Nikolay Ivanov defeated the Austrians at the Battle of Galicia. This was followed a month later by his push into the Carpathian Mountains where he surrounded Przemysl, laid it under siege and inflicted further casualties on the Austrians.

## 1914 SEA BATTLES

The naval warfare was essentially a battle between Britain, aided by France and the United States, and the German navy. German access to the oceans of the world was through the North Sea, the Straits of Dover and the English Channel. The latter two had always been controlled by Britain. At the start of the war, with Churchill as the First Lord, Prince Louis of Battenburg the First Sea Lord and Admiral Sir John Jellicoe in command of the Grand Fleet based in Scapa Flow in the Orkney Islands, Britain was well prepared. At sea, 1914 saw significant activity. The first action took place in the Mediterranean where the Germans successfully brought the battlecruiser *Goeben* and the light cruiser *Breslau* to Constantinople. This was despite the presence of the British Mediterranean Fleet in Malta, including the *Inflexible* and the *Indomitable*. As a result of this German action as well as the transfer of these ships to the Ottoman Empire, Turkey decided to join the Central Powers.

The first major action took place in the North Sea at the Battle of Heligoland Bight, where on August 28 the British Commander Tyrwhitt led the light cruisers *Fearless* and *Arethusa* together with the first and third destroyer flotillas against German ships located near the German naval base at Heligoland. Tyrwhitt came under heavy fire and called on Admiral Beatty for assistance. His arrival turned the tide of the battle and the Germans suffered significant losses. This action enhanced the status of Beatty.

Another major task of the British Navy was the protection of the trade routes worldwide and also the protection of British troop movements. In the Indian Ocean the German vessel *Emden*, with its funnel disguised to look like that of an English cruiser, sank fifteen ships before being run ashore by the Australian cruiser *Sydney*. In the West Indies, the *Karsruhe* destroyed seventeen ships before it was destroyed by an internal explosion. However, it was the Far East German Squadron under Vice Admiral Maximilian von Spee that posed the major threat to British shipping in the Indian and Pacific oceans. Through an intercepted communication the British became aware of von Spee's plan to disrupt shipping along the west coast of South America. Admiral Cradock, who commanded the naval squadron in this area, had inferior vessels. He planned to attack von Spee after receiving reinforcements. These, however, did not arrive on time and he confronted the full force of the German Squadron at Coronel off the coast of central Chile. At sunset on October 31, Cradock's fleet was attacked by von Spee. The *Scharnhorst* crippled the flagship *Good Hope* and shortly thereafter the *Monmouth*. Cradock went down with his flagship. Only the *Glasgow* and *Otranto* escaped. Coronel was the first British defeat at sea for over one hundred years. This prior defeat had occurred during the American War of 1812–1815 when the Royal Navy suffered defeats at the Battles of Lake Erie and the Thames in 1813. As a result of this defeat at Coronel Lord Fisher, who was now the first Sea Lord, sent the battlecruisers *Invincible* and *Inflexible* under Admiral Sturdee to join the other cruisers. Von Spee, unaware of this superior force, decided to attack the British station at the Falkland Islands. The Germans were defeated. The German armored cruisers *Scharnhorst* and *Gneisenau* were sunk. Also, the *Nurnberg* and *Leipzig* were sunk. Only the German vessel *Dresden* survived the battle. It sank a few months later. As a result Germany's ability to disrupt commercial trading on the high seas was brought to an end. Admiral Sturdee's reputation was also enhanced by this victory.

# 1915

## 1915 LAND BATTLES

The first major battle of 1915 along the Western Front occurred at Neuve Chappelle. This was the first British-initiated offensive of the war. In the beginning of March the Belgians held the line from the sea to Dixmuide and the French from this point to the top of the Ypres Salient. The British 1st Army under General Haig decided to engage the Germans. West of Neuve Chapelle was the IV Corps under General Rawlinson and then there was the Indian Corps under General Wilcox. On March 10 the British attacked and made significant advances. The Germans counterattacked the next day but did not make a substantial difference. At the end of the battle on March 13, the British had proven that they were a substantial force and not merely a part of the French forces.

On April 22 the Germans attacked the Allies on the Ypres Salient in what was to be the Second Ypres Battle. Its importance lies in the fact that this was the first battle where the Germans introduced poison gas, despite them having been a signatory to the 1907 Hague Convention forbidding the use of poisonous gas. In the late afternoon the Germans let loose a barrage of gas cylinders across No Man's Land. Two French Divisions were wiped out and the remaining French observing this turned and fled to Ypres, leaving the way open for the Germans. The Germans did not have the manpower to take advantage of this breech. The Canadians used wet handkerchiefs to stay in the battle. British counter-attacks could not take back any of the land and General Smith-Dorrien, who commanded the 2nd Army, decided to withdraw his troops to a more practical position by the Yser Canal and Ypres ramparts. Field Marshal French did not view this favorably and replaced him with General Herbert Plumer, who now assumed responsibility for Ypres. Fighting continued for another month before it died down with many casualties on both sides.

The British then developed their own poison gas that they used for the first time at the Battle of Loos in September. This battle was a part of the larger French Artois Offensive, Joffre's last attempt to take advantage of the Allied numerical advantage over the Germans. The British Offensive was at Loos. Although this gas was only partially successful, it was sufficient for Haig's 1st Army to overrun the German front lines. Advances of four thousand to five thousand yards were made, including capturing the town of Loos. However, the BEF suffered heavy casualties. Since General French's reserve troops were ten miles in the rear, they could not be brought up rapidly enough. This led to French's forced resignation after the battle. On the next day, September 26, the newly formed XI Corps was thrown into the battle. It suffered heavy casualties and had to be relieved by the Guards Division. However, by this stage the chance for success had passed.

The net result of 1915 activities on the Western Front demonstrated the lethality of the machine gun and artillery and the greater strength of defensive positions. It was a year of great casualties, more so on the Allied side than on the German side.

On the Eastern Front in the Carpathian Mountains, the fortress of Przemysl was still under siege under General Ivanoff. Despite German efforts, the fortress was ultimately conquered by the Russians, but not before the Austrian General, Hermann Kusmanek von Burgneustadten destroyed the city before surrendering. Meanwhile the Germans took the offensive in 1915. The German High Command disagreed as to where to attack, with Hindenburg wanting the major offensive against the Russians to be in the south and Falkenhayn wanting it in the north. In the end both offensives took place. Over the course of the year the German offensives resulted in the Russians ceding a large extent of territory three hundred miles in depth. Grand Duke Nicholas, who was in command of these armies, was relieved of his command and Tsar Nicholas II took over.

It was on the Turkish front that the most memorable events took place in 1915. On April 25 while the Second Ypres Battle was in progress, the controversial Dardanelles or Gallipoli Campaign began. In an effort to shift Axis Power resources from the deadlocked Western Front and to open up the Black Sea to secure a sea route to Russia, the Secretary of the British War Council, Colonel Hankey, submitted a plan in late 1914 to send an army against Turkey, hoping Greece and Bulgaria would lend their support. Although originally rejected by the Council, Winston Churchill did embrace the concept and modified the plan. He still indicated it should be only a naval operation. The War Council then accepted this in January. Admiral Carden was in command of the blockading force in the Dardanelles. The campaign opened in February when an Anglo-French force, including the powerful Dreadnought the *HMS Queen Elizabeth*, bombarded the coast. The main attack began on March 18 but after the British battleships *HMS Irresistable* and *HMS Inflexible*, as well as *HMS Ocean,* were sunk by mines and *HMS Lord Nelson* was damaged, the naval attack was called off. Carden's Second-in-Command, Admiral John de Robeck, indicated at that stage that the campaign would only succeed if complemented by a land force. Despite this Churchill kept up the pressure on Carden to attack, even at the expense of loss of ships and lives, if this could bring success. Carden did not want to follow through, and in March de Robeck assumed command.

After the failure of the naval attacks, the decision was taken to use land forces to eliminate the mobile Ottoman artillery. Lord Kitchener appointed Sir Ian Hamilton to command the Mediterranean Expeditionary Force. The invasion called for the 29th Division to land at Helles. The Anzacs (Australian and New Zealand Army Corps) were to land further north. Although the Turks under Mustafa Kemal were lacking in adequate manpower and ammunition they held off any meaningful British advance. There were many casualties that day. Over the course of the next few months a number of battles took place with many casualties but the Allies gained no real advantage. A trench-style warfare also developed here. British naval advantage was further diminished with the loss of the battleship *HMS Goliath* in May. Shortly thereafter *HMS Triumph* and *HMS Majestic* were sunk. A new plan for the campaign was then developed with an August offensive. On August 6 landings were made at Sulva, north of Anzac, where a strong assault also took place. On August 21 the Battle of Hill 60 began. It was the last major offensive of the Campaign. Hill 60 was a low knoll at the northern end of a range near the Sulva landing. The assault was led by the Australians. The Allies received no good artillery support and as a result large numbers were killed by the Turks. After several more attempts at taking the hill over the next week, the Ottomans in the end retained control of it. Once again the Allies were unsuccessful in achieving their goals. At this stage the campaign entered a period of inertia. Ultimately, after a personal visit by Kitchener, the decision was made to evacuate. This was successfully executed in December.

The major political repercussions of this campaign led to Fisher resigning in May because of significant disagreement with Churchill. After the campaign, as a condition for the

Conservatives to enter the government, Churchill was removed from his position as First Lord of the Admiralty. Asquith was partly blamed for the failure and in December of 1916 he was overthrown and David Lloyd George became the Prime Minister. Only in 1917 did he re-appoint Churchill as Minister of Munitions.

Also in 1915 another major change occurred. Italy was enticed to join the Allies. Although this impacted the Austro-Hungarian front mainly, it was still a setback for Germany, since it had to contend with another front. The main efforts of this front between 1915 and 1917 consisted of a series of battles along the Isonzo River. This river had a sixty-mile stretch that ran along the Italian and Austro-Hungarian border. Despite extensive efforts and high casualties, over the course of two years little was gained.

## 1915 SEA BATTLES

The only significant sea battle that took place in 1915 was at Dogger Bank. The Germans were at a loss as to how the British knew where they were at sea. They suspected that the many fishing boats in the North Sea might be providing the information. These were usually flying Dutch colors. Many were centered around Dogger Bank. Admiral Hipper was then ordered by the German Naval command to reconnoiter Dogger Bank. This message was intercepted by the British and Admiral Beatty set a trap. The fighting between the *HMS*

*Aurora* and the *Kolberg* began on January 24. Beatty and Hipper then steamed towards the action. Hipper's battlecruiser the *Seydlitz* sighted Beatty's flagship, the *HMS Lion*. The older British Battlecruiser Squadron lagged behind. Beatty placed the *Lion* in an advantageous position and opened fire. The slower moving *Blucher* was then damaged. Beatty concentrated his fire also on the *Seydlitz*. This ship was hit and a fire broke out with the loss of many German sailors. However, later in the morning the *Lion* was hit and damaged sufficiently that it began to lag behind. Other German ships were also damaged. Hipper then decided to abandon the *Blucher* and take his other damaged ships home. The *Blucher* continued to fire and put the destroyer *Meteor* out of action and damaged other vessels as well. By this time Beatty had lost control of the battle. Although it was not a decisive British victory, it boosted British morale. The Germans had a serious reversal but learned their lessons. Unfortunately the British did not, especially with the incorrect signaling that took place on the *Lion*. This had serious consequences the following year when *Lion* did a poor job of signaling at the onset of the Battle of Jutland.

The navy was also significantly involved in the Gallipoli Campaign as was described earlier under the land battles.

Another event that took place at sea in May 1915 was the German sinking of the British ocean liner *RMS Lusitania*. Over one thousand people died. It produced a worldwide outcry, especially from America.

# 1916

## THE BLOODY LAND BATTLES OF 1916

In December 1915 the Allied military leaders under the chairmanship of General Joffre agreed to develop a joint strategy against the Central Powers. This resulted in a plan to launch a united offensive by the Triple Entente and Italy. The aim was to kill more Germans than their pool could afford, to break the German lines, and then to exploit this situation. The plan developed by Joffre involved simultaneous attacks on the Western, Italian and Eastern Fronts. The Western Front plan involved joint attacks to the north and south of the Somme River. The Somme offensive would be the Anglo-French contribution to this plan. This would involve thirty-nine French and thirty British divisions. Simultaneously, Falkenhayn knew that the Germans would have to go on the offensive. The Allies were increasing their numbers faster and the naval blockade was beginning to take a toll. Since the Germans had been so successful on the Eastern Front with great losses to the Russian Army, Falkenhayn felt that a Western Front attack was the most important. Therefore he selected Verdun, a fortress city one hundred sixty miles east of Paris and split by the Meuse River, as the objective of his attack. He placed the Crown Prince in command.

The attack was planned for February 12, but bad weather delayed it. This gave the French the opportunity to bring up reinforcements. On the morning of February

21 the Germans opened up with an artillery barrage over a fifteen mile front. Later that afternoon they launched their ground attack. Although the French put up a good defense this soon began to crumble. This necessitated Joffre to send in General Pétain to lead the defense. He reorganized the French forces into four commands and also established the famous single-road supply system (The Sacred Way). Although Pétain contained the German assault he questioned the strategic value of Verdun, but after a visit in March by French President Poincaré and General Joffre, it was decided for political reasons and as a matter of national morale to make every effort to hold onto Verdun. The battle settled into one of attrition. Pétain requested more troops from Joffre, but these were not forthcoming. Despite this Pétain maintained a policy of immediate counter-attacks against all German approaches. In April the Germans launched their third main attack. Pétain was ably assisted by Generals Robert Nivelle and Charles Mangin. In May Pétain was placed in charge of an army group and Nivelle took command at Verdun. In June the Germans tried another attack. By this time they had conquered two of the forts built to defend Verdun, Douamont and Vaux. On June 23 the Germans decided to attack the remaining forts. However, they were not successful. On July 11 the Crown Prince ordered the identical attack, but with

a successful counter-attack by the Allies, the Germans could not capture Verdun. It was the July British attack on the Somme that then forced the Germans to abandon the Verdun Offensive. Falkenhayn was discredited and the Kaiser replaced him with Generals von Hindenburg and Ludendorff. Verdun was a quasi-victory for the French but at a tremendous cost. Later that year Nivelle recaptured the forts.

As a result of the German Verdun Offensive, the Allies were forced to change their strategy from that of a joint French-British offensive, to one of the British now taking the lead at the Somme. The battle was divided into five parts between July 1 and November 13. Thus on July 1 the second big offensive of 1916 on the Western front began with a heavy artillery barrage on the entrenched German forces. General Haig's offensive was planned over a twenty mile front north of the Somme River with Sir Henry Rawlinson in command of the Fourth Army. South of the Somme, the French carried out a supportive role. The goal of the artillery barrage was to have eliminated the German frontline defense. In addition three large mines were detonated under the German positions. When the British began their advance they thought it would be easy to occupy the German positions. However, the Germans were waiting with their machine guns. They slaughtered the British in No Man's Land. More men were poured in, all to no avail. There were nearly sixty thousand British casualties that day. None of the objectives had been achieved. After this Haig reorganized his attack; the next one took place on the night of July 13–14. This was more successful and they took a stretch of land of six thousand meters. Other attacks took place in September. What stands out as a signal event of the September 15 attack was the use of the tank for the first time in battle. The one used in this battle was the Mark I. Although the crews were not well-trained and there were too few of them spread over a wide area, they had a tremendous psychological impact. Haig attacked again on September 25 and made little inroad. Also the rains had begun. A final attack took place on November 13. The British advanced less than a mile. A few days later a blizzard struck and this brought the battle to an end. The battle did achieve one positive effect in that it relieved the pressure on Verdun.

An interesting side note to this period of the war was that after Winston Churchill left the cabinet in November 1915, he decided to go on active service in the Western Front where he served as a Battalion commander of the 6th Royal Scots Fusiliers. He was based near the Ploegsteert Wood, or what has now come to be known as "Plugstreet" Wood. He narrowly escaped death when his lookout post was shelled by the Germans.

On the Eastern Front, the Brusilov (or Brusiloff) Campaign was launched in June against Austria-Hungary. It was one of the most lethal battles in history and resulted in the diversion of many German troops from Verdun, as well as breaking the back of the Austro-Hungarian Army. The Russians successfully recaptured Galicia. This was also Russia's most significant victory and its proudest moment of the war.

## THE OTHER FRONTS IN 1916

On the Italian front, the Austro-Hungarians made another offensive attack in May (the Trentino Offensive), but without German support. The need to transfer troops against the Russian offensive in Galicia resulted in no change of the status quo on this front. On the Eastern front, the removal of the Grand Duke Nicholas and the assumption of command of the Russian forces by Tsar Nicholas II had a negative impact on morale and the functioning of the army. In May, in response to an Italian plea for help, General Brusilov launched his offensive in Galicia. He had significant successes against the Austro-Hungarians, who seemed near collapse. However, he faced supply problems and the offensive did not progress, and the front was saved. Although this was Russia's greatest success of the war, its ultimate goal of defeating the Austro-Hungarian army was not accomplished. After being courted by both sides the Romanians eventually joined the Allies, blocking a critical supply route for the Central Powers. In Greece, King Constantine insisted on remaining neutral, while his prime minister, Venizelos, wanted to join the Allies. In late 1916 the Allies blockaded Greece and recognized Venizelos's provisional government.

## 1916 SEA BATTLES

1916 stands out as the pivotal year for the War at Sea. This was the year when the inconclusive Battle of Jutland occurred. The battle took place on May 31 and June 1 near Jutland, Denmark. It was not only the largest naval battle of the war and involved the major fleets and battleships of both sides, but the largest naval battle in history. The German goal was to bring out the British Grand Fleet, trap them, and destroy enough of their vessels so as to break the blockade on German naval vessels. The German fleet was under the command of Vice-Admiral Reinard Scheer. In January 1916 he was given command of the High Seas Fleet. He was an aggressive leader and believed in taking the fleet to sea to engage the enemy. He did so in February, March and April. He had been preparing for an elaborate engagement for the end of May. His aim was to use the scouting group vessels of modern battlecruisers under Vice-Admiral Franz Hipper's command to lure Vice-Admiral Sir David Beatty's battlecruiser squadron to the main German fleet. Submarines were placed along this route to attack the British fleet as it approached. The British intercepted these signals and therefore Admiral Sir John Jellicoe sailed on May 30 with the Grand Fleet to meet Vice-Admiral Sir David Beatty. Thus on May 31 there was a combined German and British naval force of over two hundred fifty warships all steaming to a location near Jutland, Denmark. The combined enemy fleets included forty-four Dreadnoughts and fourteen battlecruisers. On the British side these included four of the newest and fastest *Queen Elizabeth*–class battleships.

The Battle of Jutland is probably the most analyzed of all naval battles. This is primarily because of its undecided outcome, although in time it came to be viewed as somewhat of a British victory. In essence it consisted of five different phases.

The first was the one where Beatty's Fleet made "the run to the south." The second was then his "run to the north." There were then two phases of interactions between the Dreadnoughts, and finally a fifth phase at night when the lighter vessels on each side tried to cause severe damage to the enemy fleet with torpedoes.

Beatty's reconnaissance fleet consisted of six battlecruisers, all four of the *Queen Elizabeth*–class battleships, fourteen light cruisers and twenty-seven destroyers. When he approached the German Fleet he ordered the seaplane carrier *Engadine* to launch a plane and determine the size of the enemy force. This was the first time in history that this type of reconnaissance was used in naval battle. Beatty undertook course changes, but these were not received by the last ship in the column, the *Tiger*. It, in turn, could not relay signals to Sir Hugh-Evan Thomas's 5th Battle Squadron. This led to confusion and separation of the ships, with his faster *Queen Elizabeth*–class battleships ending up farther away. The force was thus divided, denying him an overwhelming advantage in firepower in the first half hour of the battle that began when Hipper opened fire. The Germans had the first advantage when three of the six British battlecruisers were hit. A little later Beatty's flagship *Lion* took a hit on the turret. Shortly thereafter *HMS Indefatigable* took three hits and a fourth ripped it apart; it sank rapidly with the loss of over one thousand lives. As the 5th Battle Squadron eventually came into range, Hipper's situation deteriorated, but his mission to lure the British into the range of Scheer's main force was almost accomplished. During this "run to the south," the Germans inflicted damage on the *Princess Royal*, the *Queen Mary*, the *Tiger*, the *New Zealand* and the *Barham*. The Germans also suffered damage to four of their vessels.

In the late afternoon Scheer's main force sighted the distant battlecruiser action. Shortly thereafter Commodore Goodenough on the *HMS Southampton* also sighted the German main fleet of sixteen dreadnoughts and six older battleships. This came as a surprise to Jellicoe and Beatty who previously had no idea that Scheer was even at sea. At the same time a fierce destroyer action was taking place between the battlecruiser forces. Captain Barry Bingham of the *HMS Nestor* led the British attacks during which his forces destroyed two torpedo boats. Although the *Nestor* and *HMS Nomad* were later hit by Scheer's dreadnoughts, Bingham won the Victoria Cross for his leadership in this action.

Upon being sighted Beatty turned his battlecruiser force around and made the "run for the north" to bring the Germans in range of Jellicoe's Grand Fleet. Jellicoe signaled his own force to prepare for action and also sent a radio signal to the Admiralty. The battleships of the 5th Battle Squadron did not immediately get Beatty's orders to turn around and there was a delay in them doing so. They nevertheless acted as Beatty's rearguard. As a result Beatty, now being at a disadvantage relative to Hipper's superior force, withdrew his damaged ships from the fire of the enemy. The 5th Battle Squadron then received the fire and *Barham*, *Warspite* and *Malaya* were hit. Only *Valiant* remained intact.

Meanwhile, Jellicoe did not know the location of the German fleet. He was therefore not sure whether to deploy towards the eastern or western columns. This would make a critical difference since deploying to the west would bring his fleet closer to Scheer, and that would give him a distinct advantage. In what turned out to be one of the most difficult and critical tactical decisions of the entire war, Jellicoe ordered deployment to the east. Hipper had rejoined Scheer and together they headed toward Jellicoe. At the same time the British light cruisers and destroyers, as well as Rear-Admiral Arbuthnot's armored cruiser *HMS Defence* and its sister cruiser *HMS Warrior,* were all scurrying to get into their correct positions, often criss-crossing each other so closely as to barely escape collisions. This deployment became known as "Windy Corner." Arbuthnot's cruisers had no place among the dueling dreadnoughts and both the *Warrior* and *Defence* were badly hit. Hipper now moved into the range of Rear-Admiral Hood's 3rd Battlecruiser Squadron, still within range of Beatty. *HMS Indomitable* hit several German ships, but a bit later *Invincible* came into a clear target for the German vessels the *Lutzow* and *Derfflinger,* which rapidly sank it.

At about this time the two main battle fleets joined action for the first time. The Germans were taken completely by surprise. Jellicoe's flagship *Iron Duke* repetitively hit the leading German dreadnought. Realizing his impossible position Scheer ordered his fleet to turn. Concern about torpedo action against his battleships led Jellicoe to pursue a southern course rather than pursue Scheer directly. Realizing it was a while until dark and that in his current course and direction he was still in a vulnerable position, Scheer turned to the east, directly towards Jellicoe's deployed battle line. As a result Jellicoe caused severe damage to several German battleships. Scheer once again tried to turn while at the same time ordering a torpedo attack, as well as a charge by four battlecruisers. However, they came under what at that time was the heaviest ever concentration of naval gunfire released. All except one of the German battlecruisers were hit. This action allowed Scheer to get his dreadnoughts out of the range of fire. Finally just after sunset the final interaction between the capital ships took place. The British battlecruiser *Princess Royal* was the only one to get a direct hit, while the *Seydlitz* and other German ships were also hit. In the last moments of twilight *HMS King George V* exchanged fire with *SMS Westfalen*. Thus ended the first and last encounter between the two dreadnought fleets for the entire war.

Jellicoe did not want to engage in the dark, but the Germans did in several independent encounters, damaging the *Southampton* and *HMS Spitfire*, and causing the loss of the destroyers *HMS Tipperary*, *Ardent*, *Fortune*, *Sparrowhawk* and *Turbulent*. The final action took place just after midnight when the *HMS Black Prince* of the 1st Cruiser Squadron was sunk when it sailed into the German line.

In a final assessment of the battle, the British lost a greater tonnage of ships than the Germans. In addition, over six thousand British seamen were lost compared with two thousand five hundred Germans. Most importantly, the British remained in control of the North Sea. The British hope for a decisive victory was never realized. The Germans failed in their objective of destroying the British fleet. Thus, the general impression over the long term has come to be that the British had a strategic victory at that battle. Just after the

battle Jellicoe was criticized for his caution, including that by Beatty. Jellicoe was taken out of active service and became First Sea Lord, while Beatty assumed his position as commander of the Grand Fleet.

# 1917

## 1917 OPERATIONS

At the end of 1916 Herbert Asquith resigned as Prime Minister and David Lloyd George, the Liberal leader, took over and formed a new coalition government. The cabinet he appointed was designed to take total control of the war. It also instituted a state of total war, such that all citizens would be able to play their part. Under the Defense of the Realm Act it allowed this government to react quickly to events. It was also in 1917 that another dramatic event took place. The United States of America entered the war. This same year saw the collapse of the Russian Empire. These changes and events ultimately turned the tide of the war. In January, even though disliked by Lloyd George, but favored by the King, Haig was promoted to Field Marshal. The Prime Minister, however, did like General Nivelle. They agreed to a major offensive for April.

In preparation for the Nivelle Offensive a diversionary battle took place, the Battle of Arras. This was aimed at drawing the Germans away from Aisne. A key objective in this battle was Vimy Ridge, which forms a part of the Arras Sector. The Germans had held this position since 1914. The preparation for this included building a number of tunnels to bring the troops to the front line. Caves were also built to store the equipment and hold the soldiers. An air offensive just before the battle gave the British artillery the opportunity to position their guns effectively. The front covered fifteen miles, with the southern half using the Third Army under General Allenby and in the north using the First Army under General Thorne. The assault began on April 9, led by the Canadians, and by midday the Germans had lost Vimy Ridge. The other objective of diverting German troops from the Aisne was also accomplished.

On April 16 Nivelle began his offensive at Aisne. This attack was between Soissons and Reims and the objective was a ridge known as Chemin des Dames. Between April 9 and May 16 only limited gains were achieved. The Germans had been expecting this offensive and were well-prepared for it. It was at this same time that the mutinies in the French Army began. Only after Marshal Pétain instituted reforms did these settle down.

Another important action of this year was the British offensive in Flanders. The purpose of this was to break through the German lines in the Ypres salient in the section between the North Sea and the River Lys. As a result Belgium would be liberated and German lines of communication would be disrupted. The British Navy also hoped that the German submarine bases in Belgium would then be destroyed. Haig gave responsibility for this offensive to Generals Gough, Rawlinson and Plumer. First the Messine Ridge had to be taken. This was successfully accomplished by Plumer. Seven weeks later the formal campaign, which was the Third Battle of Ypres or Passchendaele, began under General Gough. Over the course of the next five months a series of eight distinct battles

occurred. These were Pilckem, Langemarck, Menen Road, Polygon Wood, Broodseinde, Poelcapelle, First Passchendaele and Second Passchendaele. The last battle ended on November 10. In the early part of the campaign the combination of destroyed dykes and rain created an impossible territory and tanks could not be utilized. A second attempt was made in August and this was even worse. Another attempt was made in late September. Then in October the rains returned. Finally, in late October and early November, at heavy cost, the British took the Passchendaele Ridge and village. This prolonged battle became the epitome of the futility of the Western Front war. At the end of this Passchendaele Battle the cost was one quarter million British soldier fatalities, many thousands of whom were never found. It earned Haig the title of "Butcher."

The last battle of the year on the Western Front took place in the north. It was the Battle of Cambrai, fought from November 20 to December 7. A large number of tanks were used in this offensive, although it was not truly a tank battle. The British Mark IV tank was used. There were initial British gains, but then the Germans counter-attacked. They regained most of the early losses to the British.

In April of 1917 the United States of America entered the war. This would ultimately play a significant role in turning the tide of war in favor of the Allies.

Meanwhile on the Eastern Front the Russian Revolution occurred, which later changed the dynamics of the war in this region. When a Provisional Government of moderate leaders was established in March, the offensive continued. The critical campaign under the political leadership of Kerensky took place in the summer, known as the Second Brusilov Offensive. The aim of this was to hold the Germans at bay while the major attack occurred against the Austro-Hungarians in Galicia. As a result of a poorly equipped and demoralized Russian army, despite good leadership, the offensive failed miserably. By the early autumn the Bolshevik Revolution dominated Russian life, with Lenin and Trotsky in charge. This was the beginning of the Communist era. War weariness was gripping both the Russian and the Central Power States.

In the Middle East the most important event of 1917 was the Battle of Jerusalem from November 17 until December 30 under the leadership of General Edmund Allenby. The British Empire's XX and XXI Corps and the Desert Mounted Corps fought in the Judean Hills. The Eighth Army fought north of Jaffa and near the Mediterranean Sea. Victories were attained in these battles, resulting in a severe setback for the Ottoman Empire. General Allenby then entered the Old City of Jerusalem. He was the first Christian leader to pass through the Jaffa Gate, which he did on foot, as a sign of respect for the holy places of the three monotheistic religions.

## 1917 WAR AT SEA

The most important naval impact of 1917 was from Germany's submarine campaign. In the early months of 1917 they instituted unrestricted warfare against the Allies with devastating effect. Over the course of a few months many hundreds of Allied merchant ships were sunk. The Allies responded by developing the convoy system, as well as what came to be known as SONAR. By the end of the year, the danger of this submarine warfare had been effectively contained.

# 1918 — The Last Year of the War

## EASTERN FRONT

In early 1918 the new Communist regime in Russia, despite Allied opposition, went on to make peace with the Central Powers. The Treaty of Brest-Litovsk of March 1918 resulted in Russia ceding Poland, Ukraine, Livonia, Estonia and Finland. Germany immediately occupied these territories. Two months later Romania, which was isolated, signed a similar treaty, ceding parts to Bulgaria and Hungary.

## WESTERN FRONT

Believing the Germans had a narrow window of opportunity, General Erich Ludendorff planned a large offensive against the Allies that came to be known as the Ludendorff Offensive. On March 21, after a five-hour artillery bombardment, one million German soldiers advanced over a fifty mile front opposite the British Third and Fifth Armies. The German armies penetrated forty miles and Gough's army was routed. There were heavy casualties on both sides. The German Army recaptured much of the territory it had lost in 1916. Bray-sur-Somme was once again the scene of fighting in this offensive. The Allied leadership adopted a unified command, with overall command of the Western Front being assigned to General Ferdinand Foch. In this desperate situation Britain instituted conscription, and over the course of the next month, between British and American new arrivals, over seven hundred thousand soldiers were added to the European Allied forces. In April Ludendorff launched a second offensive to the north in Flanders, just south of Ypres on both sides of the Lys River. His goal was the destruction of the British forces there. Although the British were pushed back their line did not break. Plumer had to withdraw the Second Army from Passchendaele Ridge to near Ypres. This was the first ever tank versus tank battle, but this did not make a significant impact on the outcome. It took place in late April during the Second Battle of Villers-Bretonnneux, which was part of the Battle of Lys. The Australians played a major role in this battle. Later Rawlinson launched a counteroffensive and drove the Germans back. At this point Ludendorff called off his offensive.

## SIMULTANEOUS NAVAL OPERATIONS

Meanwhile, also in late April, the Royal Navy launched a series of raids against Ostend and Zeebrugge, where German submarines and torpedo boats were based. Although by now the submarine threat had been contained, the action was more to support the British forces and improve morale. The operation was under the command of Admiral Roger Keyes. This operation met with only limited success.

## ONGOING LAND BATTLES

Once again at the end of April Ludendorff resumed his offensive, but now the American troops, which General Pershing had agreed to place under the overall command of Foch, were in place. The German offensive was directed at the juncture of the British and French forces. This offensive, the Third Battle of the Aisne, began on May 27. The French lines crumbled and by the end of the month they were within fifty miles of Paris, in the Marne River valley. This was near the first major battle of 1914, the Battle of the Marne. However, without supplies and with the aid of the American forces, the German advance was stopped here. Ludendorff tried to replace his troops and equipment, and on July 15 launched what became known as the Second Battle of the Marne. Parisians once again heard the artillery fire and the repeated fear of 1914 gripped the French. However, the German soldiers were deserting in large numbers. The Germans were stopped to the east of Rheims. The Allies now gained the upper hand. Foch initiated a counteroffensive that not only saved Paris, but caused the Germans to retreat.

At this stage General Pershing undertook an independent U.S. Army offensive aimed at the St. Mihiel salient. This was successful, but Foch then instructed Pershing to move in the direction of Marne. Foch's plan was to have one large offensive action extending from Ypres in the north to Verdun in the south. Thus in late September the last major offensive of the war, the Meuse-Argonne offensive, began.

## THE END

By this time Ludendorff realized the war had been lost. At the end of September he asked for a new government to begin negotiations for an armistice. Prince Max of Baden was appointed the new chancellor and he sent President Wilson a proposal that the latter arrange for an armistice followed by peace negotiations based on Wilson's Fourteen Points. Ludendorff then resigned. Finally on the eleventh day of November at 11:00 AM the guns fell silent.

CHAPTER 3

# TIMELINE of the WAR

This is a somewhat abbreviated timeline that nevertheless includes the major aspects of the war, and should be helpful when reviewing the various chapters in the book. The emphasis of this timeline is to include many of the personalities and events illustrated and described on the cards.

An asterisk in the left-hand column next to an event indicates that a corresponding card is described in the text.

**1914**

| |  |  |
|---|---|---|
| | Assassination of Archduke Franz Ferdinand of Austria, heir to the throne | June 28 |
| | Austria-Hungary declares war on Serbia, and Russia mobilizes | July 28 |
| | Germany declares war on Russia<br>Italy declares its neutrality<br>Germany and the Ottoman Empire sign a secret alliance | August 1 |
| | Germany invades Luxembourg | August 2 |
| | Germany declares war on France and Belgium | August 3 |
| | German troops enter Belgium to outflank French Army<br>Great Britain declares war on Germany | August 4 |
| | Montenegro declares war on Austria-Hungary | August 5 |
| | Austria-Hungary declares war on Russia<br>Serbia declares war on Germany | August 6 |
| * | Lord Kitchener calls for 100,000 men to enlist in British Army | August 7 |
| * | The BEF arrives in France | August 7 |
| | Montenegro declares war on Germany | August 9 |
| | France declares war on Austria-Hungary | August 11 |
| | The UK declares war on Austria-Hungary | August 12 |
| * | Battle of the Frontiers, with initial German victory | August 14–24 |
| * | Russian Army enters East Prussia, Germany attacks and fails<br>Battle of Tannenberg, further defeat for Germans | August 17–<br>September 2 |
| | Japan declares war on Germany | August 23 |
| * | Battle of Mons begins | August 23 |
| * | Germans occupy Bray-sur-Somme | Late August |
| * | Destruction of Louvain by Germans | August 25 |
| * | Battle of Landrecies and British Disaster at Le Cateau | August 26–<br>September 6 |
| | Battle of Lemberg with Russian victory | August 26–<br>September 11 |

| | | |
|---|---|---|
| * | Battle of Heligoland Bight, North Sea, British victory | August 28 |
| | First Battle of St. Quentin (Battle of Guise), Allies retreat | August 29–30 |
| * | First Battle of the Marne. German advance on Paris halted and failure of Schlieffen plan | September 5–12 |
| * | First Battle of the Aisne and Race to the Sea begins | September 13–September 28 |
| | German Army siege and capture of Antwerp, Belgium | September 28–October 10 |
| | First German plane shot down by Allies | October 5 |
| * | First Battle of Ypres<br>Included the Battles of Yser Armentieres, Messines, Langemarck, Gheluvelt and Nonne Boschen<br>Race to the Sea ends with Allies securing Calais to Dunkirk | October 19–November 22 |
| * | Battle of Coronel<br>British Navy Squadron under Cradock defeated by Von Spee | November 1 |
| | France and the UK declare war on the Ottoman Empire | November 5 |
| * | Sinking of the *Emden* by the *Sidney* | November |
| * | Battle of the Falklands. Von Spee defeated by Royal Navy | December 8 |
| | Unofficial Franco German Christmas Truce | December 24–25 |

### 1915

| | | |
|---|---|---|
| * | First Zeppelin Raid on Great Britain | January 19 |
| * | Battle of Dogger Bank | January 24 |
| | Germany begins submarine warfare against merchant vessels | February 4 |
| * | First British and French Naval attack on the Dardanelles | February 19 |
| * | Battle of Neuve Chapelle. Initial British success but then halted | March 10–13 |
| * | Second Battle of Ypres. Began with German gas attack. Ended in a stalemate | April 22–May 25 |
| | Gallipoli Campaign begins with Allied landing | April 25 |
| | German troops break through Russian lines in Galicia | May 1–3 |
| | Sinking of *Lusitania* | May 7 |
| * | Asquith forms coalition government in Great Britain | May 25 |
| * | First Zeppelin raid on London | May 31 |
| | First Battle of Isonzo on Italian front. Minimal Italian advantage gained | June 23–July 7 |
| | Second Battle of Isonzo. Italians gained a strategic foothold | July 28–August 3 |
| * | Suvla offensive begins in Gallipoli Campaign | August 6 |
| * | Battle of Hill 60, Gallipoli | August 21 |
| * | Grand Duke Nicholas Nikolayevich removed as Commander-in-Chief of Russian Army. Tsar Nicholas II assumes that role | September 8 |
| * | Battle of Loos. British offensive fails | September 25–28 |
| | Germany, Austria-Hungary and Bulgaria invade Serbia | October 6 |
| | Third Battle of Isonzo on Italian front | October 18 |
| | Fourth Battle of Isonzo | November 10 |
| * | Douglas Haig replaces John French as Commander of the BEF | December 19 |

**1916**

| | | |
|---|---|---|
| | Gallipoli Campaign ends | January 9 |
| * | Battle of Verdun begins with German offensive | February 21 |
| | Fifth Battle of Isonzo | March 9 |
| * | Battle of Jutland | May 31–June 1 |
| * | Russian Brusilov (Brusiloff) Offensive begins | June 4 |
| * | Lord Kitchener dies when *HMS Hampshire* is sunk off Orkney Islands | June 5 |
| * | Battle of Somme begins with Anglo-French offensive | July 1 |
| | Sixth Battle of Isonzo | August 6 |
| | Hindenburg becomes German Chief of Staff | August 29 |
| | Seventh Battle of Isonzo | September 14 |
| * | British tanks used for the first time at last offensive of Battle of Somme at Flers Courcelette | September 15 |
| | Eighth Battle of the Isonzo | October 10 |
| | Ninth Battle of the Isonzo | November 1 |
| | Battle of Somme ends as stalemate and with enormous casualties on both sides | November 18 |
| * | Franz Joseph I, Emperor of Austria and King of Hungary, dies | November 21 |
| * | David Beatty becomes the commander of the Grand Fleet and Jellicoe becomes First Sea Lord | November 25 |
| * | David Lloyd George succeeds Asquith as Prime Minister | December 5–7 |
| * | Robert Nivelle replaces Joffre as Commander-in-Chief of the French Army | December 13 |

**1917**

| | | | |
|---|---|---|---|
| * | Nivelle Offensive begins | | January 19 |
| * | British Arras Offensive begins | | January 19 |
| | Tsar Nicholas II abdicates. Provisional government created | | March 15 |
| | United States declares war on Germany | | April 6 |
| | Canadians capture Vimy Ridge | | April 12 |
| | Second Battle of Aisne (part of Nivelle Offensive) Ends in disaster for French and for Nivelle | | April 16–May 9 |
| * | Tenth Battle of the Isonzo | | May 12 |
| * | Pétain appointed Commander-in-Chief of Western Front | | May 15 |
| * | John Pershing in command of American Expeditionary Force | | May 19 |
| * | British capture of Messines Ridge Preparatory attack of 3rd Ypres Campaign | | June 7–8 |
| | Greece declares war on Central Powers | | June 29 |
| * | Third Battle of Ypres (or Battle of Passchendaele) begins | | July 31 |
| * | Eleventh Battle of the Isonzo | | August 19 |
| * | First Battle of Passchendaele | | October 12 |
| | Twelfth Battle of the Isonzo | | October 24 |
| | Second Battle of Passchendaele | | October 26– November 10 |
| | Bolsheviks seize power in Russia | | November 7 |
| * | Battle of Cambrai Massed tank attack. Battle ends in stalemate | | November 20– December 3 |
| * | British under Allenby enter Jerusalem | | December 8 |
| | Russia signs armistice with Germany | | December 2 |

**1918**

| | | | |
|---|---|---|---|
| * | President Wilson outlines his Fourteen Point Peace Plan | | January 8 |
| | Start of German Spring Offensive | | March 21 |
| * | Marshal Ferdinand Foch appointed Supreme Commander of Allied Forces | | March 26 |
| * | Bray-sur-Somme once again scene of battles of this Offensive | | April |
| * | Royal Air Force formed by combination of the Royal Flying Corps and the Royal Naval Service | | April 1 |
| * | First Battle of Villes Brettaneux | | March 30–April 5 |
| * | Second Battle of Villes Brettaneux. First tank against tank battle | | April 24–27 |
| | Third Battle of Aisne. German advance ultimately halted | | May 27–June 6 |
| | Second Battle of Marne. Last German offensive fails | | July 15–August 5 |
| | Battle of Amiens Beginning of final Hundred Day Offensive | | August 8–11 |
| | United States St. Mihel Offensive | | September 26 |
| | Bulgaria signs an armistice with Allies | | September 30 |
| | German High Fleet mutinies | | October 29 |
| | Kaiser William II abdicates | | November 9 |
| | Armistice begins at 11 AM | | November 11 |

# CHAPTER 4

# The INDIVIDUAL'S WAR

It is valuable to look at the war from the perspective of the citizen soldiers and the civilians of Great Britain, since many individual cards, as well as sets, under different titles, deal with this aspect of the war.

## THE SOLDIERS' WAR

Different from Germany and elsewhere in Europe, Great Britain did not have military conscription at the start of the war. It was purely a volunteer army. However, in the post-Victorian and Edwardian era, the patriotism of the average citizen was such that it was considered one's duty to enlist. Furthermore, in the persistent mindset of both the military leaders and the population-at-large, they believed this war would be of the same nature as many of "Victoria's Little Wars." Most volunteers viewed this war as just another such adventure, with it all being over by the Christmas of 1914. It was in the same spirit that the Colonies signed up for the war as well. In order to swell the ranks of the enlisted men an active recruiting program was instituted, epitomized by perhaps the most famous poster of all times, that of the elaborately mustached Lord Kitchener with his pointing finger. It was only later in the war that conscription was introduced.

However, once the first battle took place with all its horror, the myth of the adventure rapidly dissipated. It did not take long for the average soldier to become battle-seasoned. This was manifested by the many acts of heroism by individual soldiers, such that many Victoria Crosses were awarded during the first year of the war.

Traditional cavalry charges became extinct by the end of August 1914, a victim of the machine gun and of artillery shrapnel. Yet hundreds of thousands of horses were used extensively in varying capacities throughout the war. These were drawn mainly from the British farmlands. There remained a close relationship between the soldier and his horse, but in a different capacity.

The stalemate that rapidly developed with trench warfare had a significant impact on the individual soldier. Most soldiers' experience of the war was based on the small world of their squadron, platoon, or the company with whom they lived in close proximity in the trenches. The life in the trenches was one of limited communication and of boredom. Soldiers passed their time by writing many letters and postcards that found their way to and from the warfront.

The life of the soldier was perfectly described in one of the most powerful literary forms of the war with the enormous outpouring of erudite and heart-wrenching works of wartime poetry. A number of the famous World War One poets fought and even died in the trenches. They left an eternal impression of the horrors of this war. They also approached the war and its impact more at the individual level rather than at the global level. One of the most famous poems was Rupert Brooke's, written at the onset of the war when the air was filled with patriotism and long before reality had set in.

### 1914: THE SOLDIER

If I should die, think only this of me:
That there's some corner of a foreign field
That is ever England. There shall be
In that rich earth a richer dust concealed;
A dust whom England bore, shaped, made aware.
Gave, once, her flowers to love, her ways to roam,
A body of England's, breathing English air,
Washed by rivers, blest by suns of home.

A number of poets wrote about life in the trenches, for example, Ivor Gurney's "First Time In," Isaac Rosenberg's "Break of Day in the Trenches," and Richard Aldington's "In the Trenches." Siegfried Sassoon's poem "The Redeemer" described what it was like in the rainy, muddy conditions:

Darkness: the rain sluiced down; the mire was deep;
It was past twelve on a mid-winter night,
When peaceful folk in beds lay snug asleep;
There, with much work to do before the light,
We lugged our clay-sucked boots as best we might
Along the trench; sometimes a bullet sang…

Martin Armstrong described the loneliness and anonymity of the soldier in his poem "Before the Battle":

Here on the blind verge of infinity
We live and move like moles. Our crumbling trench
Gapes like a long wound in the sodden clay,
The land is dead. No voice, no living thing,
No happy green of leaves tells that spring
Wakes in the world behind us. Empty gloom
Fills the cold interspace of earth and sky.

Wilfred Owen's famous poem "Dulce et Decorum Est" described the nightmare of the effects of poisonous gas.

> Gas! GAS! Quick boys! – An ecstasy of fumbling,
> Fitting the clumsy helmets just in time,
> But someone still was yelling out and stumbling
> And flound'ring like a man in fire or lime. –
> Dim through the misty panes and thick green light,
> As under a green sea, I saw him drowning.

## THE CIVILIANS' WAR

The vast majority of the civilian population, at least at the onset of the war, was totally supportive. The press also adopted a supportive role and for most of the war did not fulfill their critical function. On the other hand, the press was censored right from the onset of the war. For cards, this can be seen in two forms. Either the card sets were deemed to contain sensitive material that the enemy could easily gain access to, and hence these were censored and not issued. Or the cards, after review, could be issued but they carried a statement indicating that they had been passed by the censors. Much later some of these unissued sets became available to collectors.

One of the major social changes that occurred during the war was the large scale employment of women. The hundreds of thousands and later millions of males who were called up to war potentially could have brought the domestic war industry as well as general industrial production to a standstill. A new source of industrial labor had to be found to fill this large void. There was the transformation of industry to a younger and significantly female workforce. They took over essentially all the work that men previously did, from heavy manual labor, to munitions work and aeronautical labor, as well as in the many service industries. As the war continued, adolescents were openly recruited and their education took second place.

Another major contemporaneous literary form was that of the cartoonist. It took two main forms: either that of biting humor and satire directed at the enemy or, in a more jocular form, self-directed at the local population and the enlisted men. Most of these were also directed at individuals.

Many of these aspects are well-illustrated in card sets. They provide significant insight into the society of the time.

CHAPTER 5

# BACKGROUND and ALLIES

## BACKGROUND

As indicated earlier, it was Benjamin Disraeli (Figs. 9a, 9b) who, in 1871, foresaw the consequences of the defeat of France and the creation of the German Empire, not in the traditional context of the danger of a powerful Germany, but rather in terms of the impact of Russian military expansion into Asia and its impact on Britain and its trade there. It was Russia's major defeat against Japan in the Russo-Japanese War of 1904–1905 that swung the pendulum in favor of Britain and allowed the British to develop alliances with Russia.

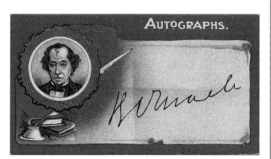

Fig. 9a. Benjamin Disraeli, Lord Beaconsfield
(Taddy, Autographs, 1910, No. 5)

Fig. 9b. Benjamin Disraeli, Lord Beaconsfield
(Wills, Builders of the Empire, 1898, No. 32)

Fig. 10a. Emperor of Japan
(Taddy, Russo-Japanese War (125), 1904, No. 2)

Fig. 10b. General Count Nodzu
(Taddy, Russo-Japanese War (26–50), 1904, No. 26)

Fig. 10c. Marquis Ito
(Taddy, Russo-Japanese War (1–25), 1904, No. 6)

Fig. 10d. General Count Nodzu
(Taddy, Russo-Japanese War (1–25), 1904, No. 2)

There were two card companies that addressed the Russo-Japanese War. Taddy and Co. produced in 1904 two fine sets of 25 cards each that illustrated both Russian and Japanese regal (Figs.10a, 10b), political (Figs. 10c), military (Figs. 10d, 10e), and naval (Fig. 10f) leaders. Also in 1904, Phillips produced a set that was reprinted in 2001 on this war that included leaders (Figs. 11a, 11b), vessels (Figs. 12a, 12b), and soldiers (Figs. 13a, 13b).

**Fig. 10e. General Kuropatkin**
(Taddy, Russo-Japanese War
(1–25), 1904, No. 19)

**Fig. 10f. Admiral Uriu**
(Taddy, Russo-Japanese War
(1–25), 1904, No. 12)

**Fig. 11a. Admiral Ito**
(Phillips, Russo-Japanese War
Series 1904, 2001 Reprint)

**Fig. 11b. Mons. L. Kurino**
(Phillips, Russo-Japanese War
Series 1904, 2001 Reprint)

**Fig. 12a. "Shikishima"
Battle Cruiser**
(Phillips, Russo-Japanese
War Series 1904, 2001
Reprint)

**Fig. 12b. "Retvisan"
Battleship**
(Phillips, Russo-Japanese
War Series 1904, 2001
Reprint)

**Fig. 13a. Japanese Infantry**
(Phillips, Russo-Japanese War
Series 1904, 2001 Reprint)

**Fig. 13b. Preobajensky Guards**
(Phillips, Russo-Japanese War
Series 1904, 2001 Reprint)

In 1910 Nugget Polish Co. issued a set titled Allied Series. This series illustrates on the front of each card a banner on the top with the name of the ally. Beneath that is an iconic building illustrative of that country. To the left is a soldier in the uniform representative of that country and to the right the flag of that country. Thus Nos. 1 and 2 are of England; Nos. 3, 4 and 5 of Scotland, Ireland and Wales; Nos. 6 and 7 of Canada and Australia; No. 8 of New Zealand (Fig. 14); No. 10 of India; Nos. 15 and 16 are of France and Russia; Nos. 17 and 18 are Italy and Belgium; No. 19 is Japan; Nos. 20, 21, 22 and 27 are of Rumania, Serbia, Montenegro and Greece; and No. 25 the United States.

**Fig. 14. New Zealand**
(Nugget Polish Co., Allied Series, No. 8, 1910)

**Fig. 15a. Sir Edward Grey**
(Morris, War Celebrities, 1916, No. 5)

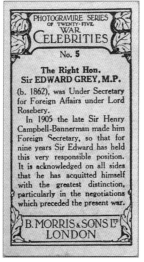

**Fig. 15b. Grey, reverse side**
(Morris, War Celebrities, 1916, No. 5)

**Fig. 15d. Sir Edward Grey**
(Bewlay & Co., War Series, 1915, No. 7)

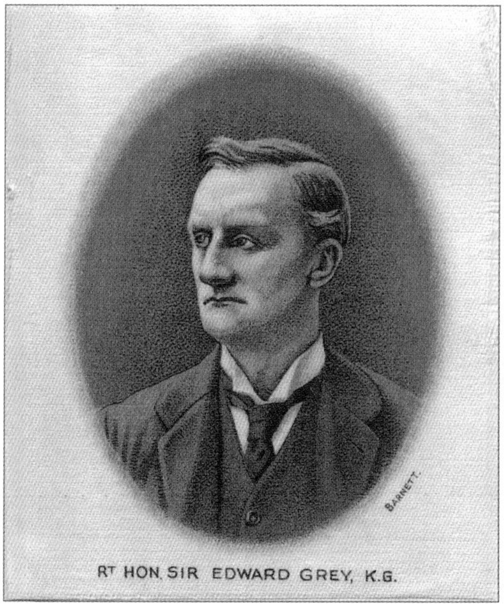

**Fig. 15c. Sir Edward Grey**
(Phillips [anonymous], Great War Leaders II, 1915)

As July 28, 1914, inexorably arrived, and the First World War began, Sir Edward Grey, the British Foreign Secretary (Figs. 15a, 15b, 15c, 15d), famously remarked "The lamps are going out all over Europe. We shall not see them lit again in our time." As the back of the Bewlay series states, "the most eloquent speech he has ever delivered was that in which he announced the British ultimatum to Germany." By November 1918, the landscape of Europe—geographical and political—had changed dramatically. In many ways, Grey's traditional world had been upended and according to his accurate prediction, the lamps were truly out.

# CHAPTER 6

# MONARCHS and POLITICAL LEADERS

## The Monarchs

In Britain, as in many European countries in 1914, the heads of state of those countries that were either involved in the war or affected by it were its kings and one queen. By the end of the war many had not only lost their historic seats of power, but in some countries the sovereignty was eliminated. The number of these illustrated on card sets is extensive. The list includes those of the European Allies, those who were initially neutral but then later joined the Allies, those who remained neutral throughout the war, as well as those of the enemy. Non-European monarchs involved in the War also found their faces and biographies on these cards. Several of the monarchs had close family ties.

Fig.16a. Queen Victoria (Salmon & Gluckstein Ltd., Her most Gracious Majesty Queen Victoria, 1901)

Fig. 16b. Queen Victoria (Alex. Jones & Co., Portrait of Queen Victoria, 1897

Fig. 17. King Edward VII (Pritchard and Burton, Royalty Series, 1902)

Fig. 18. Victoria Adelaide, German Dowager Empress (Pritchard & Burton, Royalty Series, 1902)

King George V, Tsar Nicholas II and Kaiser Wilhelm II were all closely related. King George and Kaiser Wilhelm were both grandsons of Queen Victoria (Figs. 16a, 16b), the former through his father Edward VII (Fig. 17) and the latter through a daughter Victoria Adelaide Mary, the Dowager Empress (Fig. 18). Nicholas's wife Alexandra (Figs. 19a, 19b, 19c) was Queen Victoria's granddaughter through her daughter Alice Maud Mary. There were even more family connections among this trio. Nicholas was also the nephew of Alexandra of Denmark (Fig. 20), wife of Edward VII. These interrelationships extended to the honorary military level among the countries. For example, Edward VII was an Honorary Colonel of the 5th Blucher Hussar Regiment of Prussia (Fig. 21a), Honorary Colonel of the 1st Prussian Dragoon Guards (Fig. 21b), and an Honorary Colonel of the Russian Dragoons (Fig. 21c).

**Fig. 19a. Alexandra, Czarina of Russia**
(Adkins, A Royal Favourite, 1900)

**Fig. 19b. Empress of Russia**
(Gallaher, Royalty Series, 1902)

**Fig. 19c. Empress of Russia, reverse side**
(Gallaher, Royalty Series, 1902)

**Fig. 21a. King Edward VII, as a Prussian Hussar**
(Edwards, Ringer & Bigg, Portraits of HM the King in Uniforms of the British & Foreign Nations, 1902)

**Fig. 20. Queen Alexandra**
(Murrati, Great War Leaders, Series P, 1916)

**Fig. 21b. King Edward VII, as a Prussian Dragoon Guard**
(Edwards, Ringer & Bigg, Portraits of HM the King in Uniforms of the British & Foreign Nations, 1902)

**Fig. 21c. King Edward VII, as a Russian Dragoon**
(Edwards, Ringer & Bigg, Portraits of HM the King in Uniforms of the British & Foreign Nations, 1902)

## THE ALLIES

In Britain, King George V (Figs. 22a, 22b, 22c, 22d, 22e, 22f, 22g) was crowned king in 1911 after the death of Edward VII. By his side was Mary of Teck whom he had married in 1893 (Fig. 23).

**Fig. 22a. King George V**
(Westminster Tobacco Co. Ltd, The Great War Celebrities, 1916, No.1)

**Fig. 22b. King George V**
(Anstie (silk), c. 1915)

**Fig. 22c. King George V**
(Wix, Builders of the Empire, 1937)

**Fig. 22d. King George V, reverse side**
(Wix, Builders of the Empire, 1937)

**Fig. 22e. King George V**
(Major Drapkin, Celebrities of the Great War, 1916)

**Fig. 22f. King George V**
(Clarke, Nicholas and Coombs, Great War Leaders, 1916)

**Fig. 22g. King George V**
(B.A.T., War Leaders and Scenes, 1916)

**Fig. 23. King George V and Queen Mary**
(Phillips, Great War Leaders, 1916)

In Eastern Europe King George's relative, Tsar Nicholas II (Figs. 24a, 24b, 24c, 24d), was ruler of the vast but dysfunctional Russian Empire. As Winston Churchill wrote of him, "He was neither a great captain nor a great prince. He was only a true simple man of average ability." The Bolsheviks assassinated him and his family in July 1918.

**Fig. 24a. Czar Nicholas II**
(Cohen Weenen, War Series –
Leaders of the War, 1915, No. 28)

**Fig. 24b. Czar Nicholas II, reverse side**
(Cohen Weenen, War Series –
Leaders of the War, 1915, No. 28)

**Fig. 24c. Czar Nicholas II**
(Wills Overseas, Royalty, Notabilities and Events in Russia, China and South Africa, 1900- 1902)

**Fig. 24d. Czar Nicholas II**
(Westminster Tobacco, The Great War Celebrities, 1916, No. 37)

Meanwhile, small Belgium, the country Germany decided to invade because it was the only open pathway to its real enemy, France, was ruled by King Albert I, born in 1875 (Figs. 25a, 25b). His wife was Queen Elizabeth of Bavaria (Fig. 26). The Belgian Monarchy survived after the War.

**Fig. 26. Queen of Belgium**
(Phillips, Great War Leaders and Celebrities IV, Extra Large, 1916)

**Fig. 25a. King Albert I**
(Phillips [anonymous], Great War Leaders II, 1915)

**Fig. 25b. King Albert I**
(Major Drapkin, Celebrities of the Great War, 1916)

Another ruling member of the Allies was Peter I, King of Serbia (Figs. 27a, 27b). It was the assassination on June 28, 1914, in Sarajevo of the Archduke Franz Ferdinand of Austria, the heir presumptive to the throne ever since the suicide of the Emperor's son, that became the immediate cause of the War. After the War, the monarchy was reduced to a parliamentary one. Montenegro was an ally of the Serbs, and they fought mainly the Austrians during the war. The ruler of this small country was King Nicholas I (Figs. 28a, 28b, 28c). After the War the monarchy was deposed.

**Fig. 27a. King Peter I**
(British American Tobacco Co.. (B.A.T.), War Leaders and Scenes, 1916)

**Fig. 27b. King Peter I**
(Muratti Cigarettes, Great War Leaders Series P, 1916)

**Fig. 28a. King Nicholas I**
(Morris, War Celebrities, 1916, No. 18)

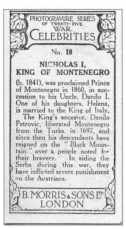

**Fig. 28b. King Nicholas I, reverse side**
(Morris, War Celebrities, 1916, No. 18)

**Fig. 28c. King Nicholas I**
(Colton, War Portraits, 1916, No. 49)

**Fig. 29a. King Constantine I**
(Muratti, Crowned Heads, 1912, No. 23)

**Fig. 29b. King Constantine I, reverse side**
(Muratti, Crowned Heads, 1912, No. 23)

**Fig. 29c. King Constantine I**
(B.A.T., War Leaders and Scenes, 1916)

The ruler of Greece was King Constantine I (Figs. 29a, 29b, 29c). He was a brother-in-law to Kaiser William. He kept Greece neutral, despite the opposition of his Prime Minister, Venizelos. He died in 1917. The Monarchy was deposed in 1924.

At the beginning of the war, Italy decided to remain neutral. Its ruler was Victor Emanuel III (Fig. 30). His wife was Elena of Montenegra (Fig. 31). The Triple Entente (Great Britain, France, Russia) convinced him to enter the war on the Allies' side, which the Italian government agreed to after being promised certain territories. The Monarchy survived after the War.

**Fig. 31. Queen of Italy**
(American Tobacco Co., Famous Queens, 1910)

**Fig. 30. King Victor Emanuel III**
(Phillips, Great War Leaders II, Extra Large Size, 1915)

**Fig. 32a. Ferdinand, King of Romania**
(Wills, Allied Army Leaders, 1917, No. 35)

**Fig. 32b. Ferdinand, reverse side**
(Wills, Allied Army Leaders, 1917, No. 35)

In the Balkan theater of the war, among the Central Powers was King Carol I, born Prince Karl of Hohenzollen, of Rumania. He was an ardent supporter of Austria. However, with his death in October 1914 his nephew Ferdinand became king (Figs. 32a, 32b, 32c). The British sovereign family relationships extended to this small country as well. The back of this card describes how "he married the beautiful Princess Marie of Edinburgh, a cousin of King George V" (Fig. 33). Despite having had a secret treaty with the Triple Alliance (Germany, Austria-Hungary, Italy) since 1883, the Romanian public and government wanted to join the Triple Entente. Rumania also remained neutral until 1916, when it joined the Allies. Ferdinand facilitated this. The Monarchy continued after the War.

**Fig. 32c. Ferdinand, King of Romania**
(Phillips, Great War Leaders and Celebrities IV,
Extra Large Size, 1916)

**Fig. 33. Queen of Rumania**
(Phillips, Great War Leaders and
Celebrities IV, Extra Large, 1916)

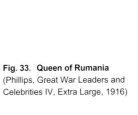

Haakon VII was the king of Norway (Fig. 34). He reigned from 1905 until 1957. Although the country remained neutral during the war, the people had strongly anti-German attitudes.

The Netherlands, under the sovereignty of Queen Wilhelmina (Fig. 35), remained neutral during the war. It suffered under the British blockade of Germany, since the Netherlands was included in the blockade. After the war she gave asylum to the Kaiser.

**Fig. 35. Queen Wilhelmina**
(Phillips, Great War Leaders and Celebrities IV, Extra Large Size, 1916)

**Fig. 34. King Haakon VII**
(Phillips, Great War Leaders and Celebrities IV, 1916)

In the Far East an important ally of the Triple Entente was His Majesty, Yoshihito, Emperor of Japan (Figs. 36a, 36b). In early August 1914 the British government requested Japanese assistance in destroying the German Imperial Navy located in Chinese waters. The Japanese agreed and declared war on Germany. Japan also quickly occupied German-leased territories in the region.

A colonial ally in India was the ruler of the small princely city state of Gondal, part of the larger state of Gujarat, His Highness Thakur Sahib (Figs. 37a, 37b). He was educated in Edinburgh and Oxford. Other Indian principality rulers who were British allies were His Highness the Maharaja Dhira ja Holkar of Indore (Fig. 38) and the Maharaja of Gwalior (Fig. 39). All of these are illustrated in the Major Drapkin series of Great War Celebrities.

Fig. 36a. HM Yoshihito
(B.A.T., War Leaders and Scenes, 1916)

Fig. 36b. HM Yoshihito
(Cohen Weenen, War Series – Leaders of the War, 1916, No. 48)

Fig. 37a. His Highness Thakur Sahib
(Major Drapkin, Celebrities of the Great War, 1916)

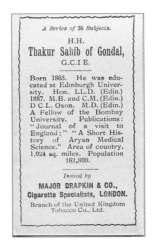

Fig. 37b. Thakur Sahib, reverse side
(Major Drapkin, Celebrities of the Great War, 1916)

Fig. 38. Maharaja Dhira ja Holkar
(Major Drapkin, Celebrities of the Great War, 1916)

Fig. 39. Maharaja of Gwalior
(Major Drapkin, Celebrities of the Great War, 1916)

## THE CENTRAL POWERS AND THEIR ALLIES

In the more central European region, another joint relative of both the British and Russian rulers was Kaiser Wilhelm II (Figs. 40a, 40b, 40c, 40d, 40e 40f, 40g). The Cohen Weenen set describes him as follows: "of all the European Monarchs, the German Emperor is more absolutely ruler than any other." It is this aspect that manifested itself a decade after the issue of the last of the above sets when he was the force pushing towards war. He had ruled Germany since 1888. Shortly after he was crowned he had dismissed the great German Chancellor, Otto von Bismarck (Fig. 41), and embarked on his bellicose path leading up to that fateful day of late July 1914. A trade card set Goodies Limited issued in 1973 titled Wicked Monarchs has an illustration of the Kaiser (Fig. 42) and describes his encouragement of his people in their faith in "Prussian Militarism." This was among the factors that led to the First World War.

Fig. 40a. Kaiser Wilhelm II
(Cohen Weenen, Celebrities, 1900)

Fig. 40b. Kaiser Wilhelm II
(Kinnear Ltd., Royalty, 1897)

**Fig. 40c. Kaiser Wilhelm II**
(Gallaher, Royalty Series, 1902, No. 13)

**Fig. 40d. Kaiser Wilhelm II**
(BAT, Historical Figures, 1st Series, 1961, No. 7)

**Fig. 40e. Kaiser Wilhelm II**
(Wills, Royalty, Notabilities & Events, 1902)

**Fig. 40f. Kaiser Wilhelm II**
(Muratti, Crowned Heads, 1912)

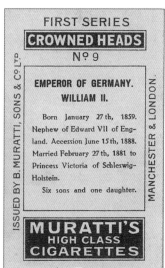

**Fig. 40g. Kaiser Wilhelm II, reverse side**
(Muratti, Crowned Heads, 1912)

**Fig. 41. Otto von Bismarck**
(Ogdens Guinea Golds Numbered, Set 71-S, No. 24)

**Fig. 42. Kaiser Wilhelm II**
(Goodies Limited, Wicked Monarchs, 1973)

Franz Joseph, the Emperor of Austria and King of Hungary, who died during the war (1916), is illustrated on only a few cards (Figs. 43a, 43b, 43c, 43d, 43e). He was a reactionary and had a tragic personal life, with his son and heir's suicide in 1889, and as the reverse of the card describes, his wife's assassination in 1898.

Mohammed V, Sultan of Turkey (Figs. 44a, 44b), had succeeded his deposed brother in 1909. He died a few months before the end of the war on July 3, 1918, and was succeeded by his brother Mohammed VI, who was the last Sultan before the Ottoman sultanate was abolished in 1922.

This set by Muratti issued in 1912 is beautifully illustrated and has an image of essentially every monarch in Britain and Europe in the early twentieth century.

**Fig. 43a. Emperor Franz Joseph**
(Lever Bros., Celebrities, 1905)

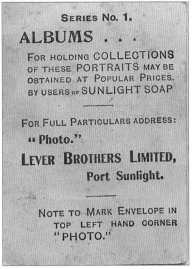

**Fig. 43b. Emperor Franz Joseph, reverse side**
(Lever Bros., Celebrities, 1905)

**Fig. 43c. Emperor Franz Joseph**
(Muratti, Crowned Heads, 1912, No. 6)

**Fig. 43d. Emperor Franz Joseph**
(Wills Overseas, Royalty,
Notabilities and Events in Russia,
China and South Africa, 1900-
1902)

**Fig. 43e. Emperor Franz Joseph,
reverse side**
(Wills Overseas, Royalty, Notabilities
and Events in Russia, China and
South Africa, 1900-1902)

**Fig. 44a. Sultan Mohammed V**
(Muratti, Crowned Heads, 1912, No. 29)

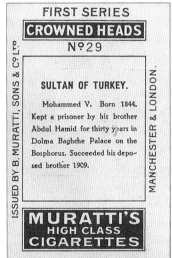

**Fig. 44b. Sultan Mohammed V, reverse side**
(Muratti, Crowned Heads, 1912, No. 29)

# Political Leaders

## THE ALLIES

In Britain at the onset of the war, Herbert Henry Asquith (Figs. 45a, 45b, 45c, 45d, 45e) was the prime minister leading the Liberal Party. As a result of an arms production crisis, and following the Gallipoli Campaign failure, his cabinet was brought down. Rather than face an election he formed a coalition government with the Conservative Party. However, by 1916 the coalition collapsed, mainly over dissatisfaction with the Battle of the Somme. The political maneuverings that caused this were led by Andrew Bonar Law (Fig. 46a, 46b), leader of the Conservative Party, and by David Lloyd George (Figs. 47a, 47b, 47c, 47d) from the Liberal Party. The former did not have the widespread support to become the new prime minister and therefore Lloyd George, who had great support, became the new prime minister.

**Fig. 45a. Herbert Asquith** (Colton, War Portraits, 1916, No. 2)

**Fig. 45b. Herbert Asquith** (Bouchere's Firm, War Portraits, 1916, No. 2)

**Fig. 45c. Herbert Asquith** (Westminster Tobacco, The Great War Celebrities, 1914, No. 3)

**Fig. 45d. Herbert Asquith** (Adkin and Sons, Notabilities, 1915, No. 5)

**Fig. 45e. Herbert Asquith** (Henry Welfare & Co., Prominent Politicians, c. 1911)

**Fig. 46a. Andrew Bonar Law** (Henry Welfare & Co., Prominent Politicians, c. 1911)

**Fig. 47a. David Lloyd George** (Godfrey Phillips, Personalities of Today, 1927, No. 10)

**Fig. 46b. Andrew Bonar Law**
(Phillips, Great War Leaders II, 1915)

**Fig. 47b. David Lloyd George**
(Hill, Great War Leaders, 1919, No. 6)

**Fig. 47c. David Lloyd George**
(B.A.T., War Leaders and Scenes, 1916)

**Fig. 47d. David Lloyd George**
(Henry Welfare & Co., Prominent Politicians, c1911)

**Fig. 48. Horatio Herbert Kitchener**
(Cereal Food, Famous People and Places, 1949, No. 22)

**Fig. 49a. Horatio Herbert Kitchener**
(Singleton and Cole, Famous Officers, 1915, No. 1)

**Fig. 49b. Kitchener, reverse side**
(Singleton and Cole, Famous Officers, 1915, No. 1)

Kitchener, the Secretary of State for War, is variously titled in different cards depending on when they were issued. Thus he is known as Earl Kitchener of Khartoum, Field Marshal Earl Kitchener, F-M Lord Kitchener or Lord Kitchener (Figs. 48, 49a, 49b, 50a, 50b, 51). Kitchener first came to prominence when he won the Battle of Omdurman in 1898 (Fig. 52). During the Anglo-Boer War he was chief of staff (Fig. 53a) to Lord Roberts (Fig. 53b). Asquith appointed him as the Secretary of State for War. He ran the war until his death in 1916 when the *HMS Hampshire*, on which he was a passenger on a mission to Russia, was sunk by a mine in the Atlantic Ocean.

**Fig. 50a. Horatio Herbert Kitchener**
(Hill, Great War Leaders, 1919, No. 3)

LORD KITCHENER

**Fig. 50b. Horatio Herbert Kitchener**
(Phillips, Great War Leaders &
Celebrities, anonymous)

Field-Marshal EARL KITCHENER.
Copyright.

**Fig. 51. Horatio Herbert Kitchener**
(Anonymous Tobacco, Set M1, 1915)

Gen-Kitchener

**Fig. 53a. Horatio Herbert Kitchener**
(Churchman, Boer War Generals
(CLAM), (black front), c1901)

**Fig. 53b. Frederick Roberts**
(Ogden's Guinea Golds, Set 71-S,
No. 100)

In 1911 Winston Churchill, then only thirty-seven years old, was appointed First Lord of the Admiralty (Figs. 54a, 54b, 54c, 54d). He had already held political office and cabinet positions, first in the Conservative party and then in the Liberal Party. In this position he, together with Lord Fisher, had the British Navy well-prepared for the war. Churchill had been a guest of the Kaiser several years earlier and watched German troop maneuvers with him (Figs. 55a, 55b).

**Fig. 52. Horatio Herbert Kitchener**
(John Player, The Sirdar Lord Kitchener of Khartoum, c. 1898)

**Fig. 54a. Winston Churchill**
(A. and B.C., Winston Churchill, 1965, No. 11)

**Fig. 54b. Winston Churchill**
(A. and B.C., Winston Churchill, 1965, No. 13)

**Fig. 54c. Winston Churchill**
(Westminster Tobacco, the Great War Celebrities, 1914, No. 4)

**Fig. 54d. Winston Churchill**
(Lever Bros., Celebrities [Black Border], 1905)

**Fig. 55a. Churchill and Kaiser**
(A. and B.C., Winston Churchill, 1965, No. 4)

**Fig. 55b. Churchill and Kaiser, reverse side**
(A. and B.C., Winston Churchill, 1965, No. 4)

**Fig. 56. Arthur Balfour**
(Great War Leaders II (anonymous), 1915)

**Fig. 57. Sir Edward Carson**
(Phillips, Great War Leaders and Celebrities, 1915)

After Churchill left the cabinet in 1915, following Gallipoli, Arthur Balfour (Fig. 56) took over the position of First Lord of the Admiralty in the new coalition government. He held this position for only one year when Sir Edward Carson (Fig. 57) was appointed to replace him.

With Britain's declaration of war, all dominions of the British Empire were automatically involved in the war. They were called upon to fight by Britain's side. They had no choice. At the outset of the war Joseph Cook briefly served as Prime Minister of Australia. Shortly thereafter Andrew Fisher (Fig. 58) became the country's leader. He was followed by W. M. Hughes (Fig. 59). In South Africa Louis Botha (Figs. 60, 61) became prime minister when the union was formed in 1910.

During the war he commanded the South West African campaign. Botha first came to the forefront during the Anglo-Boer War when he led the effective guerilla campaign against Britain (Fig. 62). Together with General Jan Christian Smuts (Figs. 63a, 63b), his Minister of Defense, he attended the Paris Peace Conference. Canada was an active participant in the War. Her prime minister at the time was the Rt. Hon. Sir Robert Laird Borden (Figs. 64a, 64b).

**Fig. 58.  Andrew Fisher**
(B.A.T., War Leaders and
Scenes, 1916)

**Fig. 59.  W. M. Hughes**
(Phillips, Great War Leaders II, Extra Large Size,
1916)

**Fig. 60.  Louis Botha**
(Colton, War Series, 1916,
No. 26,)

**Fig. 61.  Louis Botha**
(Wix, Builders of the Empire, 1937,
No. 20)

**Fig. 62.  Louis Botha**
(Taddy, Boer War Leaders,
1901, No. 10)

**Fig. 63a.  Jan Christian
Smuts**
(Wills, Allied Army Leaders,
1917, No. 27)

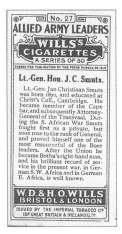

**Fig. 63b.  Smuts, reverse side**
(Wills, Allied Army Leaders,
1917, No. 27)

**Fig. 64a.  Sir Robert Laird
Borden**
(B.A.T., War Leaders and
Scenes, 1916)

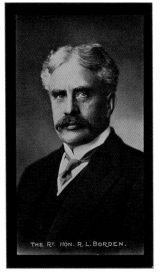

**Fig. 64b.  Sir Robert Laird Borden**
(Major Drapkin, Celebrities of the Great
War, 1916)

France, the primary country to be attacked by Germany, and Britain's major ally, had not had a monarch since the death of Napoleon III in 1870 when the Third Republic was formed. In the years preceding the war, Theophile Delcasse (Fig. 65), as France's Foreign Minister, was noted for his strongly anti-German feelings. He was responsible for adhering closely to the alliance with Russia, for improving relations between France and Italy, and for concluding the Entente Cordiale with Great Britain. At the onset of the war Raymond Poincaré was the President of the French Republic (Figs. 66a, 66b, 66c). An interesting comment on the descriptive back of the sample card in the Lea set indicates that "This series of War Portraits is produced in an emergency, as deliveries of the regular series cannot be obtained." The descriptive back of the card with his portrait from the Major Drapkin set of Celebrities of the War describes Poincaré as "…the strong man of France. He is very tactful and a clear and eloquent speaker. At the age of 27 he was elected a Deputy." He remained president throughout the war. He was largely responsible for the increase in military spending in the few years prior to the War and investing in chief of the General Staff Joseph Joffre's offensive deployment plan.

**Fig. 65. Theophile Delcasse**
(B.A.T., War Leaders and Scenes, 1916)

**Fig. 66a. Raymond Poincaré**
(Lea, War Portraits, 1915, No.7)

**Fig. 66c. Raymond Poincaré**
(Muratti, Great War Leaders, Series P, 1916)

**Fig. 66b. Raymond Poincaré**
(Phillips, Great War Leaders and Celebrities IV, Extra Large Size, 1916)

Algerian born Rene Viviani (Fig. 67) was the prime minister at the onset of the war. After Viviani, Georges Clemenceau (Figs. 68a, 68b) became the Prime Minister of France. The back of the card includes his nickname "The Tiger" for his determination as a war leader. The description also states that he was the President of the Paris Peace Conference where the Treaty of Versailles was signed. Paul Cambon (Fig. 69) was the French Ambassador to England. He was instrumental in laying the groundwork for the Entente Cordiale. Alexander Millerand (Figs. 70a, 70b) was appointed French War Minister at the outbreak of War. The reverse side of the card indicates he had served in multiple cabinet positions before his wartime appointment.

**Fig. 67. Rene Viviani**
(The Picture House, War Series, 1916, No. 33)

**Fig. 68a. Georges Clemenceau**
(Hill, Great War Leaders, 1919, No. 8)

**Fig. 68b. Clemenceau, reverse side**
(Hill, Great War Leaders, 1919, No. 8)

**Fig. 69. Paul Cambon**
(Parodi, War Series, 1916, No. 50)

**Fig. 70a. Alexander Millerand**
(Hignett, Military Portraits, 1914, no. 18)

**Fig. 70b. Alexander Millerand**
(Wills [Scissors], Military Portraits, 1917, No.18)

Russia was essentially an autocracy with an emasculated Duma (Russian Parliament). She was ill-prepared for war in 1914 and after reversals in Galicia more civilians were brought into the administration of the war, including in the Duma. During war the Russian premier was Goremykin (Fig. 71). Sazanoff (Fig. 72) was the War Minister. The Duma, however, remained ineffective.

Eleftherios Venizelos (1864–1936) (Fig. 73), the charismatic Greek leader, was responsible for the creation of the modern Greek state. He opposed Greece's neutrality at the onset of the war, but ultimately managed to bring her into the war on the side of the Allies.

Although the United States only entered the war in 1917, President Wilson (Figs. 74a, 74b) played a significant role at the Peace Conference. He enthusiastically promoted the idea of the formation of the League of Nations, the precursor to the United Nations formed after the Second World War.

**Fig. 71.  M. Goremkyn**
(B.A.T., War Leaders and Scenes, 1916)

**Fig. 72.  M. Sazanoff**
(A. Parodi, War Portraits, 1916, No. 16)

**Fig. 74a.  President Woodrow Wilson**
(Phillips, Great War Leaders and Celebrities IV, 1916)

**Fig. 73.  Eleftherios Venizelos**
(Muratti, Great War Leaders, 1916)

**Fig. 74b.  President Woodrow Wilson**
(John Scerri (Malta), Prominent People, 1930, No. 73)

# CHAPTER 7

# MILITARY, NAVAL and AVIATION LEADERS

## Military Leaders

War leaders are extensively covered in all the card sets. Although they are too numerous to list and describe aspects of all of them, most of the important ones will be briefly mentioned. Some of those shown played a more important role than others. Many of the military leaders of the various subdivisions of the British Army first established their reputations in the earlier Anglo-Boer War of 1899 to 1902. A review of the card sets from this war will show a number of the same faces as in the First World War card sets. Some of the card illustrations from this earlier war will be included.

Fig. 75a. Richard Haldane
(B.A.T., Notabilities, 1917, No. 17)

Fig. 75b. Haldane, reverse side
(B.A.T., Notabilities, 1917, No. 17)

Fig. 76. Henry Campbell-Bannerman
(Carreras, British Prime Ministers, 1928, No. 21)

### BRITAIN

A brief review of the organizational structure of the British Army is helpful in understanding the role played by the military leaders. At the onset of the war the British Expeditionary Force (BEF), made up of volunteers, consisted of those forces that were sent to France. This type of force was originally conceived after the Anglo-Boer War. Richard Haldane originally carried out the planning for the BEF (Figs. 75a, 75b). He was appointed Secretary of State for War in 1906 after the Liberals, under Henry Campbell-Bannerman (Fig. 76), came to power. He implemented wide-ranging reforms of the army. The BEF was the main element of these reforms. Initially it consisted of six infantry divisions and five cavalry brigades.

The infantry were divided into several corps. I Corps consisted of First and Second Divisions. These contained infantry brigades, mounted troops, artillery and engineers. Included in the Second Division was a brigade of the Kings Guard of Regiments. II Corps consisted of the Third and Fifth Divisions, similarly made up as the other two. III Corps was made up of the Fourth and Sixth Divisions. In October 1914 the 7th Infantry Division came to France.

The First through Fourth Cavalry Brigades were initially grouped together to form a division, but in September the Third and the newly added Fifth Brigades were separately formed into the Second Cavalry Division. By the end of the First Battle of Ypres in November of 1914 the original BEF, after having successfully halted the German advance, was essentially eliminated.

Over the course of the war the original BEF changed from its initial six divisions to include the entire forces of the British Empire. This necessitated a reorganization of the British Army with the creation of a number of Armies. In December 1914 the First and Second Armies were formed. In July 1915 the Third Army was formed, followed by the Fourth Army in February 1916 and the Fifth Army in May 1916.

At the supreme organizational level was the General Headquarters where Field Marshal Sir John French (Figs. 77a, 77b, 77c, 77d, 77e) was appointed as Commander-in-Chief of the original BEF. He was also a hero of the Anglo-Boer War where he led the relief of the Siege of Kimberley (Figs. 78a, 78b). He was ultimately made the First Earl of Ypres in 1922. His Chief of Staff was Lieutenant-General Sir A. J. Murray (Fig. 79). Many of the senior officers he appointed were also his colleagues during the Anglo-Boer War, where they had been cavalrymen and Sandhurst graduates, and lesser rank officers then. Many of them died in this war.

**Fig. 77a. John French**
(Singelton & Cole, Famous Officers, 1915, No. 2)

**Fig. 77b. John French**
(B.A.T., War Leaders and Scenes, 1916)

**Fig. 77c. John French**
(Maypole, War Series, 1915, No. 8)

**Fig. 77d. John French**
(Ardath, Great War Series, first, 1916)

**Fig. 77e. John French**
(Prudhoe, Army Pictures, Cartoons etc., 1916)

**Fig. 78a. John French**
(Salmon and Gluckstein, Heroes of the Transvaal War, 1901)

**Fig. 78b. John French**
(Richard Lloyd, Boer War Celebrities, 1901)

**Fig. 79. Lt.-Gen. Sir A. J. Murray**
(Wills, Allied Army Leaders, 1917, No. 20)

Lieutenant-General Sir Douglas Haig commanded the First Army (Figs. 80, 81a, 81b, 81c). In December of 1915 he replaced French as the Commander-in-Chief. He too fought in the Anglo-Boer War. In 1917 he was promoted to Field Marshal (Figs. 82a, 82b, 82c). He remained in this position throughout the War. Although for many decades he was praised as a leader, later historians blamed him for the excessive loss of life during the various battles.

**Fig. 80. Douglas Haig**
(Westminster Tobacco, The Great War Celebrities, 1914, No. 27)

**Fig. 81a. Douglas Haig**
(B.A.T., Britain's Defenders, 1914, No. 17)

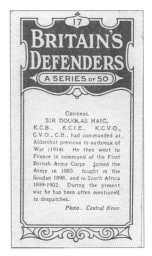

**Fig. 81b. Haig, reverse side**
(B.A.T., Britain's Defenders, 1914, No. 17)

**Fig. 81c. Douglas Haig**
(B.A.T., War Leaders and Scenes, 1916)

**Fig. 82a. Douglas Haig**
(John Player, Straight Line Caricatures, 1926, No. 26)

**Fig. 82b. Douglas Haig**
(Wills, Allied Army Leaders, 1917, No. 18;)

**Fig. 82c. Haig, reverse side**
(Wills, Allied Army Leaders, 1917, No. 18;)

Sir Horace Smith-Dorrien commanded the Second Army (Figs. 83a, 83b). He was one of French's colleagues during the Anglo-Boer War. In 1915 he was succeeded by Lieut.-Gen Sir Herbert Plumer (Fig. 84), another leader in the Anglo-Boer War (Figs. 85, 86). He remained in this position until 1917. It is of cartophilic interest that both the Hignett and the B.A.T. sets of Military Portraits, issued three years apart, have the identical subject matter in the same order but with updated photographs. Similarly the Wills (Scissors) issue of 1917 has the same photographs. Of further interest is that the latter two sets have printed above the front of the card "Passed for Publication by the Press Bureau, London, 11/1/17" (e.g., Fig. 84).

**Fig. 83a. General Sir Horace Smith-Dorrien**
(Singleton and Cole, Famous Officers, 1915, No. 6)

**Fig. 83b. General Sir Horace Smith-Dorrien**
(Hignett Bros., Military Portraits, 1914, No. 10)

Fig. 84. Lt.-Gen. Sir Herbert Plumer
(B.A.T., Military Portraits, 1917, No. 8)

Fig. 85. Lt.-Col. Plumer
(J.F. Sporting Collectibles, Boer War Officers, 2008, No. 8)

Fig. 86. Lt.-Col. Plumer
(Gallaher, The South African Series, 1901, No. 153)

Fig. 87. Sir Charles Monro
(Wills, Allied Army Leaders, No. 19)

Fig. 88. Ian Hamilton
(Parodi, War Portraits, 1916, No. 6)

Sir Charles Monro commanded the Third Army (Fig. 87). This followed his stint in Gallipoli where he took over from Sir Ian Hamilton (Fig. 88), another of French's contemporaries of the Anglo-Boer War (Figs. 89a, 89b). In 1915 he was appointed by Kitchener to command the Mediterranean Expeditionary Force. In this capacity he was responsible for the Dardanelles and hence the Gallipoli campaign. Under him was General Birdwood (Fig. 90), who was responsible for the Australian and New Zealand troops in the Dardanelles.

Fig. 89a. Ian Hamilton
(Goodbody, Boer War Celebrities [CAG], 1900)

Fig. 89b. Hamilton, reverse side
(Goodbody, Boer War Celebrities [CAG], 1900)

Fig. 90. General Birdwood
(Hill, Great War Leaders, 1919, No. 19)

**Fig. 91a. Edmund Allenby**
Pattreiouex, Builders of the
Empire, 1929, No. 48)

**Fig. 91b. Allenby, reverse
side**
Pattreiouex, Builders of the
Empire, 1929, No. 48)

**Fig. 91c. Edmund Allenby**
(Hill, Great War Leaders, 1919, No. 11)

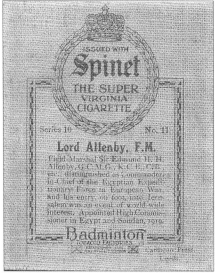

**Fig. 91d. Allenby, reverse side**
(Hill, Great War Leaders, 1919, No. 11)

**Fig. 91e. Edmund Allenby**
(Major Drapkin, Celebrities of the
Great War, 1916)

**Fig. 92. Sir Henry
Rawlinson**
(Wills, Allied Army Leaders,
1917, No. 23)

Hamilton was succeeded by Field Marshal Sir Edmund Allenby (Figs. 91a, 91b, 91c, 91d, 91e) to lead the Third Army. He held this position until 1917 when he was placed in charge of the Egyptian/Palestine Army. It was in this latter role that he achieved his greatest victory over the Turkish Army, conquering Jerusalem in 1917.

In the latter part of the war General Sir Henry Rawlinson led both the Fourth and Fifth Armies (Fig. 92). Brigadier-General Gough had led these armies prior to his taking command of the Fifth Army in October 1916 (Fig. 93).

**Fig. 93. Brigadier-General Gough**
(Phillips, Great War Leaders and Celebrities, B.D.V. Extra-Large Size, 1916)

Field Marshal the Earl Roberts (Figs. 94a, 94b, 94c) was placed in command of the Colonial Volunteer Forces. As the description on the back of the Morris Celebrities series correctly states, his illustrious military career began in the Indian Mutiny of 1857, where he won the Victoria Cross (Fig. 95). This card describes how he was "Awarded the VC for capturing a Standard from two rebel sepoys during the Indian Mutiny 1857." He went on to distinguish himself in the Second Anglo-Afghan War where he relieved Kandahar at the Battle of Kandahar. He then went on to command the British forces in the Second Anglo-Boer War until Kitchener succeeded him (Fig. 96). He died of pneumonia in France in November 1914 while visiting the Indian troops.

Fig. 94a. Frederick Roberts
(Phillips, Great War Leaders II, 1915)

Fig. 94b. Frederick Roberts
(Colton, War Portraits, 1916, No. 10)

Fig. 94c. Frederick Roberts
(Cohen Weenen, Silhouettes of Celebrities, 1905)

Fig. 95. Frederick Roberts
(Taddy, Victoria Cross Heroes - Boer War, 1902, No. 41)

Fig. 96. Frederick Roberts
(Gallaher, The South African Series, 1901, No. 101)

## FRANCE

Unlike the initial BEF, the French Army was made up of conscripts. In 1914 it consisted of ten armies, each of which had several commanders throughout the course of the war. The military leader commanding all of these armies was the Commander-in-Chief. There were three such leaders throughout the course of the war. At the start of the war in 1914 it was Marshal Joseph Joffre (Figs. 97a, 97b, 97c, 97d, 98). He was considered a great organizer. After the First Battle of the Marne in September 1914 he was successful in halting the month-long German offensive. However, following at first the tremendous losses at Verdun in 1916, and then also those from the Somme offensive in the latter part of that year, he was replaced by General Georges Nivelle (Fig. 99) in December 1916. He held this position until late 1917. As a result of the widespread mutinies in the French Army following the disastrous Second Battle of the Aisne, which was a part of the Nivelle Offensive, Philippe Pétain replaced him (Figs. 100a, 100b). While still a general, he commanded the vastly outnumbered French army during the long-lasting Battle of Verdun in 1916.

Fig. 97a. Joseph Joffre
(Lea, Chairman's War Portraits, 1915, No.19)

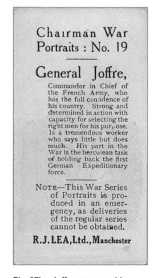

Fig. 97b. Joffre, reverse side
(Lea, Chairman's War Portraits, 1915, No.19)

**Fig. 97c. Joseph Joffre**
(Phillips, Great War Leaders
and Celebrities II, 1916)

GENERAL JOFFRE

**Fig. 97d. Joseph Joffre**
(The Picture House, War
Portraits, 1916, No. 18;
Pascal, War Portraits, 1920)

**Fig. 98. Joseph Joffre**
(Ardath, Great War Series,
No. 2, 1916)

**Fig. 99. General Georges
Nivelle**
(Wills, Allied Army Leaders,
1917, No. 8)

**Fig. 100a. General Philippe
Pétain**
(Wills, Allied Army Leaders,
1917, No. 11)

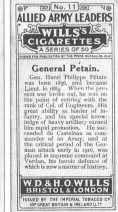

**Fig. 100b. Pétain, reverse
side**
(Wills, Allied Army Leaders,
1917, No. 11)

Joffre's Chief-of-Staff at the outset of the war was General Ferdinand Foch (Fig. 101). Late in the war Pétain, who was then the Commander-in-chief, appointed him as the Chief of the General Staff. It was in this capacity that he successfully halted the German advance on Paris during the Second Battle of the Marne in the spring of 1918. General Paul Pau (Fig. 102), at the age of seventy, was recalled from retirement by Marshal Joffre to lead the "Army of Alsace," a part of the French plan to defeat the Germans. However, after his defeat, Joffre disbanded his army. General Joseph Gallieni (Figs. 103a, 103b, 103c) was recalled from retirement and appointed Military Governor of Paris to defend the city before the First Battle of the Marne. He then went on to become Minister of War before retiring again in 1916.

**Fig. 101. General Ferdinand Foch**
(Singleton and Cole, Famous Officers, 1915, No. 17)

**Fig. 102. General Paul Pau**
(The Canterbury Electric Theatre, War Portraits, 1916, No. 48)

**Fig. 103a. General Joseph Gallieni**
(Hignett, Military Portraits, 1917, No. 17)

**Fig. 103b. General Joseph Gallieni**
(Singleton and Cole, Famous Officers, 1915, No. 20)

**Fig. 103c. General Joseph Gallieni**
(B.A.T., Military Portraits, 1917, No. 17)

General Albert D'Amade (Figs. 104a, 104b, 104c) was in command of forces to oppose the original German offensive. Later he commanded the French forces in the Dardanelles Campaign during the landing in April 1915 and with the trench warfare that followed this. Other French army leaders illustrated on cards were Generals Mangin, Roques and Sarrail. The former is on the Hill's card, and all are illustrated and described in the Wills Allied Army Leaders set (Figs. 105, 106a, 106b).

**Fig. 104a. General Albert D'Amade**
(Picture House Harrogate, War Portraits, 1916, No. 39)

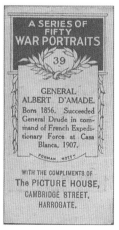

**Fig. 104b. D'Amade, reverse side**
(Picture House, War Portraits, 1916, No. 39)

**Fig. 104c. General Albert D'Amade**
(Prince's Hall, War Portraits, 1916, No. 39)

**Fig. 105. General Maurice Sarrail**
(Hill, Great War Leaders, 1919, No. 21)

**Fig. 106a. Generals Mangin, Roques, Sarrail**
(Wills, Allied Army Leaders, 1917, Nos. 7, 9 and 10)

**Fig. 106b. Mangin, Roques, Sarrail, reverse side**
(Wills, Allied Army Leaders, 1917, Nos. 7, 9 and 10)

## RUSSIA

The Commander-in-Chief of the Russian forces was the Grand Duke Nicholas (Figs. 107a, 107b, 107c, 107d). The Grand Duke placed onto the battlefield twelve Russian armies. Kitchener described him as "not only a great military leader, but a great man" (Fig. 108). General Paul von Rennenkampf (Figs. 109a, 109b) was commander of the First Army for the invasion of East Prussia. He had a few successes but more failures, and was then forced to resign in October 1915. He was executed by the Bolsheviks in 1918. The B.A.T. card once again indicates above the illustration that this set was "Passed for Publication by the Press Bureau, London, 11/1/17."

**Fig. 107a. The Grand Duke Nicholas**
(Murray and Sons, War Series, series K, 1915)

**Fig. 107b. The Grand Duke Nicholas**
(Singleton and Cole, Famous Officers, 1915, No. 9)

**Fig. 108. The Grand Duke Nicholas**
(Major Drapkin, Celebrities of the Great War, 1916)

Fig. 107c. The Grand Duke Nicholas
(Hignett, Military Portraits, 1914, No. 19)

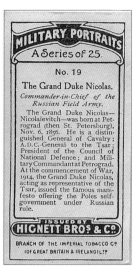

Fig. 107d. The Grand Duke Nicholas, reverse side
(Hignett, Military Portraits, 1914, No. 19)

Fig. 109a. General Paul von Rennenkampf
(B.A.T., Military Portraits, 1917, No. 20)

Fig. 109b. General Paul von Rennenkampf
(Singleton and Cole, Famous Officers, 1915, No. 19)

General Nicolai Russky (Figs. 110a, 110b) was the commander of the Third Army in 1914. He achieved great popularity after successfully entering Lvov (Lemberg). He too was most likely murdered by the Bolsheviks. One of the most successful Russian generals in the early part of the war was General Ivanoff (Fig. 111). The reverse side of the card describes how he "…commanded the Russian Armies operating in Russian Poland, 1914. It was, however, the brilliant campaign culminating in the capture of Przemysl, March 21, 1915, with about 120,000 officers and men, which brought Ivanoff into prominence. For that he received from the Tsar the Order of St George."

Fig. 110a. General Nikolai Russky
(Cohen Weenan, War Series – Leaders of the War, 1915, No. 32)

Fig. 110b. General Nikolai Russky
(Singleton and Cole, Famous Officers, 1915, No. 22)

Fig. 111. General Ivanoff
(Wills, Allied Army Leaders 1917, No. 44)

General Radko Dimitrieff (Fig. 112) followed General Russky in 1915 in commanding the Third Army. General Brusiloff (Fig. 113a, 113b) commanded the army operating in Galicia in 1914. He planned the famous and highly successful Brusiloff Offensive against Austria-Hungary in June 1916. This card also has on the reverse side that it was "Passed for Publication by the Press Bureau, 28.12.16."

**Fig. 112. General Radko Dimitrieff**
(Wills, Allied Army Leaders 1917, 2000 Reprint, No. 43.)

**Fig. 113a. General Alexey Brusiloff**
(Wills, Allied Army Leaders, 1917, No. 41)

**Fig. 113b. Brusiloff, reverse side**
(Wills, Allied Army Leaders, 1917, No. 41)

**Fig. 114. H.R.H. Prince Alexander of Serbia**
(Wills, Allied Army Leaders, 1917, No. 49)

## SERBIA

The back of the Wills card describes His Royal Highness, Prince Alexander, the Crown Prince of Serbia (Fig. 114) and second son of King Peter. It indicates that when Serbia mobilized against Austria in July 1914 he took supreme command. Further description indicates how during the "disastrous retreat over the mountains in November 1915, he went on foot like the humblest of his men, and shared in their hardships."

**Fig. 115a. General Baron Wahis**
(Home and Colonial Stores, War Pictures, 1915)

**Fig. 115b. Wahis, reverse side**
(Home and Colonial Stores, War Pictures, 1915)

**Fig. 116. General Mathieu Leman**
(Colton, War Portraits, 1916, No. 10)

## BELGIUM

General Baron Wahis was the Belgian Commander-in-Chief (Figs. 115a, 115b, 115c). General Mathieu Leman is described in Colton's War Portraits (Fig. 116) as "the Belgian general who made history by his heroic defence of Liege, 1914." This was at the time when the Germans invaded Belgium on their way to France at the onset of the war. He is also illustrated on Bewlay and Co.'s War Series (Figs. 117a, 117b)

Fig. 115c. General Baron Wahis
(Phillips, War Pictures, 1915, No. 8)

Fig. 117a. General Mathieu Leman
(Bewlay and Co. War Series, 1915,
No. 4)

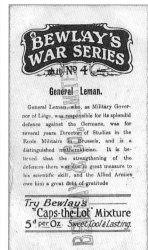

Fig. 117b. Leman, reverse side
(Bewlay and Co. War Series, 1915,
No. 4)

## ITALY

When Italy declared war in 1915 the Commander-in-Chief was General Count Luigi Cadorno (Figs. 118a, 118b).

There are many other officers of Britain and the Allies who have not been mentioned here, but who are illustrated and described in the many sets. They held various leadership positions in subdivisions of the various armies. The descriptive backs of all these cards give brief biographical histories of the individuals and, in keeping with the patriotic fervor demonstrated in all these descriptions, speak of their military skills in glowing terms, even though some of them had less than stellar performances during the war.

Fig. 118a. General Count Luigi Cadorno
(Phillips, Great War Leaders II, 1915)

Fig. 118b. General Count Luigi
Cadorno
(Wills, Allied Army Leaders 1917,
2000 Reprint, No. 32)

 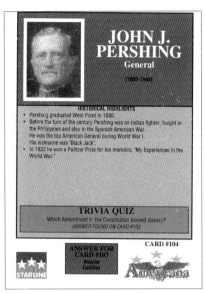

## UNITED STATES OF AMERICA

When the United States entered the war on the side of the Allies in 1917, General John Pershing (Figs. 119a, 119b) was in command of the United States forces.

**Fig. 119a. General John J. Pershing**
(Starline USA, Americana, 1992, No. 104)

**Fig. 119b. Pershing (reverse side)**
(Starline USA, Americana, 1992, No. 104)

**Fig. 120a. Archduke Frederick of Austria**
(Hignett, Military Portraits, 1914, No. 23)

**Fig. 120b. Gen. Hoetzendorff**
(Hignett, Military Portraits, 1914, No. 24)

**Fig. 120c. F.M. Lt. Wenzel Wurm**
(Hignett, Military Portraits, 1914, No. 25)

**Fig. 121. General von Falkenhayn**
(Brasella, German Heroes & Leaders of the World War, No. 49)

## CENTRAL POWERS

Among the Austrian Army leadership shown on cards are the Archduke Frederick (Fig. 120a), General Baron von Hoetzendorff (Fig. 120b), and Field Marshal Wenzel Wurm (Fig. 120c), all on Hignett's Military Portraits. A German cigarette set by Brasella titled German Heroes of the World War has a portrait of General von Falkenhayn (Fig. 121).

# Naval Leaders

For Britain, the Royal Navy was the major offensive and defensive division of the armed forces. Under good political and naval leadership, it was well-prepared for combat in August 1914. This pride in the Navy was manifested at the cartophilic level by the issuing of a number of card sets dedicated specifically or predominantly to naval leadership and vessels. One set was dedicated only to Admirals. It is mainly from these sets that the various naval leaders and, in the later section the warships, will be referenced. However, many more naval leaders are included in these sets than can be described. They include leaders who were at the organizational and administrative level as well as those who commanded fleets or individual warships.

Before describing the various leaders, it is worthwhile to briefly outline the organizational structure of the Admiralty, since many of the leaders shown on cards filled these various positions. The mission of the Admiralty was to command the Royal Navy. The governing body was the Board of Admiralty. There was the office of the Lord High Admiral that was exercised by a Board of Admiralty. This consisted of a number of Lords Commissioners known otherwise as Naval Lords or Sea Lords, and Civil Lords, who were usually politicians. The president of this Board was the First Lord of the Admiralty, who also was a member of the British cabinet. These Lord Commissioners commanded the Royal Navy. There were five Sea Lords. They had responsibility for naval staff, personnel, shipbuilding and maintenance, supplies, and in the twentieth century for naval air services.

**Fig. 122a. Lord Fisher**
(Taddy, Admirals and Generals – The War, c. 1915)

**Fig. 122b. Fisher, reverse side**
(Taddy, Admirals and Generals – The War, c. 1915)

**Fig. 122c. Lord Fisher**
(Maypole, War Series, 1959, No.1)

**Fig. 122d. Fisher, reverse side**
(Maypole, War Series, 1959, No.1)

**Fig. 122e. Lord Fisher**
(Cope, British Admirals, 1915, No. 23)

Lord Fisher of Kilverstone (Figs. 122a, 122b, 122c, 122d, 122e) had an illustrious naval career. From 1904 to 1910 he was First Sea Lord of the Admiralty. He was known as a reformist and is perhaps the most important naval figure after Lord Nelson.

On October 30, 1914, Fisher was re-appointed to that position, following the resignation of Prince Louis of Battenberg (Figs. 123a, 123b). In the Murray and Sons War Series, series K, 1915 set, the Prince is described as "The Kitchener of the Navy." He was a German Prince related to the British Royal Family who had an illustrious career of over forty years in the British Royal Navy. He was forced to resign his position at the onset of the war because of strong public anti-German feeling. The family subsequently changed its name to Mountbatten. In his role as First Sea Lord, Fisher worked closely with Winston Churchill, then the First Lord of the Admiralty (Fig. 124a, 124b, 124c), but the two strong personalities often fought bitterly. He eventually resigned in 1915 as a result of the failure of the Gallipoli Campaign.

**Fig. 123a. Prince Louis of Battenberg**
(Lambert and Butler, Naval Portraits, 1915, No. 11)

**Fig. 123b. Battenberg, reverse side**
(Lambert and Butler, Naval Portraits, 1915, No. 11)

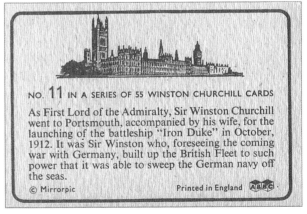

**Fig. 124c. Churchill, reverse side**
(A&BC, Winston Churchill, 1965, No. 11)

**Fig. 124a. Winston Churchill**
(Major Drapkin, Celebrities of the Great War, 1916)

**Fig. 124b. Winston Churchill**
(A&BC, Winston Churchill, 1965, No. 11)

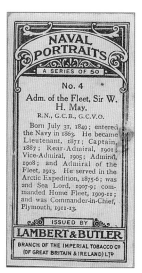

**Fig. 125a. Sir William Henry May**
(Lambert & Butler, Naval Portraits, 1914, No. 4)

**Fig. 125b. May, reverse side**
(Lambert & Butler, Naval Portraits, 1914, No. 4)

**Fig. 125c. Sir William Henry May**
(Phillips, British Admirals [anonymous issue], 1915)

Sir William Henry May (Figs. 125a, 125b, 125c) was appointed Admiral of the Fleet in 1913, the highest rank in the British Royal Navy. Prior to this he had served as the Commander-in-Chief, Plymouth from 1911. During his entire career he never saw any active service during any war.

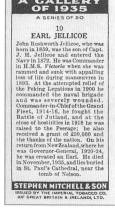

**Fig. 126. Sir George Callahan**
(Lea, War Portraits, 1915, No. 23)

**Fig. 127a. Admiral John Jellicoe**
(Phillips, Real Photo Series – Admirals and Generals of the Great War, 1916)

**Fig. 127b. Admiral John Jellicoe**
(John Player, Straight Line Caricatures, 1926, No. 30)

**Fig. 128a. Admiral John Jellicoe**
(Stephen Mitchell and Son, A Gallery of 1935, 1936, No. 10)

**Fig. 128b. Jellicoe, reverse side**
(Stephen Mitchell and Son, A Gallery of 1935, 1936, No. 10)

Until the onset of the war, Admiral Sir George Callaghan (Fig. 126) was Commander of the Home Fleet. In August 1914, he was succeeded by one of the most well-known Admirals of the Fleet, John Jellicoe, the First Earl of Jellicoe (Figs. 127a, 127b, 128a, 128b). At the outbreak of war Jellicoe was Commander-in-Chief of the Home Fleets. In this capacity he was the supreme commander in the North Sea. As Admiral of the Fleet, he is best remembered today for his command of the Grand Fleet during the famous Battle of Jutland in June 1916. It was fought in the North Sea near Jutland against the German High Seas Fleet, the enemy's main fleet. His leadership role and the outcome of that battle has remained a controversial issue. Winston Churchill, when writing about the war in his multi-volume set *The World Crisis*, stated "Jellicoe was the only man on either side who could lose the war in an afternoon."

Equally well-known, but with less of a controversial career, was Admiral Sir David Beatty (Figs. 129, 130a, 130b, 130c). He had a dramatic rise in the navy. He served as Winston Churchill's Naval Secretary from 1911 to 1913 and then was appointed as Commander of the Battle Cruiser Squadron of the Grand Fleet at the outbreak of war. In this capacity he had early and dramatic successes at Heligoland Bight. This was followed up by another success at Dogger Bank in early 1915 against the German Admiral Hipper and his vessel *Blucher*. However, like Jellicoe, but for different reasons, his name is most associated with the Battle of Jutland. At the onset of the battle he vigorously attacked the German Grand Fleet, where he both inflicted and suffered significant losses until the arrival of the British Grand Fleet. Jellicoe was subsequently removed from his position as Admiral of the Fleet and moved to First Sea Lord. The dashing Beatty was seen as a natural successor. It was Beatty who accepted the surrender of the German High Fleet in November 1918. In 1919 he was honored by being made an Earl.

**Fig. 129. Admiral Sir David Beatty**
(Phillips, Real Photo Series – Admirals and Generals of the Great War, 1916)

**Fig. 130a. Admiral Sir David Beatty**
(B.A.T., Naval Portraits, 1917, No. 9; Cope, British Admirals, 1915, No. 12)

**Fig. 130b. Beatty, reverse side**
(B.A.T., Naval Portraits, 1917, No. 9)

**Fig. 130c. Admiral Sir David Beatty**
(Cope, British Admirals, 1915, No. 12)

Admiral Tyrwhitt (Figs. 131a, 131b, 131c) also fought in the Battle of Heligoland Bight. Tyrwhitt's role in this battle and that of his armored cruiser *Arethusa* are well described on the back of the card. Commander R. J. B. Keyes (Figs. 132a, 132b) commanded the submarine flotilla at this battle. He was also involved in the Dardanelles or Gallipoli Campaign. Commodore W. E. Goodenough (Fig. 133) commanded the *HMS Southampton* that also took part in the Heligoland raid.

**Fig. 131a. Admiral R. Y. Tyrwhitt**
(Lambert and Butler, Naval Portraits, 1915, No. 37)

**Fig. 131b. Tyrwhitt, reverse side**
(Lambert and Butler, Naval Portraits, 1915, No. 37)

**Fig. 131c. Admiral R. Y. Tyrwhitt**
(Sniders and Abrahams, Great War Leaders and Warships, 1915)

**Fig. 132a. Commander R. J. B. Keyes**
(Sniders and Abrahams, Great War Leaders and Warships, 1917)

**Fig. 132b. Keyes, reverse side**
(Sniders and Abrahams, Great War Leaders and Warships, 1917)

**Fig. 133. Commodore W. E. Goodenough**
(Wills [scissors], Britain's Defenders, 1914, No. 8)

**Fig. 134. Admiral A. G. H. W. Moore**
(Cope, British Admirals, 1915, No. 2)

**Fig. 135. Vice-Admiral Somerset Gough-Calthorpe**
(Lambert and Butler, Naval Portraits, 1915, No. 7)

Admiral A. G. H. W. Moore (Fig. 134) was a Lord Commissioner of the Admiralty. He was appointed to this position in 1912. Vice-Admiral Somerset Gough-Calthorpe (Fig. 135) was appointed a Second Sea Lord in 1916.

**Fig. 136a. Rear Admiral Sir Christopher Cradock**
(Phillips, British Admirals, anonymous issue, 1915)

**Fig. 136b. Rear Admiral Sir Christopher Cradock**
(Lambert and Butler, Naval Portraits, 1915, No. 33)

**Fig. 136c. Rear Admiral Sir Christopher Cradock**
(Taddy, Admirals and Generals, The War, 1914)

**Fig. 136d. Cradock, reverse side**
(Taddy, Admirals and Generals, The War, 1914)

Rear Admiral Sir Christopher Cradock (Figs. 136a, 136b, 136c, 136d) commanded the Royal Navy squadron off the coast of Chile, where he was defeated by Vice-Admiral Graf Maximilian von Spee at the Battle of Coronel. Cradock died in this battle when his ships *HMS Good Hope* and *HMS Monmouth* were sunk. In classical non-critical patriotic terms of the descriptions on the early card sets, Cradock's role in Coronel is described as being "in command of the British Squadron that 'most gallantly contested' the engagement with a much stronger German Squadron."

**Fig. 137a. Admiral Sir F. C. D. Sturdee**
(Colton War Portraits, 1915, No. 14)

**Fig. 137b. Admiral Sir F. C. D. Sturdee**
(B.A.T., Britain's Defenders, 1915, No. 24)

**Fig. 138a. Rear-Admiral John M. De Robeck**
(Muratti, War Series II, 1917, No. 21)

**Fig. 138b. Rear-Admiral John M. De Robeck**
(Taddy, Admirals and Generals – The War, c1915, No. 38)

After this defeat Lord Fisher then sent Admiral Sir F. C. D. Sturdee (Figs. 137a, 137b) there to head off a powerful squadron under Von Spee. Sturdee had earlier distinguished himself at Heligoland Bight. Von Spee's squadron that was defeated by Sturdee in the Falklands battle included the armored cruisers *SMS Scharnhorst* and *Gneisenhau*. For his victory at the Falklands Sturdee was created a baronet in 1916. He then saw service as commander of the fourth Battle Squadron at the Battle of Jutland.

Rear-Admiral John M. De Robeck (Figs. 138a, 138b) succeeded Admiral Carden as commander of the British Fleet at the Dardenelles. In the Taylor War Series, 1915 set, it described Rear Adm. J. M. De Robeck as an "authority on torpedo and submarine warfare."

**Fig. 139. Admiral Gregovitch**
(Sniders and Abrahams Great War Leaders and Warships, 1915)

**Fig. 140a. Admiral Augustin Boue de Lapeyrere**
(Sniders and Abrahams Great War Leaders and Warships, 1915)

**Fig. 140b. Admiral Sir George Patey**
(Sniders and Abrahams Great War Leaders and Warships, 1915)

**Fig. 140c. Admiral Sir George Patey**
(Phillips British Admirals, 1915)

## THE ALLIES

There are extremely limited cards of naval leaders of British Allies. In the card set of Sniders and Abrahams Great War Leaders and Warships, 1915 there is a card of a Russian Admiral Gregovitch (Fig. 139), but it is without any description. In the same set is a card of a French Admiral Augustin Boue de Lapeyrere (Fig. 140a). At the outbreak of war he was Commander-in-Chief of the French Mediterranean Force. However, no large battles occurred. He did, however, let the German ships *Goeben* and *Breslau* escape to Turkish waters. In this set too is a card of Admiral Sir George Patey (Figs. 140b, 140c) who, although British and enlisted in the Royal Navy, was in command of the Australian Fleet. He is also illustrated in Phillips British Admirals, 1915 issue.

## THE CENTRAL POWERS

There are also only a minimal number of cards of the naval leaders of the Central Powers. Scerri issued a large set titled Prominent People. There is a card of Grand Admiral Alfred von Tirpitz. He was the Secretary of State of the German Imperial Naval Office (Fig. 141). After the Battle of Jutland and the controversy over the submarine warfare, he was dismissed from office.

**Fig. 141. Admiral Alfred von Tirpitz**
(Scerri, Prominent People, c1930, No. 96)

# Aviation Leaders

Although tethered "air machines" had been used since the late nineteenth century, World War I was the first war where aircraft played a significant role. In the ten years since the Wright brothers (Figs. 142a, 142b, 142c, 142d, 142e) flew their first plane, aircraft played a role from the outset of the war and this increased over the next few years. The French were initially ahead of the British in airplane manufacture. At first air reconnaissance was the most important use of planes. Air combat only became important later in the war.

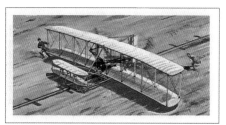

**Fig. 142a. Wright Flyer**
(Brooke Bond Tea, History of Aviation, 1972, No. 4)

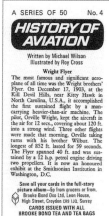

**Fig. 142b. Wright Flyer, reverse side**
(Brooke Bond Tea, History of Aviation, 1972, No. 4)

**Fig. 142c. Orville and Wilbur Wright**
(Barratt & Co. Ltd, History of Air, 1960, No. 9)

**Fig. 142d. Orville and Wilbur Wright**
(Trucards, History of Aircraft, 1970, No. 2)

**Fig. 142e. Wright Aeroplane, 1903**
(Lambert & Butler, History of Aviation, (green front), 1932, No. 9)

In 1911 the Committee of Imperial Defence established the Royal Flying Corps. It consisted of a military wing and a naval wing. At the outbreak of war Brigadier-General David Henderson (Figs. 143a, 143b) was originally appointed to command this service. Major Frederick Sykes had responsibility for the military wing and Commodore Charles Rumney Samson was in command of the naval wing. Flight Commander Grahame-White (Fig. 144) was appointed Flight Commander for Special Services in 1914. In the early years of the war, from the public perspective, greater awareness and interest was in the air aces rather than the leaders. As such the few cards that are available on the air force are mainly those of the fighter pilots.

**Fig. 143a. Brigadier-General David Henderson**
(Westminster Tobacco, The Great War Celebrities, 1914, No. 30)

**Fig. 143b. Brigadier-General David Henderson**
(Parodi, War Portraits, 1916, No. 12)

**Fig. 144. Flight Commander Grahame-White**
(The Picture House, War Portraits, 1916, No. 44)

**Fig. 145. Hugh Trenchard**
(Ardath, Empire Personalities, 1937, No. 22)

**Fig. 146a. Hugh Trenchard**
(Godfrey Phillips In the Public Eye, 1935, No. 11)

**Fig. 146b. Trenchard, reverse side**
(Godfrey Phillips In the Public Eye, 1935, No. 11)

In France, Hugh Trenchard (Figs. 145, 146a, 146b) was the commander of the Royal Flying Corps from 1915. In 1917 after the bombing of London General Jan Smuts was given the task of investigating British air services. His report recommended the establishment of an independent air service. In January 1918 Trenchard was appointed Chief of the Air Staff of the newly formed Royal Airforce, a combination of the Royal Flying Corps and the Royal Naval Air Service.

Sir Edward Leonard Ellington (Fig. 147) was appointed to the Royal Flying Corps in 1913. He was one of the first airmen to go to France. He was soon brought back to the war office.

HM King George V became the Colonel-in-Chief of the Royal Flying Corps (Naval and Military wings) and of the Royal Air Force in 1918. This is described on the back of the card in the Ardath set (Figs. 148a, 148b).

**Fig. 147. Sir Edward Leonard Ellington**
(Ardath, Empire Personalities 1937, No. 21)

**Fig. 148a. H.M. King George V**
(Ardath, Silver Jubilee, 1935, No. 10)

**Fig. 148b. H.M. King George V, reverse side**
(Ardath, Silver Jubilee, 1935, No. 10)

CHAPTER 8

# WAR SCENES

In a manner similar to the war poets, who through their individual poems of aspects of the War conveyed the whole mood and perspective of that conflict, card companies took a similar approach to the specific details of the war, particularly at the battlefront. Rather than attempting to provide an overview of the war by illustrating and describing the various battles that took place on the land, on the sea and in the air, the companies chose to illustrate on the card sets they issued, instead, vignettes of these battles and descriptions of particular incidents. They also laid emphasis on what life was like on the battlefront. These illustrations and descriptions were of individuals, small military units, or occasionally of regiments. In reviewing these sets it becomes obvious as to why this approach was adopted and why it was so successful. There was a significant and intense patriotic and even perhaps jingoistic element to these cards. The consumers (cigarette smokers and others) could comprehend the acts of bravery of individuals and small components of the army more easily than trying to understand the grand strategy of the war and the tactics of the battles between the armies. Thus the imagery on these cards, rather than trying to relay the history of war at the greater strategic and tactical levels, successfully distilled major battles into a single scene or a variety of scenes on a series of related cards, while still conveying the larger narrative of these aspects of the war. Furthermore, since the vignettes that were described were so extensive on the large number of sets illustrating and describing life at the battlefront, an excellent insight is gained into the larger aspects of the war and of its progress.

Where possible and where appropriate, these cards are illustrated and described according to the sequence of events as the war evolved. Since card production diminished significantly during the latter half of the war, most of the card sets concentrate on events of 1914 to 1916. Sets issued in the latter part of the war or after the war, however, still covered, although to a lesser extent, the last two years of the war. Correlating these war incidents with the section on the Timeline of the War is helpful to appreciate the extent of the detailed coverage of the war on these cards.

Individual war scenes involved all components of the armed services. At the highest level His Royal Highness, King George V is shown on a number of cards. These clearly illustrate both his interest and concern in the specifics of the war. Several cards show him either visiting locations on the home front or on the battlefield. In a set issued by International Tobacco, titled Gentleman, The King!, issued in 1937, he is shown in a number of war scenes. Card No. 32 illustrates him inspecting a new bomb near the fighting line in 1917. He was accompanied by the Prince of Wales, who had been on the staff of Sir John French in 1914, when he was the Commander-in-Chief (Fig. 149). Card No. 33 shows the king inspecting a new tank in 1918 (Fig. 150). No. 35 is of one of his wartime visits to the Fleet. He is shown standing between the guns of the *H.M.S. Queen Elizabeth* in 1917 (Fig. 151). A poignant scene is illustrated and described on No. 37 (Fig. 152). It shows the king at the hospital bedside of a wounded soldier. The individual is rifleman Simmons, who is receiving a decoration from the King while he was visiting the Whipps Cross War Hospital. The description states how at every spare moment throughout the War the King made informal visits. Card No. 47 shows the King on Armistice Day 1919 laying a wreath in front of a temporary Cenotaph (Fig. 153).

**Fig. 150. King George V Inspecting a Tank**
(International Tobacco, Gentleman, The King, 1939, No. 33)

Fig. 149. King George V
Inspecting a Bomb
(International Tobacco,
Gentleman, The King, 1939,
No. 32)

Fig. 151. King George V
Between Guns
(International Tobacco,
Gentleman, The King, 1939,
No. 35)

Fig. 153. King
George V Laying
Wreath
(International
Tobacco, Gentleman,
The King, 1939,
No. 47)

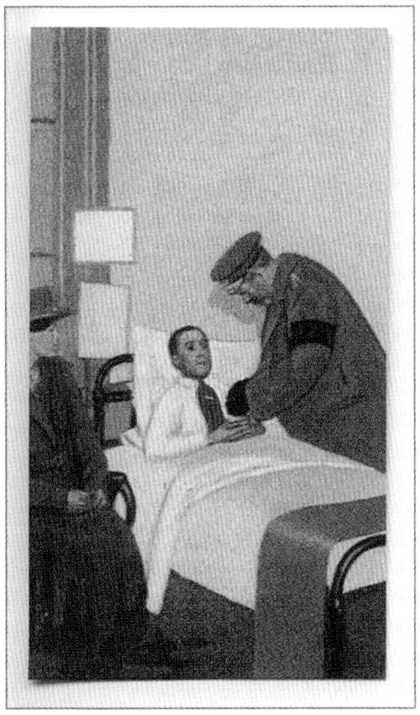

Fig. 152. King George V
at Hospital
(International Tobacco,
Gentleman, The King,
1939, No. 37)

Fig. 154. King George V
and King Albert
(Godfrey Phillips, War
Photos, 1916, No. 53)

Godfrey Phillips issued a set of War Photos in 1916. One card illustrates King George V and King Albert inspecting Belgian troops (Fig. 154). In two variations of the same title, two cards from this set show King Albert conversing with a French general. On the one card the two are standing opposite each other. On the variation card, one is on a horse in a different area (Figs. 155a, 155b). Three cards from the Liebig set of King Albert show him at the beginning of the war, sometime during the war, and then just after the war (Figs. 155c, 155d, 155e). In the American Tobacco Co. set of World War I Scenes a card illustrates "The Czar of Russia off to the Front" (Fig. 156).

A full description of the four years of the war on land is first given, followed by the four years of events at sea and then in the air. The individual cards selected show many aspects of the war fought on all these fronts.

Fig. 155a. King Albert and French General
(Godfrey Phillips, War Photos, 1916, No. 62)

Fig. 155b. King Albert and French General
(Godfrey Phillips, War Photos, 1916, No. 63)

Fig. 155c.  King Albert, 1914
(Leibig, King Albert of Belgium,
1936, No. 3)

Fig. 155d.  King Albert, During War
(Leibig, King Albert of Belgium, 1936, No. 4)

Fig. 156.  The Czar Off to Front
(American Tobacco Co., World War I
Scenes, 1917-18, No. 159)

Fig. 155e.  King Albert, After War
(Leibig, King Albert of Belgium, 1936, No. 6)

# Incidents from Land Battles

## 1914

With the German invasion of Belgium and the declaration of war on Germany by Britain, the BEF was immediately dispatched to France. Among the early events illustrated and described on cards are the transfer and landing of the British Expeditionary Force (BEF) in France.

The first one is in the Wills War Incidents (1st Series), 1916 issue (Fig. 157a), where it also illustrates the landing of the BEF in France in August 1914. Bewlay's War Series of 1915 shows specifically the Seaforth Highlanders arriving at Boulogne (Fig. 157b). The one from the Smith War Incidents, 1st Series 1914 set (Fig. 157c) illustrates them having arrived at Boulogne. The reverse description states "The transport of the Expeditionary Force across the Channel, which was effected with great secrecy and 'without a single casualty,' was a triumph of organization on the part of Lord Kitchener and his staff."

Fig. 157c.  BEFin France
(Smith War Incidents, 1st Series, 1914, No. 9)

Fig. 157b.  BEF, Seaforth Highlanders
(Bewlay, War Series, 1915)

Fig. 157a.  BEF Landing in France
(Wills War Incidents (1st Series),
1916, No. 7)

Fig. 159.  Cathedral in Louvain
(Lea, War Pictures Series 1, 1915,
No. 1)

Fig. 158a.  Belgian Artillery, Louvain
(Smith's War Incidents 1st Series, 1914, No. 15)

Fig. 158b.  Belgian Artillery, Louvain
(Smith's War Incidents 1st Series, 1914, No. 16)

Fig. 158c.  Belgian Artillery, Louvain
(Smith's War Incidents 1st Series, 1914, No. 17)

A number of cards are devoted to the invasion of Belgium and its consequences on the local population. Smith's War Incidents (1st Series) 1914 set illustrated the Belgian artillery in action at Louvain and then the soldiers fighting there (Figs. 158a, 158b, 158c). Louvain was attacked in late August. According to the descriptions, it was a small town near Tirlemont where the Allies checked the German advance. It is about fifteen miles from Brussels and the gallant defense there was the "key to Brussels." The description on No. 16 indicates that "Though hopelessly outnumbered by the hordes of the invaders, the Belgians effectually delayed the German advance, and enabled the main body of the Belgian Army to retreat in safety." Another set by Lea titled War Pictures Series 1, 1915 illustrates the Hotel de Ville and Cathedral of St. Pierre in Louvain (Fig. 159). It describes the founding of Louvain and indicates how the town hall was spared, but that the cathedral was in ruins.

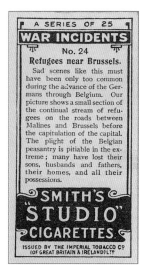

Fig. 160a. Refugees Near Brussels
(Smith's War Incidents 1st Series, 1914, No. 24)

Fig. 160b. Refugees Near Brussels, reverse side
(Smith's War Incidents 1st Series, 1914, No. 24)

Fig. 161. Refugees Leaving Louvain
(Sniders and Abrahams, European War Series, 1916)

Fig. 162. Belgian Soldiers' Funeral (Smith, Series War Incidents 2nd Series, 1915, No. 2)

Fig. 163. Germans in Brussels (Smith, Series War Incidents 2nd Series, 1915, No. 23)

The human toll of this invasion is shown on a number of cards. One in the Smith's set titled "Refugees Near Brussels" (Fig. 160a, 160b) illustrates the all too frequent sad scene of "a small section of the continual stream of refugees on the roads between Malines and Brussels before the capitulation of the capital." A similar card is illustrated in Sniders and Abrahams set of European War Series, 1916, titled "Belgian Refugees Leaving Louvain" (Fig. 161). It illustrates a family pulling a cart with members of the family both in the cart and walking by its side. The Smith's 1915 2nd Series War Incidents illustrates a military funeral procession passing through the streets of Ostend (Fig. 162). Another card in this set (Fig. 163) shows the Germans in Brussels on August 20.

Fig. 164. Battle of Mons
(My Weekly, Battle Series, 1916)

The My Weekly Battle Series set of 1916 consists of nine cards, each one describing a different battle of the War. There are several sets that have a number of cards that illustrate and describe individual battles that formed a part of the larger Battle of the Frontier. From this set there is a card on the Battle of Mons (Fig. 164). Its description is "The first great battle of the World War began on August 22nd, 1914, on Belgian soil close to the town of Mons. Five German Army Corps were launched against the BEF – 'That Contemptible little Army' of which the Kaiser spoke so scathingly. Bit by bit our troops were compelled to fall back. Their gallant stand checked the German advance on Paris, and led to the great victory of the Marne." Lea's War Pictures Series 1 illustrates a scene from this same battle (Fig. 165). The reverse description indicates that

"Mons is in the north-east of France and it was in this neighborhood that the British Expeditionary Force was first concentrated, and where our soldiers came in for the heaviest fighting within a few hours of landing on French soil." The Bewlay War Series card shows a different scene from the Mons engagement (Figs. 166a, 166b). The reverse-side description gives good details of the battle. "In the four days battle which began August 23rd and ended August 28th, the British Army offered a determined resistance in the face of tremendous odds and though our losses amounted to 5,000 or 6,000 men, they were trifling in comparison to those suffered by the enemy. This illustration represents a night scene in the Arras region where for hours the British lines were swept by the enemy's searchlights followed by great gusts of shrapnel."

**Fig. 165. Battle of Mons**
(Lea, War Pictures Series 1, 1915, No. 24)

**Fig. 166a. Battle of Mons**
(Bewlay, War Series
(Photogravure War Pictures,)
1915, No. 3)

**Fig. 166b. Battle of Mons,
reverse side**
(Bewlay, War Series
(Photogravure War Pictures),
1915, No. 3)

**Fig. 168. Shoulder to Shoulder**
(Wills War Incidents, 1st Series,
1916, No. 28)

**Fig. 167. Coldstream at Landrecies**
(Wills War Incidents, 1st Series, 1916, No. 17)

**Fig. 169. At Battle of Marne**
(Bewlay, War Series
(Photogravure War Pictures),
1915, No. 7)

**Fig. 170. British
and French
Sharing Cigarettes**
(Smith, War
Incidents 2nd
Series, 1915,
No. 1)

**Fig. 171. Trenches
in Paris**
(Smith, War
Incidents 2nd
Series, 1915,
No. 13)

Another early event of the war is illustrated in the Wills War Incidents 1st Series set on a card titled "Coldstream at Landrecies" (Fig. 167). It involved a skirmish between the British I Corps under General Haig and the German Fifth Army on August 25, 1914, at Landrecies in northern France. This event was part of the larger Battle of Le Cateau in late August. It involved the exhausted Coldstream Guards, who, according to the description, "after having fought at and retired from Mons, were given leave to rest, but were then attacked by the German 9th Army Corps. Springing suddenly to arms, and fighting gallantly in the narrow streets the Guards took heavy toll of their disturbers."

A card in this same Wills set is of political interest in that it is titled "Shoulder to Shoulder" and illustrates British soldiers fighting with French soldiers (Fig. 168). The description indicates that "the reality of the 'Entente Cordiale' cemented by the late King Edward between England and France, has been proved over and over again in this present war. At the Battle of the Marne, British and French troops fought side by side with the utmost enthusiasm, and helped to stem the advance on Paris." A card in the Bewlay War Series set illustrates an aspect of this battle, where there is "The Turn of the Tide" (Fig. 169). On the reverse side it describes that at this battle "General Joffre had decided that the time had come to take the offensive, and drive the enemy back. He therefore ordered the advance of the Allies. After desperate fighting the Germans retreated at every point along the line and at the end of four days they had been pushed back fifty miles."

A card of no military or historical significance but illustrating the personal side of the war is from the Smith's 2nd Series 1915 War Incidents. It illustrates and is titled "British giving French soldiers Pinewood Cigarettes" (Fig. 170). No. 13 of this same set illustrates a scene in the Forte Maillot in Paris, where trenches were being dug in the defense of Paris (Fig. 171).

The Battle of the Marne card of the My Weekly Battle Series (Fig. 172) describes how the "Battle of the Marne definitely turned the tide of the war. Von Kluck, German Commander, was out-generalized and the great advance upon Paris was stopped by the British and French troops." The battle was fought between September 5 and 12. Following this battle there was the First Battle of the Aisne that began on September 13. The card of the My Weekly Battle Series set on the Battle of the Aisne describes on the reverse side a typical example of clearly defined patriotism (Fig. 173). "Despite the overwhelming numbers of the enemy and the desperate character of their attack, the Allied Armies stood firm and emphasized the victory gained earlier at the Marne." On a card from the Bewlay War Series set titled "Saving a Battery" there is a description of a "thrilling incident" in this battle (Fig. 174). One of the batteries was shelled before the drivers had time to unlimber." The horses stampeded and three of the seven guns were upset. Four teams broke away and galloped towards the enemy. Half-a-dozen men went after them and three quarters of a mile from the Germans caught up with them. Some of the horses had to be shot, but all the guns were rescued and only one man was hit."

**Fig. 172. Battle of Marne**
(My Weekly, Battle Series, 1916)

**Fig. 173. Battle of the Aisne**
(My Weekly, Battle Series, 1916)

**Fig. 174. Saving a Battery**
(Bewlay, War Series [Photogravure War Pictures], 1915, No. 18)

**Fig. 175. First Battle of Ypres**
(My Weekly, Battle Series, 1916)

After the "Race to the Sea," when the Belgians held the small strip north of Ypres to the ocean, the Germans still persisted in trying to reach the coast. Thus began on October 18 the First Battle of Ypres. The My Weekly set of Battle Series has a card on both the First and Second Battles of Ypres in 1914 and 1915 (Fig. 175). In the same Wills War Incidents, 1st Series, 1916 issue, a card illustrates the charge of the London Scottish at Messines, near Ypres during the First Ypres Battle at the end of October 1914 (Fig. 176). It was the first infantry battalion in action against the Germans. The card description states "…(it) will rank as one of the most brilliant events of the war." As a part of the First Battle of Ypres, in the Battle of the Yser, the Germans failed to secure the Yser Canal and that portion of Belgium. A card from the American Tobacco Co. set World War One Scenes shows "French snipers at work from a tree top" during the Battle of the Yser (Fig. 177).

By the end of 1914, the situation had stabilized and the Western Front became well established with the line of trenches extending from the North of Belgium near the North Sea to near the border with Switzerland. Edwards, Ringer and Biggs produced two different sets in 1916 titled War Map of the Western Front. They have the same content on the front of the cards, but in different colors. These are sectional maps consisting of fifty-six cards each. When placed sequentially next to each other, they cover the area that includes the North Sea and the territories of Holland, Belgium, parts of France and Germany, and even a portion of Switzerland (Fig. 178).

**Fig. 176. London Scottish at Messines**
(Wills War Incidents, 1st Series, 1916, No. 6)

**Fig. 177. French Snipers, Battle of Yser**
(American Tobacco Co., World War One Scenes, 1917-18, No. 231)

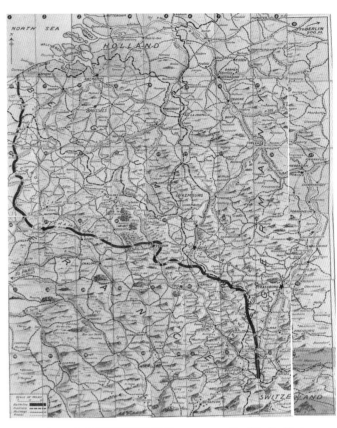

**Fig. 178. The Western Front**
(Edwards, Ringer and Bigg, War Map of the Western Front, 1916)

**Fig. 179a. Russians Mobilizing**
(Smith, War Incidents 1st Series, 1914 No. 1)

**Fig. 179b. Russians Mobilizing**
(Smith, War Incidents 1st Series, 1914 No. 2)

On the Eastern Front, the Smith War Incidents (1st Series), 1914 showed on two cards the Russians entraining after mobilization in late July 1914, and then marching more heavily clad than their British counterparts and carrying their greatcoats over their shoulders (Figs. 179a, 179b). Emblematic of how, at the beginning of the war, the military mindset was still set in the nineteenth century, Lea's War Pictures Series 1 No. 2 is of "Cossacks Reconnoitering" (Fig. 180a). The card describes these "fearless riders on Scout duty in German Poland. They serve the Czar of Russia with the utmost zeal and devotion...." Another card of the same set illustrates a "Cossack from the Ural Mountains" mounted on his horse (Fig. 180b). Still another card is of "A soldier of the famous Czar's Cuirassier Guard" (Fig. 180c).

**Fig. 180a. Cossacks Reconnoitering**
(Lea, War Pictures Series 1, 1915, No. 2)

**Fig. 180b. Cossack from Urals**
(Lea, War Pictures Series 1, 1915, No. 8)

**Fig. 180c. Czar's Cuirassier Guard**
(Lea, War Pictures Series 1, 1915, No. 20)

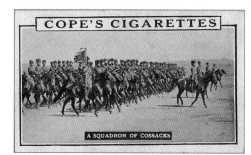

Fig. 181a. Squadron of Cossacks (Cope Bros., War Pictures, 1916 No. 6)

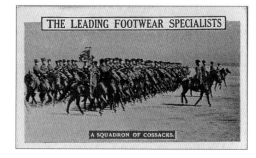

Fig. 181b. Squadron of Cossacks (W & E Turner, War Pictures, 1916)

Fig. 182. Russian Artillery (Godfrey Phillips, War Photos, 1916, No. 28)

In the Cope Bros. Set of War Pictures, 1916 a card is titled "A Squadron of Cossacks" (Fig. 181a). It describes how "A large portion of Russia's Army consists of these burly horsemen. In the present war (1914), they have proved their valor against the Germans, and like the British Cavalry, they are armed with rifles." The same illustration in color is found in the W & E Turner 1916 set of War Pictures (Fig. 181b). In the Godfrey Phillips, War Photos set is a card showing the "Russian Artillery in Action" (Fig. 182), while in the American Tobacco Co. set of World War I Scenes, a card is titled "Result of Russian Bombardment" (Fig. 183). The illustration shows a street in a town in East Prussia that has been wrecked by the Russian bombardment. It states on the description. "By this time 'Belgium' must have been brought home to the Germans." Another card in this set is of "Siberian Infantrymen Arrive in Warsaw in Time to Check German Attack" (Fig. 184).

Fig. 183. Russian Bombardment (American Tobacco Co., World War I Scenes, 1917-18, No. 233)

Fig. 184. Siberian Infantrymen (American Tobacco Co., World War I Scenes, 1917-18, No. 248)

## 1915

In March the Battle of Neuve Chapelle took place. The My Weekly Battle Series set has a card on this battle (Fig. 185a). It description is as follows: "Early in the morning of 10th March, 1915, the British Army made a great forward move in Flanders which was very successful. All day long the battle raged fiercely, and by dusk we had captured Neuve Chapelle and the whole labyrinth of German trenches on a front of 4,000 yards. Over 1,000 prisoners were taken." The Amalgamated Press set of Great War Deeds (M32) has a card titled "Indian Gallantry at Neuve Chapelle" (Fig. 185b). The reverse description indicates how "the Indians charged against the German trenches and managed to capture four lines of trenches within three hours. The next day the Germans counter-attacked and succeeded in driving them from their trenches. However, the Indians later returned and retook the position in a dashing bayonet charge."

In the late 1920s Amalgamated Press issued a comprehensive series of six card sets with various titles, but all related to aspects of events in the war. These sets provide an excellent insight into a wide range of individual incidents during the war. Many examples from these sets are illustrated and described.

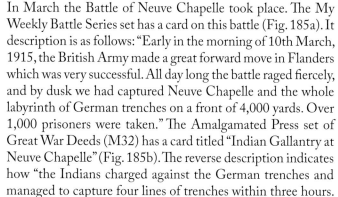

Fig. 185a. Battle of Neuve Chapelle (My Weekly, Battle Series, 1916)

1915 stands out for the major Allied failure of the Gallipoli Campaign. There are many cards from several different sets on this campaign. The cards concentrate particularly on the heroic role played by the ANZACS (Australian New Zealand Army Corps). Leibig issued a set of six cards in French in 1911 titled Les Dardanelles. It illustrated a series of scenes from the Turkish perspective. These are different aspects of civilian and military life. The first card has an inset map of the Dardanelles with many warships in one of the harbors (Fig. 186). In the initial stage of the campaign the dreadnought *HMS Queen Elizabeth* was part of the force used to bombard the coast. In March, Admiral De Roebeck was placed in command of the initial attempt to secure the Dardanelles Straits. Periodical issued a set of large cards in 1917 titled Great War Pictures. One of the cards is of the *HMS Queen Elizabeth* with an inset portrait of Admiral de Roebeck (Fig. 187a, 187b). The rear of the card describes the vessel, but at the end it indicates how de Roebeck replaced Vice-Admiral Carden who was "incapacitated through illness."

**Fig. 185b. Indian Gallantry at Neuve Chapelle**
(Amalgamated Press, Great War Deeds (M32), 1927, No. 14)

**Fig. 186 The Dardanelles**
(Liebig, The Dardanelles, 1911)

**Fig. 187a. HMS Queen Elizabeth and Admiral de Roebeck**
(Periodical, Great War Pictures, 1917)

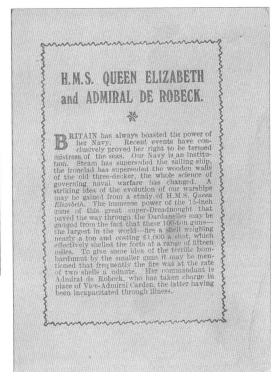

**Fig. 187b. HMS Queen Elizabeth and de Roebeck, reverse side**
(Periodical, Great War Pictures, 1917)

A card in the Wills War Incidents (1st Series) set illustrates and describes the "Australians in the Dardanelles" (Fig. 188a). Their landing on a strip of beach was efficient. A card in the Amalgamated Press, Heroic Deeds of the Great War set is titled "Australians at the Dardanelles." The description states "Of the soldiers who fought at the Dardanelles none showed greater courage than the Australians. The difficult nature of the country in which they fought is shown in this picture of reinforcements of the 3rd Australian Brigade struggling up a rock-strewn defile from the sea under fire from snipers and shrapnel" (Fig. 188b). Similarly, a card in the Wills War Incidents (2nd Series) set No. 7, titled "Wonderful Climbing," illustrates the Australians climbing the heights at Suvla Bay "in the face of murderous fire" (Fig. 188c). No. 8 is titled "Jam Cakes in the Valley of Death" and illustrates and describes how the Australian and Indian soldiers soon became loyal comrades at Gallipoli (Fig. 189). No. 9 illustrates the Australians and New Zealanders landing at the difficult Suvla Bay shore that was rocky and had insurmountable cliffs (Fig. 190). According to the description, they accomplished this almost impossible feat under heavy fire.

**Fig. 188a. Australians Landing at Dardanelles**
(Wills, War Incidents (1st Series), 1916, No. 38)

**Fig. 188b. Australians at Dardanelles**
(Amalgamated Press, Heroic Deeds of the Great War, 1927, No. 27)

**Fig. 188c. Australians Climbing at Suvla**
(Wills, War Incidents (2nd Series), 1917, No. 7)

**Fig. 189. Australians and Indians at Gallipoli**
(Wills, War Incidents (2nd Series), 1917, No. 8)

**Fig. 190. Anzacs landing at Suvla Bay**
(Wills, War Incidents (2nd Series), 1917, No. 9)

No. 10 illustrates how the Anzacs used dummies to lure the Turkish snipers (Fig. 191). No. 12 illustrates the charge of the Australian Light Horse at Gallipoli (Fig. 192a, 192b). Similar to the Western Front, the Allies had to dig trenches. Card No. 11 of this set describes how "it has been difficult for the Empire troops to dig trenches in the hard stony ground and still harder to hold them in the face of the fearfully hot fire of the Turks, whose own trenches, built under German guidance, have proved well-nigh impregnable" (Fig. 193). One of the late but major assaults of the Gallipoli Campaign was the Battle of Hill 60. It was located at the northern end of the range that dominated Suvla Bay. It was important to capture this hill to secure the Suvla landings. The Wills set card No. 30 titled "The Bravest of the Brave" describes how they were "attacked again and again, [yet] the Australians grimly held on, at Hill 60 in Gallipoli, in spite of heavy losses. But superior numbers prevailing, they were forced back, all except 2nd Lieut. Throssell, whose seven feet of gallant manhood refused to budge in spite of wounds and danger [Fig. 194]. He kept his position and gained the V.C." A number of other cards in this 2nd Series issue illustrate and describe aspects of the Gallipoli campaign.

**Fig. 191. Luring Turkish Snipers**
(Wills, War Incidents (2nd Series), 1917, No. 10)

**Fig. 192a. Charge of ALH at Gallipoli**
(Wills, War Incidents (2nd Series), 1917, No. 12)

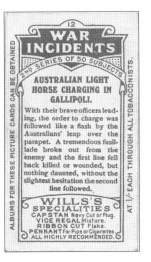

**Fig. 192b. Charge of ALH at Gallipoli, reverse side**
(Wills, War Incidents (2nd Series), 1917, No. 12)

**Fig. 193. Digging Trenches at Gallipoli**
(Wills, War Incidents (2nd Series), 1917, No.11)

**Fig. 194. Lieut. Throssell at Hill 60**
(Wills, War Incidents (2nd Series), 1917, No. 30)

**Fig. 195. Poison Gas**
(Gallaher, Great War, 2nd Series, 1915 No. 116)

Reverting once again to the Western Front, the Second Battle of Ypres is described in the My Weekly Battle Series card titled "Ypres" (see Fig. 175). After briefly describing the First Battle of late 1914 it describes the Second Battle as follows: "…and the second from the 22nd April to 24th May. In the second battle the Canadians greatly distinguished themselves. The official report says 'they saved the situation.'" It was in this battle that the Germans first used poison gas. In the Gallaher Great War, 2nd Series set, a card illustrates a soldier wearing a "Poison Gas Mask" (Fig. 195). The description indicates "The Allies were taken by surprise, and at first suffered a great deal from these attacks. It was not long, however, before an efficient respirator was devised. A type used by the French is shown in the picture."

Also in the My Weekly, Battle Series set there is a card titled "Loos" that has a description of the battle (Fig. 196a). "After a twenty-five day bombardment a great British and French offensive was launched against the enemy on the 25th September, 1915. Thus began the Battle of the Loos, where the British attacking south of La Bassee Canal, penetrated the German lines to a distance of 4,000 yards and captured the village of Loos, part of Hulluch and Hill 70. The French gain was two and a half miles on a fifteen mile front, while 22,000 prisoners and 70 guns were taken by the Allies." In the Amalgamated Press 1927 Great War Deeds (M16) set, card No. 4 is of "The Storming of Loos" by the London Territorials (Fig. 196b). The reverse side describes this battle that lasted from September 25 to mid-October. It states "The battle was noted for its fierce hand-to-hand fighting, and none was of more desperate character than in the streets of Loos itself." In the Amalgamated Press Great War Deeds (M32) set a card is titled "Masked Territorials Charge at Loos" (Fig. 1196c). The reverse side describes the role of this regiment in the attack. Despite these descriptions of great valor, this was not a successful battle for the Allies. General French was forced to resign and by December Douglas Haig replaced him.

**Fig. 196a. Battle of Loos**
(My Weekly, Battle Series, 1916)

**Fig. 196b. Storming of Loos**
(Amalgamated Press, Great War Deeds
(M16), 1927, No. 4)

**Fig. 196c. Masked Territorials at Loos**
(Amalgamated Press, Great War Deeds (M32), 1927, No. 6)

**Fig. 197. Churchill on the Western Front**
(A and BC, Winston Churchill, 1965, No. 12)

## 1916

After the failure of the Gallipoli Campaign, Churchill resigned as Lord of the Admiralty. He desired to serve on the battlefront. Although he could not join his old regiment, the Queen's Own Oxfordshire Hussars, he was assigned as a major of the Grenadier Guards for a while. Subsequently he was appointed Lieutenant-Colonel of the 6th Brigade of the Royal Scots Fusiliers. It was positioned at Ploegseert (or Plugstreet, as the British soldier termed the place), at the southern part of Ypres, although not actually a part of the Ypres Salient. The A and BC, Winston Churchill, 1965 set has an illustration of him in his battlefront uniform wearing a winter trench coat and helmet (Fig. 197).

One of the major battles of 1916 is also illustrated and described in the My Weekly, Battle series set. It is Verdun (Fig. 198). The battle is described on the reverse of the card as follows: "Perhaps the outstanding feature of the whole war has been the brilliant defence, by the French, of Verdun. It was on Feb. 21st that a huge German army, commanded by the Crown Prince, began to batter at the French defences. They lost half-a-million men and achieved relatively nothing. Verdun still bars the road to Paris."

**Fig. 198. Battle of Verdun**
(My Weekly, Battle Series, 1916)

**Fig. 199. Battle of the Somme**
(My Weekly, Battle Series, 1916)

Next in the My Weekly, Battle Series set is the card titled "The Somme" (Fig. 199). This was the largest Allied offensive to-date. The description of the battle on the card indicates that "under Generals Haig and Foch, the Anglo-French forces began a great forward movement on July 1st. The region of the advance was that of the River Somme. The German trenches were first blasted by shellfire and then stormed and captured. Many prisoners were taken and much booty fell into the hands of the Allies." In the last two and a half months of the four and a half month Battle of the Somme, the Canadians participated with the British. Their efforts were noteworthy in that they achieved all the objectives that were set for them. In the Amalgamated Press, Thrilling Scenes from The Great War, 1927, one card is titled "Bravo, the Canadians!" (Fig. 200). It relates to their actions at Courcellete in the latter half of the four and a half month long Somme offensive. The card illustrates the desperate close quarter fighting. The reverse side describes how "in the course of the very heavy fighting they took over 1200 prisoners, including thirty-two officers, together with two guns, a large number of machine-guns, and several trench-mortars, and also inflicted very heavy losses upon the enemy." Today there is a Canadian War Memorial at Courcellete.

The tank first made its appearance during the Battle of the Somme in 1916. In a card titled "No Match for the Tank," the Amalgamated Press, Exploits of the Great War, 1929 set illustrates the beneficial use of the tank (Fig. 201). The description on the card states "After the first attack quite a number were left derelict on the battleground. Others, however, not only did great execution on their own account, but acted as a protective shelter for parties of infantry, who were able to march practically up to the enemy trenches before they came under fire."

**Fig. 200. The Canadians at the Somme**
(Amalgamated Press, Thrilling Scenes from The Great War, 1927, No. 30)

**Fig. 201. The Tank**
(Amalgamated Press, Exploits of the Great War, 1929, No. 8)

## 1917

During the run up of the Nivelle Offensives, the Battle of Arras took place beginning in April 1917. This image from the Lychgate Press 3rd series issue of Images of the Great War shows the ruins of the beautiful Arras Cathedral, destroyed by the Germans in April 1917 (Fig. 202).

On the Italian front the Tenth, Eleventh and Twelfth Battles of the Isonzo took place.

In the Amalgamated Press Great War Deeds (M32) set a card, titled "No Surrender," illustrates how the Italian and British troops, despite being forced to retreat from the Isonzo River after a combined German and Austrian army attack, directed their efforts at slowing and hampering the enemy (Fig. 203). The illustration "shows a group of brave Italian artillerymen making their last stand on the heights beyond the Isonzo. The gun had been wrecked, but around it are clustered its crew, fighting their last gallant fight with a machine gun and a few rifles, whilst the unstoppable hordes of Austro-Germans pour on to overwhelm them."

Fig. 202. Destruction of Arras Cathedral
(Lychgate Press, Images of the Great War, 4th series, No. 3, 2013)

Fig. 203. The Italian Front
(Amalgamated Press, Great War Deeds (M32), 1927, No. 8)

Fig. 204b. Constructing a Road
(Schuh Tobacco Co., Official War Photographs, 1918, No. 4)

Fig. 204a. Messines Ridge
(Schuh Tobacco Co., Official War Photographs, 1918, No. 21)

Fig. 204d. Difficulties Near Ypres
(Schuh Tobacco Co., Official War Photographs, 1918, No. 14)

Fig. 204c. German Flame Thrower
(Schuh Tobacco Co., Official War Photographs, 1918, No. 9)

Fig. 204e. Australian Howitzer at Ypres
(Schuh Tobacco Co., Official War Photographs, 1918, No. 20)

In preparation for the 3rd Ypres Campaign the British captured Messines Ridge. In the Schuh Tobacco Co. Official War Photographs of 1918 set, a scene from this ridge is depicted on a card titled "Entrance to the Catacombs near Messines" (Fig. 204a). It illustrates a number of soldiers standing at the entrance. Several other cards from this set show various scenes during the Third Battle of Ypres, also known as Passchendaele. Card No. 4 is titled "Constructing a Corduroy Road near Ypres" (Fig. 204b). No. 9 is "A Captured German Flame Projector, Ypres" (Fig. 204c). No. 14 is "In Difficulties near Ypres, Autumn 1917" (Fig. 204d). No. 15 illustrates an "Australian 8 in. Howitzer Near Ypres, 1917" (Fig. 204e).

**Fig. 205a.  British Tank at Cambrai**
(Lychgate Press, Images of the Great War, 4th series,
No. 9, 2013)

**Fig. 205b.  Downed German Plane at Cambrai**
(Lychgate Press, Images of the Great War, 4th series, No. 3, 2013)

**Fig. 206.  Officers' Mess,
Palestine**
(Lychgate Press, Images of the
Great War, 4th series, No. 6, 2013)

Lychgate Press in its 4th series of Images of the Great War illustrates a number of scenes from the Battle of Cambria in November. Many tanks participated in the battle and several are illustrated. One illustrates a tank making its way across a German trench (Fig. 205a). Another illustrates a downed German plane sent to reconnoiter following the surprise tank attack (Fig. 205b).

During this time, in the Middle East the Palestinian campaign was being fought. In this same series there is a card of an officers' mess dug out in the side of a wadi (Fig. 206). From the 3rd series of the Lynchgate Press issues, card No. 8 illustrates planes of the R.F.C. arriving in Mesopotamia (Fig. 207a, 207b).

**Fig. 207a.  R.F.C. in Mesopotamia**
(Lychgate Press, Images of the
Great War, 3rd series, No. 8, 2013)

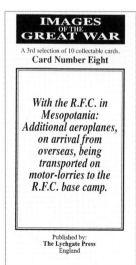

**Fig. 207b.  R.F.C. in
Mesopotamia, reverse side**
(Lychgate Press, Images of the
Great War, 3rd series, No. 8, 2013)

**Fig. 208. Unexploded Shell**
(Lychgate Press, Images of the Great War, 2013, No. 2)

**Fig. 209. Trench Mortar, Bray-sur-Somme**
(Amalgamated Press, The Great War 1914-1918,
1928, No. 16)

**Fig. 210. Gassed Australians**
(Schuh Tobacco Co., Official War Photographs, 1918, No. 3)

## 1918

A card from Lychgate Press, Images of the Great War illustrates and describes "British and Belgian officers having their photograph taken next to a huge German unexploded shell or 'dud,' behind the lines in Flanders in 1918. Shells usually fail to explode due to a fault in their internal mechanism" (Fig. 208).

Bray-sur-Somme had been occupied by the Germans since 1914. In August 1918 it was liberated by the Australians. The Amalgamated Press set, The Great War 1914-1918, 1928 has a card that illustrates the use of the trench mortar by the Australians in the attack of Bray-sur-Somme (Fig. 209). The reverse side description indicates how "the trench mortar was introduced during the Great War owing to the difficulty of getting field guns and howitzers close up to the trenches."

Although poisonous gas had been first introduced as a destructive weapon by the Germans in 1915, a set issued by the Australian Schuh Tobacco Co. issued in 1918 and titled Official War Photographs showed the devastation caused by this weapon. Card No. 3 illustrates a field of wounded and possibly some dead Australians. It is titled "Gassed Australians near Villers Brettoneux" (Fig. 210). This was the location of two battles in April where the Australians fought with great distinction. This village now houses the Australian War Memorial in France.

# General Land War Scenes

Horses remained an important form of transportation in the war, as well as fulfilling many other important functions. Two card examples illustrate this aspect of the war. An unnumbered card from Edmondson's War Series set of 1916 is titled "Royal Horse Artillery Galloping" (Fig. 211a). It illustrates six horses with three mounted artillerymen pulling two guns. In the 1927 Amalgamated Press set Great War Deeds a card titled "Good-Bye, Old Man!" illustrates a poignant scene of a fallen horse with its soldier holding its head (Fig. 211b). The description on the reverse side sums it up. "No words can tell as graphically as this famous picture by P. Matana what true comradeship existed between the soldiers and their horses… This scene, which actually happened on a road in Southern Flanders, shows a gun driver stopping to bid a last farewell to the mount that was fatally wounded by a shell while helping to drag the gun to its position." However, as an example of the futility of the horse in this war, the Meadow Dairy Company 1915 set of War Series has a card that illustrates the "Cavalry Coming Out of Cover" (Fig. 211c). The reverse description is of interest in that it indicates the military mindset was still in the era when the horse cavalry was considered an important part of war. "Cavalry is essentially an arm of defence. Being mounted it is able to cover a long distance in a short time, thus being able to embrace attack with surprise." In the era of trench warfare, barbed wire in no-man's-land and devastating firepower of artillery and machine guns, the horses were obviously of no value in this form of military operation.

**Fig. 211a. RHA Galloping**
(Edmondson, War Series, 1916)

"GOOD-BYE, OLD MAN!"

**Fig. 211b. "Good-Bye, Old Man"**
(Amalgamated Press, Great War Deeds, 1927, No. 2)

**Fig. 211c. Cavalry**
(Meadow Dairy Company, War Series, 1915, No. 17)

The critical functions performed by the various auxiliary medical services are well illustrated and described in a number of sets. An important card in the Wills War Incidents 1st Series set illustrates the Royal Army Medical Corps in action (Figs. 212a, 212b). The card describes how "the annals of the R.A.M.C. abound in cases of quiet heroism. 'First-aid' is generally administered to the wounded where they fall, but sometimes this is impossible. It is the duty of the ambulance men to search for such cases. The work calls for courage as well as skill, for the Germans show little respect for the Red Cross." In Wills' Britain's Part in the War, 1917, there is a card of a Field Ambulance of the R.A.M.C (Fig. 212c). It illustrates and describes how members of the Field Ambulance go into the field of battle to assist and evacuate wounded soldiers. The Amalgamated Press, Heroic Deeds of the Great War 1927 set also paid tribute to these heroes with a card titled "Rescue Work in No Man's Land" (Fig. 212d). It illustrates how the R.A.M.C. crawls into this area under fire to rescue wounded soldiers. Another card is of a similar type, titled "Heroic Stretcher-Bearers" (Fig. 212e). It is of a drawing by the famous war artist F. Matana, who witnessed the event of two stretcher-bearers and described in his own words how "The Barrage-fire was screaming in the air, smoke and earth were flying everywhere, and, in the midst of it, I saw two figures, the only two living souls to be seen. A shell burst in front of them, and they disappeared. The smoke cleared away, and I saw them crouching. Another rain of shells, and still they were alive. With their painful load I watched them vanishing and reappearing as the shells burst around them."

Fig. 212a. RAMC
(Wills, War Incidents 1st Series, 1916, No. 19)

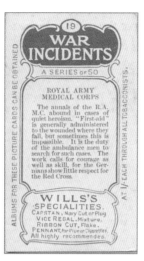

Fig. 212b. RAMC, reverse side
(Wills, War Incidents 1st Series, 1916, No. 19)

Fig. 212c. RAMC Field Ambulance
(Wills, Britain's Part in the War, 1917 No. 6)

Fig. 212e. Stretcher Bearers
(Amalgamated Press, Heroic Deeds of the Great War, 1927, No. 16)

Fig. 213a. The Red Cross
(Wills, Britain's Part in the War, 1917, No. 19)

Fig. 212d. Rescue Work of RAMC
(Amalgamated Press, Heroic Deeds of the Great War, 1927, No. 10)

Fig. 213b. Red Cross Hospital Ship
(Wills, War Incidents, 1st Series, 1916, No. 47)

Fig. 213c. Canine Member, French Red Cross
(American Tobacco Co. World War I Scenes, 1917-18, No. 88)

A card in the Wills Britain's Part in the War set illustrates and describes specifically the Red Cross (Fig. 213a). It is titled "A Tribute to the Red Cross." It shows a wounded soldier lying on a stretcher with his wounds being bandaged by a member of the Red Cross. Still dealing with the Red Cross, card No. 47 of the Wills War Incidents, 1st Series, is of a strongly propagandist nature, where it mocks the Kaiser on this same subject of the Red Cross (Fig. 213b). It illustrates a Red Cross Hospital ship being blown up and describes how "the Germans no longer respect the rule of law. While the Kaiser travels in a Red Cross train to save his own skin, his officers fire on and permit fire on Red Cross parties and hospitals, and recently a German submarine launched torpedoes at one of our Red Cross Hospital ships." The American Tobacco Co. World War I Scenes, 1917–18 has a card titled "A Canine Member of the French Red Cross" (Fig. 213c). It illustrates a dog with the white wrap around its body on which is a large red cross. The animal is next to a wounded soldier.

In illustrating life in the trenches and the toll of the war a simple photo card, issued by Godfrey Phillips in the 1916 set War Photos, 1916 is titled "Wounded British Soldier Writing Home" (Fig. 214a). It illustrates a soldier with both hands bandaged writing a letter with the paper resting on his knee. There are several cards in different sets that illustrate those who survived to reach a medical facility. In this War Photos set a card illustrates nurses taking care of Belgian and British soldiers in a hospital (Fig. 214b). It shows them playing cards. A card in the Sniders and Abrahams 1916 European War Series set illustrates "British Troops in Hospital in Holland" (Fig. 214c).

**Fig. 214a. Wounded British Soldier**
(Godfrey Phillips, War Photos, 1916, No. 13)

**Fig. 214b. Belgian and British Soldiers in Hospital**
(Godfrey Phillips, War Photos, 1916, No. 22)

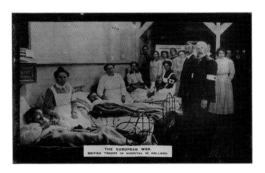

**Fig. 214c. Soldiers in Hospital in Holland**
(Sniders and Abrahams, European War Series, 1916)

Yet another signature card illustrative of the devastation of the war is from the Trucards World War I, 1970 set. It is titled "Toll of War" (Fig. 215a). The illustration is of a drawing in color of a cemetery with many simple crosses. The one in the front has a helmet on it. The description provides a summary of this toll: "There have been many attempts to make an estimate of the total lives lost in the Great War, but the best and the nearest figures must be those given in a statement in the House of Commons in May 1921: Great Britain lost 743,702 men, with 1,693,262 wounded, whilst Germany lost 2,050,466 men, with 4,202,028 wounded." Lychgate Press issued a set in 2013 on Images of the Great War. In a similar vein, one card illustrates a British Officer tending the graves of his fallen countrymen in a French graveyard. The description states that "Each cross bears a name and identification tablet, and the epitaph 'Here lies a British Soldier, R.I.P.'" (Fig. 215b).

**Fig. 215a. Toll of War**
(Trucards, World War I, 1970, No. 30)

**Fig. 215b. Tending Graves**
(Lychgate Press, Images of the
Great War, 2013, No. 1)

A card in the Godfrey Phillips War Photos set illustrates the defining nature of the warfare so specific to this war. It is an illustration of French soldiers in the trenches (Fig. 216a). The Gallaher Great War Series, 1915 set, has a card titled "Shelter Trenches." It gives a good description of one trench type (Fig. 216b). "When not liable to interruption by the enemy, elaborate entrenchment is possible. A roof of planks covered by bags of earth and supported by props provides protection against shrapnel. At regular intervals there are loopholes splayed on the outside to an angle of about 60 degrees, with sandbags in between." Other cards illustrate and describe different types of trenches (Figs. 216c, 216d, 216e). The Lychgate Press issue of Images of the Great War, 3rd series illustrates a mechanism widely used to cross trenches. (Figs. 216f, 216g).

**Fig. 216a. French Soldiers in Trenches**
(Godfrey Phillips, War Photos, 1916, No. 34)

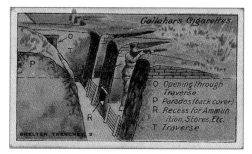

**Fig. 216b. Shelter Trenches**
(Gallaher, Great War Series, 1915, No. 51)

**Fig. 216c. Other Trenches**
(Gallaher, Great War Series, 1915, No. 57)

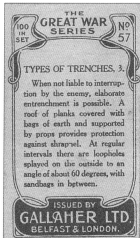

**Fig. 216d. Other Trenches, reverse side**
(Gallaher, Great War Series, 1915, No. 57)

**Fig. 216e. Other Trenches**
(Gallaher, Great War Series, 1915, No. 65)

**Fig. 216f. Crossing a Trench**
(Lychgate Press, Images of the Great War, 3rd series, No. 9, 2013)

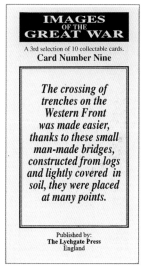

**Fig. 216g. Crossing a Trench, reverse side**
(Lychgate Press, Images of the Great War, 3rd series, No. 9, 2013)

Fig. 217a.  Trench Periscope
(Gallaher, Great War Series, 1915,
No. 66)

Fig. 217b.  Trench Gate
(Lychgate Press, Images of the
Great War, 2013, No. 3)

Fig. 218a.  Winter in the Trenches
(Wills, War Incidents 2nd Series,
1917, No. 20)

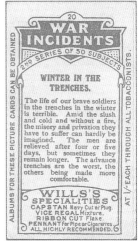

Fig. 218b.  Winter in the Trenches,
reverse side
(Wills, War Incidents 2nd Series,
1917, No. 20)

One card in the Gallaher Great War series set illustrates how a device similar to a submarine periscope was used in trenches (Fig. 217a). A card from the Lychgate Press shows the mechanism used to protect against a trench raid. It describes how "…the gate is lowered when a raid is expected. Although looking like a portcullis, this device has nevertheless proved most successful" (Fig. 217b). In the Wills War Incidents 2nd Series set is one card illustrating the misery of trench warfare (Fig. 218a). Titled "Winter in the Trenches," it illustrates three men bundled up next to each other in the trench and obviously shivering, with snow all around. The description on the reverse side clearly brings out the terrible conditions. It is factual and disturbing (Fig. 218b).

Fig. 219a. Field
Telegraph
(William Clarke,
Army Life, 1915,
No. 4)

Fig. 219b. Field
Telegraph Office
(William Clarke,
Army Life, 1915,
No. 9)

Communications on the battlefront, although still limited to an extent, had nevertheless made great strides during this war. Apart from the use of reconnaissance aircraft, described elsewhere, wireless telegraphy and field telephones played an important part, even though they had their limitations. In the William Clarke set of Army Life, a card is titled "Laying a Field Telegraph" (Fig. 219a). Another card is of a "Field Telegraph Office" (Fig. 219b). In the Gallaher Great War Series, 1915 set, a card illustrates a field telephone (Fig. 219c). The reverse side describes how "sometimes the wire is laid on the ground, but where liable to be ridden over by artillery or other heavy traffic, temporary poles forked at the top are used." In the second series of this same set, another card is of a "Field Wireless" (Fig. 219d). It describes how "Wireless Telegraphy has become almost indispensible in modern warfare. The apparatus consists of two parts, the transmitter and the coherer." Despite these communication advances, there was often a breakdown in the necessary rapid transmission of information from the front line to headquarters and vice versa. Often it took hours to transfer the message. At the front, even though telephone wires were buried, they were often hit. Thus, communication-wise the First World War existed in its own "no-man's-land" between older wars, where direct visualization with the naked eye was necessary for all activities, and effective wireless communication of later wars.

The historian John Keegan summed up the technological advances of this war as being trapped between that capable of mass destruction, but limited by lack of flexibility to perhaps limit this mass destruction of life.

Fig. 219c. Field
Telephone
(Gallaher, Great War
Series, 1915, No. 7)

Fig. 219d. Field
Wireless
(Gallaher, Great War
Series, 2nd series,
1915, No. 165)

# Incidents from Naval Warfare

A number of card sets illustrate the many types of warships from the First World War period. Among these are the many individual vessels that participated in the various naval battles, particularly between 1914 and 1916.

## 1914

According to the description on a card in Smith's 1st Series War Incidents titled "Naval Barracks, Portsmouth": "On Sunday and Monday Aug. 2 and 3, the Military and Naval Reserves received orders to mobilize immediately. Inspiring scenes were witnessed at all the great naval centres, where the mobilization orders were acted upon with speed…" (Figs. 220a, 220b). The illustration shows all the sailors passing through the gates of the Naval Barracks at Portsmouth. In the first action of the war in the Mediterranean, the Germans successfully brought their battlecruiser *Goeben* to Constantinople (Figs. 221a, 221b). This was despite the presence of the British Mediterranean Fleet at Malta (Fig. 222).

**Fig. 220a.  Naval Barracks, Portsmouth**
(Smith, War Incidents, 1st Series, 1914, No. 20)

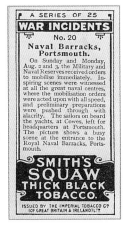

**Fig. 220b.  Naval Barracks, reverse side**
(Smith, War Incidents, 1st Series, 1914, No. 20)

**Fig. 221a.  Goeben**
(Churchman, Silhouettes of Warships, 1915, No.40)

**Fig. 221b.  Goeben, reverse side**
(Churchman, Silhouettes of Warships, 1915, No.40)

**Fig. 222.  Mediterranean Fleet**
(Phillips, British Warships, 1915, No. 10).

Fig. 223a. Fearless
(Mitchell, British Warships, First Series, 1915, No. 3)

Fig. 223b. Arethusa
(Mitchell, British Warships, Second Series, 1915, No. 49)

In the North Sea Battle of Heligoland Bight in August 1914, Admiral Tyrwhitt led the light cruiser *Fearless* (Fig. 223a) together with other ships, particularly well-known being his armored cruiser *Arethusa* (Fig. 223b). Commodore W. E. Goodenough was in command of the *HMS Southampton* (of the Chatham Class of light cruisers) (Figs. 223c, 223d). They successfully sank the German cruisers. The Amalgamated Press set of Great War Deeds (M32) has a card that illustrates and describes the German losses. Titled "The Sinking of the *Mainz*," the descriptive back indicates how this vessel, together with two German cruisers and a destroyer, was sunk at this battle (Fig. 224).

Fig. 223c. HMS Southampton
(Churchman, Silhouettes of Warships, 1915, No. 9)

Fig. 223d. HMS Southampton, reverse side
(Churchman, Silhouettes of Warships, 1915, No. 9)

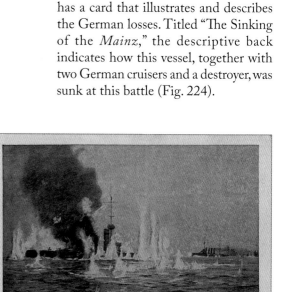

Fig. 224. The Sinking of the Mainz
(Amalgamated Press, Great War Deeds (M32), 1927, No. 2)

Fig. 225a. Emden
(Churchman, Silhouettes of Warships, 1915, No. 43)

Fig. 225b. Sinking of Emden by Sydney
(Amalgamated Press, Heroic Deed of the Great War, 1927, No. 11)

Fig. 225c. Sinking of Emden by Sydney, reverse side
(Amalgamated Press, Heroic Deed of the Great War, 1927, No. 11)

In the Indian Ocean the German vessel *Emden* (Fig. 225a) created havoc with Allied shipping. For three months after the outbreak of war, the Germans were successfully interrupting British shipping lines. The *Emden* alone had sunk fifteen vessels. In the Amalgamated Press Heroic Deeds of the Great War set there is an illustration of the sinking of the *Emden* by the Australian light cruiser *Sydney* (Figs. 225b, 225c).

In the latter part of the year the Royal Navy squadron, under Rear Admiral Sir Christopher Cradock, was defeated by Vice-Admiral Graf Maximilian von Spee, at the Battle of Coronel off the coast of Chile. Cradock died in this battle when his ships *HMS Good Hope* and *HMS Monmouth* were sunk. The *Glasgow* was one of only two British ships that escaped (Fig. 226).

At the Battle of the Falklands, the British squadron under Admiral Sturdee included the battlecruisers *HMS Invincible* (Figs. 227a, 227b) and *Inflexible* (Fig. 227c) as well as the armored cruisers *HMS Carnavon*, *Cornwall* (same class as

Fig. 226. Glasgow (Mitchell, British Warships, Second Series 1915, No. 27)

Fig. 227a. Invincible (Sniders and Abrahams, Great War Leaders and Warships, 1915)

Fig. 228a. Cornwall (Churchman, Silhouettes of Warships, 1915, No. 7)

Fig. 227b. Invincible (Wills, World's Dreadnoughts, 1910, No. 6)

Fig. 228b. Kent (Mitchell, British Warships, Second Series, 1915, No. 34)

Fig. 227c. Inflexible (Mitchell, British Warships, First Series, 1915, No. 11)

Fig. 229a. Bristol (Phillips, British Warships, 1915, No. 9)

*Monmouth*) (Fig. 228a) and *Kent* (Fig. 228b), and the light cruisers *HMS Bristol* (Fig. 229a) and *Glasgow* (Fig. 229b). Even though the British were initially caught by surprise by von Spee when he attempted to raid the British supply base at Stanley, the larger British squadron under Sturdee did subsequently engage von Spee's squadron. Outgunned and outmaneuvered by Sturdee, almost the entire German squadron was sunk. The British had only minor casualties. The German armored cruisers *Scharnhorst* and *Gneisenau* were sunk. Also the *Nurnberg* and *Leipzig* were sunk. Only the German vessel *Dresden* (Fig. 230) survived the battle. It was sunk a few months later.

Fig. 229b. Glasgow (Mitchell, British Warships, Second Series, 1915, No. 27)

Fig. 230. Dresden (Churchman, Silhouettes of Warships, 1915, No .43)

## 1915

In 1915 the only significant battle at sea occurred at Dogger Bank, located halfway between Germany and Britain in the North Sea. This battle was against the German Admiral Hipper, who the month before had successfully approached the British coastline and caused death and damage at Scarborough, Whitby and Hartlepool. At this battle Beatty managed to sink the *Blucher* on January 24 (Fig. 231). On the reverse side of the card it describes how over two hundred fifty of the crew were saved by Admiral Beatty's men. The Germans in turn damaged Beatty's flagship, *Lion* (Figs. 232a, 232b, 232c). Other vessels illustrated from this battle include Admiral Hipper's battlecruiser the *Seydlitz* (Fig. 233) that was hit by Beatty's flagship, *HMS Lion*.

**Fig. 231. Blucher**
(Wills Australian issue of War Incidents, 1st Series, No. 4)

**Fig. 232a. Lion**
(Sniders and Abrahams, Crests of British Warships, 1915)

H.M.S. LION
Battle Cruiser 26,350 tons

**Fig. 232b. Lion**
(Sniders and Abrahams, Great War Leaders and Warships, 1915)

**Fig. 232c. Lion**
(Mitchell, British Warships, 2nd Series, 1915, No. 35)

**Fig. 233. Seydlitz**
(Churchman, Silhouettes of Warships, 1915, No. 39)

**Fig. 234a. HMS Queen Elizabeth**
(Mitchell, British Warships, Second Series, 1915, No. 46)

**Fig. 234b. HMS Queen Elizabeth**
(Wills, Warships, 1926, No. 6)

**Fig. 234c. HMS Queen Elizabeth, reverse side**
(Wills, Warships, 1926, No. 6)

As on the land, the major naval event of 1915 was a part of the Gallipoli or Dardanelles Campaign. In February the *HMS Queen Elizabeth* (Figs. 234a, 234b, 234c) bombarded the forts of the Dardanelles. It was Britain's most powerful ship, a dreadnought, launched in 1913. With the main attack on March 18, the *HMS Inflexible*, a battlecruiser built in 1908, was one of several ships sunk that day (Fig. 235a). The *Irresistible*, from the same Gallaher set, was another battleship sunk that day (Fig. 235b). The *HMS Lord Nelson* was damaged (Fig. 235c).

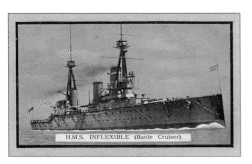

**Fig. 235a. HMS Inflexible**
(Gallaher, British Naval Series, 1914, No. 29)

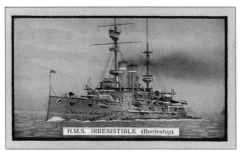

**Fig. 235b. Irresistible**
(Gallaher, British Naval Series, 1914, No. 39)

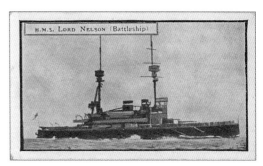

**Fig. 235c. HMS Lord Nelson**
(Sniders and Abrahams, Great War Leaders and Warships, 1915)

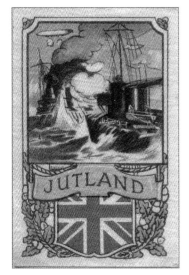

**Fig. 236a. Battle of Jutland**
(My Weekly, Battle Series, 1916)

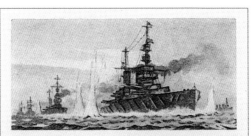

**Fig. 236b. Battle of Jutland**
(Sweetule Products, Naval Battles, 1959, No. 17)

NAVAL BATTLES
A SERIES OF 25

No. 17
JUTLAND 1916
Apart from actions between smaller forces of the rival British and German Fleets, this was the only time the main battle fleet met in full force. Although the action was inconclusive, the German Fleet never came out in full force again and was eventually scuppered and sunk in Scapa Flow.

ISSUED BY
SWEETULE PRODUCTS LTD.
RADCLIFFE·MANCHESTER ENGLAND

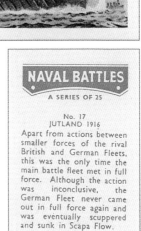

**Fig. 236c. Battle of Jutland, reverse side**
(Sweetule Products, Naval Battles, 1959, No. 17)

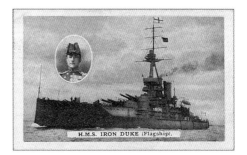

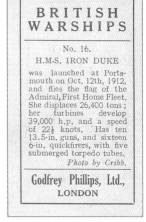

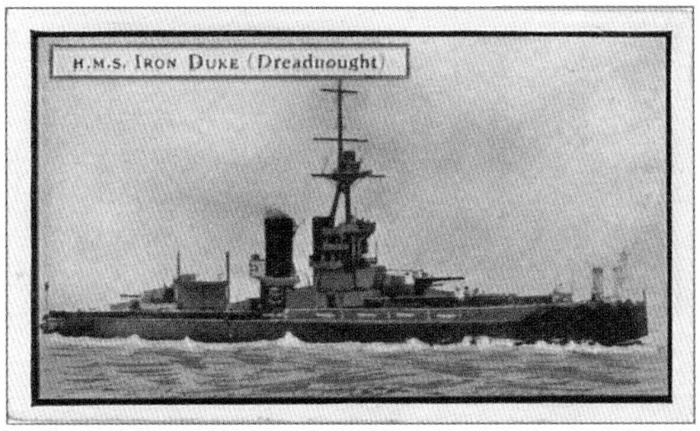

**Fig. 237a. Iron Duke**
(Sniders & Abrahams, Great War Leaders and Warships, 1915)

**Fig. 237b. Iron Duke**
(Phillips, British Warships, 1915, No. 16)

BRITISH WARSHIPS

No. 16.
H.M.S. IRON DUKE
was launched at Portsmouth on Oct. 12th, 1912, and flies the flag of the Admiral, First Home Fleet. She displaces 26,400 tons; her turbines develop 39,000 h.p. and a speed of 22½ knots. Has ten 13.5-in. guns, and sixteen 6-in. quickfirers, with five submerged torpedo tubes.
*Photo by Cribb.*

Godfrey Phillips, Ltd.,
LONDON

**Fig. 237c. Iron Duke, reverse side**
(Phillips, British Warships, 1915, No. 16)

## 1916

The My Weekly Battle Series set has a card on the Battle of Jutland (Fig. 236a). It describes it as "the greatest naval battle since Trafalgar. It was fought on May 31st, 1916 when Admiral Beatty, with the first Battle-cruiser Squadron engaged the German High-Seas Fleet and inflicted upon it serious losses. On the arrival of the British Grand Fleet, the Germans fled." This is a somewhat simplistic and inaccurate description, but one obviously aimed at boosting British morale. In the Sweetule Products set of Naval Battles there is also a card of the Battle of Jutland (Fig. 236b). This card provides a more accurate summary of the battle (Fig. 236c). It was from this major sea battle of World War I that the largest number of warships is illustrated on card sets. Admiral Jellicoe's flagship *Iron Duke* is illustrated on the Sniders & Abrahams set (Fig. 237a). The Phillips, British Warships, 1915 set also illustrates this vessel, as well as illustrating as an insert a portrait of Jellicoe on the card (Figs. 237b, 237c).

The *HMS Indefatigable* was hit early in the battle and rapidly sank (Figs. 238a, 238b, 238c). The *Queen Mary* (Fig. 239a) and the *HMS Tiger* (Fig. 239b) were damaged during the "Run to the South."

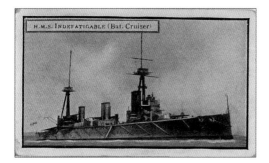

**Fig. 238a. HMS Indefatigable**
(Sniders and Abrahams, Great War Leaders and Warships, 1915)

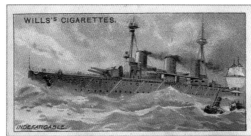

**Fig. 238b. HMS Indefatigable**
(Wills, World's Dreadnoughts, 1910, No. 4)

WILLS'S CIGARETTES
4
THE WORLD'S DREADNOUGHTS
British Cruiser
"INDEFATIGABLE."
Displacement: 18,000 tons.
Commenced 1908.
Completed 1910.
Guns: 8—12 inch.
16— 4 inch.
3 torpedo tubes.
Armour: 7 in.—4 in. belt.
10 in. turrets.
Speed: 27 knots.
The *Indefatigable* is an improved *Invincible*, and will, when completed, be the fastest armoured cruiser afloat.
W. D. & H. O. WILLS.
BRISTOL & LONDON.
ISSUED BY THE IMPERIAL TOBACCO Co (OF GREAT BRITAIN & IRELAND) LTD
ALBUMS FOR THESE PICTURE CARDS CAN BE OBTAINED
AT 1/- EACH FROM ALL TOBACCONISTS.

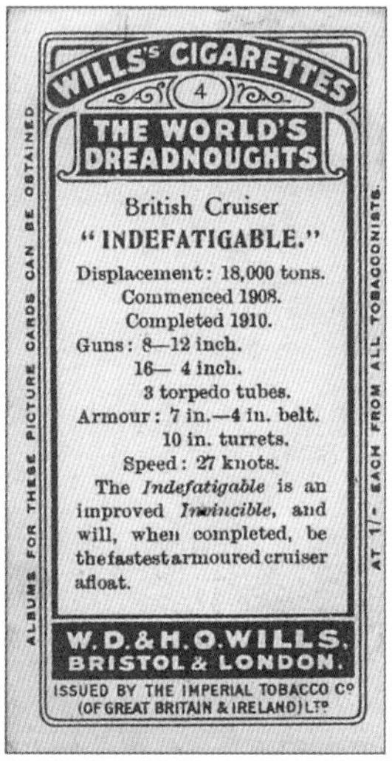

**Fig. 238c. HMS Indefatigable, reverse side**
(Wills, World's Dreadnoughts, 1910, No. 4)

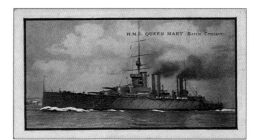

**Fig. 239a. Queen Mary**
(Mitchell and Son, British Warships, 1st Series, No. 21)

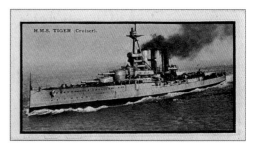

**Fig. 239b. HMS Tiger**
(Mitchell and Son, British Warships, 2nd Series, No. 47)

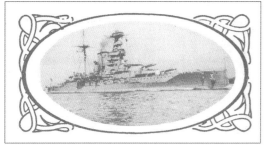

**Fig. 240a. HMS Malaya**
(Abbey Grange Hotels, Fighting Vessels, 1986, No. 3)

**Fig. 240b. Barham**
(Wills, Warships, 1926, No. 17)

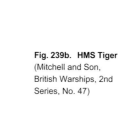

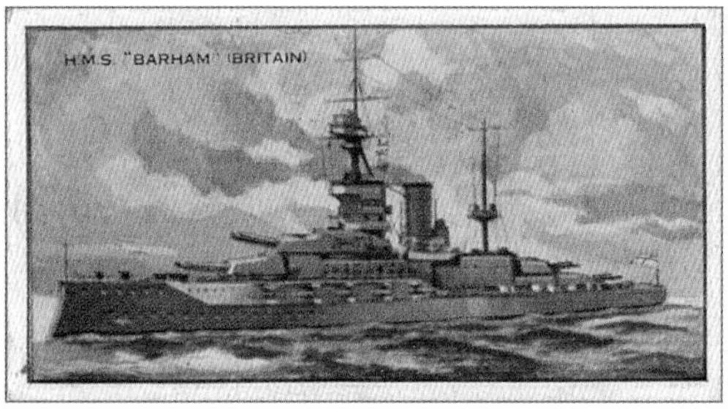

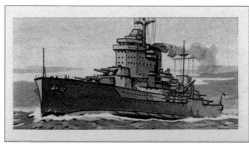

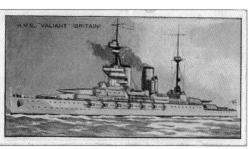

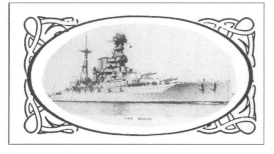

**Fig. 240c. Barham**
(Abbey Grange Hotel, Fighting Vessels, 1986, No. 1)

**Fig. 240d. HMS Warspite**
(Rington, Ships of the Royal Navy, 1961, No. 3)

**Fig. 241. HMS Valiant**
(Wills, Warships, 1926, No. 5)

The *HMS Malaya* (Fig. 240a) and the *Queen Elizabeth*–class battleships *Barham* (Figs. 240b, 240c) and the *HMS Warspite* (Fig. 240d) were three of the vessels in Beatty's 5th Battle Squadron that were hit by Hipper during the "Run to the North." Only the *HMS Valiant* remained intact in this attack (Fig. 241).

*HMS Invincible* was also sunk by Hipper's battlecruiser squadron (Fig. 242). *HMS Southampton* (Fig. 243), a Chatham class light cruiser under Commodore Goodenough, sighted the main German fleet of sixteen dreadnoughts in the late afternoon. The *HMS King George V* (Figs. 244a, 244b) and the German battlecruiser *S.M.S. Westfalen* (Fig. 245) were two of the ships engaged against each other in the last moments of the battle.

Fig. 244a. HMS King George V (Mitchell and Sons, British Warships, 1st Series, 1915, No. 2)

Fig. 242. HMS Invincible (Sniders and Abrahams, Great War Leaders and Warships, 1915)

Fig. 244b. HMS King George V (Sunny Boy, British Naval Series, 1960, No. 2)

Fig. 243. HMS Southampton (Churchman, Silhouettes of Warships, 1915, No. 9)

Fig. 245. SMS Westfalen (Wills, the World's Dreadnoughts, 1910, No. 13)

Other naval aspects illustrated and described on cards include the Morris and Sons, War Pictures set that shows a number of general naval scenes. No. 1 (Fig. 246) is of sailors signaling with a heliograph. Nos. 2 and 6 (Figs. 247a, 247b) are of different-sized naval guns. No. 8 illustrates a seaplane and describes it as "The British Navy's Eye" (Fig. 248). The Meadow Dairy Company 1915 set of War Series, No. 28 is of the "Naval Base, Malta" (Fig. 249). It describes how this base was used as a re-fitting and repairing base for the British Mediterranean Fleet.

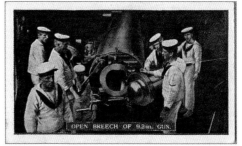

Fig. 247b. 9.2-inch Gun (Morris & Sons, War Pictures, 1915, No. 6)

Fig. 246. Heliographic Signalling (Morris & Sons, War Pictures, 1915, No. 1)

Fig. 248. Seaplane (Morris & Sons, War Pictures, 1915, No. 8)

Fig. 247a. 6-inch Gun and Crew (Morris & Sons, War Pictures, 1915, No. 2)

Fig. 249. Naval Base, Malta (Meadow Dairy Company, War Series, 1915, No. 28)

# Incidents from Air Warfare
# 1914–1918

Meadow Dairy Co. War Series 1915 set has a card titled "Types of Army Aeroplanes" (Fig. 250). The description gives a good indication of their early uses in the War. "Dispatches from Sir John French have told of the most valuable service rendered by our Airplanes by ascertaining the position and strength of the enemy."

Prior to the use of the airplane in the war, the Zeppelin was an established form of transportation and at the onset of war was used as a fighter airship. Barratt & Co. Ltd., in its set of History of the Air, illustrates and describes a Zeppelin (Figs. 251a, 251b). The first dirigible was designed by the famous Count von Zeppelin, who was an inventor and aviator. "The Zeppelin was hailed by the Germans as the conqueror of the air and was used by them during the 1914-1918 war to bomb London, but proved to be very vulnerable to bad weather, as well as offering an easy target to fighter aircraft." In the earlier stages of the war the Germans used Zeppelin airships to attack not only London, as described in the card above, but all of Great Britain. The first raid took place in January 1915 and the first raid on London took place at the end of May of that year (Fig. 252a). In the defense of Antwerp, the Germans used Zeppelins to bomb the city. In the Lea's War Pictures, Series 1 set a card illustrates British cavalrymen firing on a Zeppelin (Fig. 252b). In the 1927 Amalgamated Press issue of Heroic Deeds of the War there is a card of "The Wrecking of Zeppelin 'L15'" (Fig. 253). The reverse side of the card describes how "Zeppelins dropped destructive bombs upon London and other towns…The Zeppelin 'L 15' was discovered in the mouth of the Thames on April 1, 1916…"

Fig. 250. Types of Army Airplanes (Meadow Dairy Co., War Series 1915, No. 4)

Fig. 252a. Firing on a Zeppelin (Lea , War Pictures, Series 1, 1915 No. 14)

THE WRECKING OF ZEPPELIN "L.15"

Fig. 253. Wrecking of a Zeppelin (Amalgamated Press, Heroic Deeds of the War, 1927, No. 6)

**HISTORY of THE AIR**
SET OF 48

**No. 8 — 1900**
**The Zeppelin**

This illustration shows the first dirigible designed by the famous Count von Zeppelin, an inventor and aviator of international repute. This picture shows the dirigible flying over Lake Constance. The Zeppelin was hailed by the Germans as the conqueror of the air and was used by them during the 1914-1918 war to bomb London, but proved to be very vulnerable to bad weather, as well as offering an easy target to fighter aircraft.

Issued by

**BARRATT & CO.LTD**
LONDON · N22
PRINTED IN ENGLAND

Fig. 251a. Zeppelin
(Barratt & Co. Ltd., History of the Air, 1960, No. 8)

Fig. 251b. Zeppelin, reverse side
(Barratt & Co. Ltd., History of the Air, 1960, No. 8)

Fig. 252b. Zeppelin Raid on London
(Anonymous Tobacco, UK, Great War Incidents, 1916)

**Fig. 254. An Aerial Duel**
(Amalgamated Press, Great War Deeds (M32),
1927, No. 5)

**Fig. 255. Captured at 12,000 Feet**
(Amalgamated Press, Great War Deeds (M32),
1927, No. 10)

**Fig. 256. Strafing Enemy Trenches**
(Amalgamated Press, Great War Deeds (M32),
1927, No. 18)

The Amalgamated Press, Great War Deeds (M32) set has several cards illustrating aspects of the air warfare. One is titled "An Aerial Pistol Duel" (Fig. 254). It indicates the limited capabilities of inter-air battles at this stage of the war. The card illustrates and describes how in September 1914 a "German airman found himself pursued by a British biplane which was flying 1,000 feet higher. The biplane swooped down to close quarters, and its pilot and observer attacked the German with pistols, the only weapons with which the machine was equipped." Another card titled "Captured at 12,000 Feet" describes how most fights between airplanes were a battle to the death (Fig. 255). Sometimes, however, a crippled machine would break off a fight and glide to earth. This card illustrates the case of a British pilot who captured an enemy plane in mid-air. The card indicates how this was unique in aerial history. The German's guns jammed, and he threw up his hands in surrender and allowed himself to be shepherded back to earth as a prisoner. However, later in the war air battles became more effective. Card No. 18, "Strafing the Enemy's Trenches," illustrates British planes diving towards German trenches firing their guns (Fig. 256). The description elaborates on the process. Just before the Allied infantry went "over the top" the planes would drop bombs on the dugouts from where the Germans had their firing lines. This forced them to rush into the trench where they were met by a storm of bullets from the scouting planes. Meanwhile the British troops advanced and reached the enemy trenches. Yet another card illustrates and describes aerial warfare between two planes (Fig. 257). Titled "Fight Between Aerial Stunters," it describes how the outcome of such battles was more the result of pilot technique than the airplane. "As the planes maneuvered around each other, the fellow with the cleverest stunts worked himself into such a position that he had his rival at his mercy."

**Fig. 257. Fight Between Two Stunters**
(Amalgamated Press, Great War Deeds (M32),
1927, No. 32)

Illustrating the advancement in airplane weaponry that rapidly evolved during the war, a card in the Morris and Sons, War Pictures set shows a Lewis automatic quick-firing gun located in a position below the pilot and how the operator of the gun had an unobstructed view (Figs. 258a, 258b).

From the earliest stage of the war, airmen would sometimes undertake longer distance missions. Such a one occurred on November 21, 1914, when three airmen flew from Belfort, in the northeastern region of France, on a bombing mission to Germany. In the Cohen Weenen set of War Series – Leaders of the War there is a card illustrating one of the airmen on this mission (Fig. 259). He was Flight-Lieut. S. V. Sippe. Their mission was to attack the Zeppelin factory. The reverse of the card describes the raid as follows: "He took part in the brilliant air raid on the Zeppelin Factory at Friedrichshafen. It was a daring flight of 120 miles into German Territory. Despite bad weather and heavy firing of the Germans, Lieut. Sippe and his two comrades succeeded in damaging the Zeppelin Headquarters."

Fig. 258a. Gun Position (Morris and Sons, War Pictures, 1915, No.7)

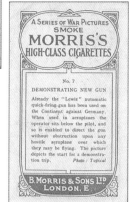

Fig. 258b. Gun Position, reverse side (Morris and Sons, War Pictures, 1915, No.7)

Fig. 259. Flight-Lieut S. V. Sippe (Cohen Weenen, War Series – Leaders of the War, 1915, No. 31)

Fig. 260. Baron von Richtofen (Amalgamated Press, Exploits of the Great War, 1929, No. 12)

Fig. 261. M. Pegoud (Carlton Picture House, War Portraits, ? year, No. 45)

Fig. 262. Lieut. Warneford, V.C. (Sinclair, Great War Heroes, 1915)

The most famous pilot in the Imperial German Army Air Force was Manfred von Richtofen, who is officially credited with having won eighty air victories. He was finally shot down and killed in a fight near the Somme on April 21, 1918. The Amalgamated Press, 1929 set Exploits of the Great War has a card that illustrates and describes "Richtofen's Last Fight" (Fig. 260). The illustration is of the air battle and the description states that "Richtofen was a name that was respected in the British Air Force, for even though the owner was a German with an incredibly long list of British victims to his credit, he was admired as a daring skillful and clean fighter…On the 21st of April he and other Germans were engaged in a battle with a number of British machines when his machine swooped to earth and crashed. He had been shot near the heart by a

British machine-gun bullet." A couple of other air aces have also been illustrated. In the Carlton Picture House set of War Portraits, No. 45 is of M. Pegoud (Fig. 261). The description on the reverse side states that he was "previously in a French Cavalry Regiment (the Chasseurs d'Afrique). Served in the Morocco Campaign under the French general d'Amade. The first Airman to 'Loop the Loop.'" Sinclair, Great War Heroes set has a silk card of Lieut. Warneford V.C. who, according to the description below his portrait, "on June 7, 1915 attacked single-handed and destroyed a large Zeppelin as it was flying over Ghent. Killed later testing an aeroplane" (Fig. 262).

Since air warfare was mainly of secondary importance in the war, there are only a limited number of cards detailing more specific air force involvement in individual battles.

# CHAPTER 9

# VICTORIA CROSS AWARDS

Although it can safely be assumed that all types of military and naval awards were given during the war, all the card manufacturers concentrated only on the most prestigious award of all, the Victoria Cross. A number of cigarette and trade companies issued sets specifically on this subject. However, among all of them, none equaled the output of cards of Gallaher Ltd. Between 1915 and 1918 it issued a total of eight sets, each consisting of twenty-five cards. Thus, covering a good portion of the war, these cards illustrate and describe two hundred recipients of this award. There was also a significant number of other company issues related to the war, with two in 1926 and 1930 respectively. This chapter will be devoted to describing and illustrating a representative example of the recipients. In so doing, these descriptions will also add another facet to the war, particularly at the individual level. It will also complement the descriptions provided in some of the other chapters. The details of the actions leading to the award to the individual are taken directly from the reverse description on each card. The reasons for many of these awards highlight an important aspect of the battlefront fighting. To individual soldiers, the larger issues of the strategic and political reasons for war bore little importance to their actions during the heat of battle. Their lives and actions were not only intimately linked to those of their comrades, but their deeds of bravery were frequently carried out knowing they were placing their own lives in grave danger. Oftentimes this was in order to save the lives of comrades.

Taddy's Medals and Ribbons, 1912 has a card that illustrates the Victoria Cross (Fig. 263). In the British American Tobacco Co. set of War Incidents, a card is titled "Gaining the V.C." (Fig. 264). The description explains that "The Victoria Cross has proved a splendid incentive to courage, though unfortunately in the endeavor to win it so many men get killed. It can only be gained by acts of bravery under the enemy's fire." Perhaps a little misrepresentative of the motive for the act of bravery, this card nevertheless describes and aptly illustrates one of a number of circumstances whereby this most prestigious of all honors was awarded. Ideas produced a series of extra large cards on a number of Great War Leaders. One card is a composite of five individuals who won the Victoria Cross (Fig. 265).

**Fig. 263. The Victoria Cross**
(Taddy, British Medals and Ribbons, 1912, No. 40)

**Fig. 264. Gaining the Victoria Cross**
(British American Tobacco Co., War Incidents, 1916, No. 18)

**Fig. 265. Five V.C. Heroes**
(Ideas, Great War Leaders, Unknown publication date)

The two earliest awards illustrated and described in Gallaher's Victoria Cross Heroes, 1st Series of 1915, are for events that took place on August 23, 1914. Card No. 4 describes Lance-Corporal C.A. Jarvis of the Royal Engineers who won his award for working in full view of the enemy, exposed to hostile fire, for one and half hours to lay and fire charges that resulted in the successful destruction of a bridge (Fig. 266a). The second award that day was to Private S. F. Godley of the 4th Batt. Royal Fusiliers (Fig. 266b). During the Battle of Mons, when, "although severely wounded, he continued to fire his machine gun for over two hours." The next day, Capt. F. O. Grenfell of the 9th Lancers won his honor for two acts of bravery (Fig. 267a). First he showed great gallantry when opposed to an unbroken line of enemy infantry at Ardregenies. Later the same day he successfully helped withdraw to safety the guns of the 119th battery Royal Field Artillery, near Doubon. There are two similar stories to that of Godley. Brigadier-General J. H. S. Dimmer was a Lieutenant in the 2nd Batt. King's Royal Rifles at the time he won his V.C. on November 12, 1914 (Fig. 267b). Although wounded by two bullets and three pieces of shrapnel he continued to operate his machine gun, only ceasing to do so when the gun had been destroyed. The other similar type of award was that of Sepoy Khudadad of the 129th Baluchis, who won this honor on October 31, 1914, at Hollebeke, Belgium (Figs. 267c, 267d). After the British officer in charge was wounded, Sepoy Khudadad, also wounded, "continued to operate his machine gun until all his comrades were killed by enemy fire."

**Fig. 266a.  Lance-Corporal C. A. Jarvis**
(Gallaher, Victoria Cross Heroes, 1st Series, 1915, No. 4)

**Fig. 266b.  Private S. F. Godley**
(Gallaher, Victoria Cross Heroes, 1st Series, 1915, No. 5)

**Fig. 267a.  Capt. F. O. Grenfell**
(Gallaher, Victoria Cross Heroes, 1st Series, 1915, No. 2)

**Fig. 267b.  Brig.-Gen. J. H. S. Dimmer**
(Gallaher, Victoria Cross Heroes, 1st Series, 1915, No. 7)

**Fig. 267c.  Sepoy Khudadad**
(Gallaher, Victoria Cross Heroes, 2nd Series, 1915, No. 34)

**Fig. 267d.  Sepoy Khudadad, reverse side**
(Gallaher, Victoria Cross Heroes, 2nd Series, 1915, No. 34)

On February 1, 1915, L-Corpl. M. O'Leary of the 1st Batt. Irish Guards, while fighting at Cuinchy in the Pas-de-Calais region near the border of Belgium, "rushed ahead of his storming party and killed eight Germans, captured two barricades and made two prisoners, practically gaining the position himself, saving the rest of his party from enemy fire." For this act of bravery he was awarded the V.C. (Fig. 268). During the Battle of Neuve Chapelle on March 15, 1915, Private E. Barber of the 1st Batt. Grenadier Guards won his award when he "dashed to the front of his company and hand-bombed the enemy so effectively that many quickly surrendered" (Fig. 269). Perhaps the first V.C. awarded to a pilot was to the late 2nd Lieut. Wm. B. Rhodes-Moorhouse of the Royal Flying Corps (Fig. 270). When flying near Coutral on April 26, 1915, he dropped his bombs on the railway line near the station. "He was mortally wounded in the effort but succeeded in flying thirty miles back to report his success."

**Fig. 268.  L.-Corpl. M. O'Leary**
(Gallaher, Victoria Cross Heroes, 1st Series, 1915, No. 11)

**Fig. 269.  Pvt. E. Barber**
(Gallaher, Victoria Cross Heroes, 1st Series, 1915, No. 21)

**Fig. 270.  2nd Lt. Wm. B. Rhodes-Moorhouse**
(Gallaher, Victoria Cross Heroes, 2nd Series, 1915, No. 39)

Many awards were given to soldiers who exposed themselves to great danger in order to save one of their colleagues. One such was to Drummer W. Kenny (2nd Batt. Gordon Highlanders), who faced death to rescue five wounded comrades near Ypres on October 23, 1914. His subsequent conduct when saving machine guns and carrying messages under fire was highly exemplary (Fig. 271a). Similarly, Bandsman Tomas E. Rendle of the 1st Batt. Duke of Cornwall's Light Infantry won the V.C. at Wulverghem on November 20, 1914, "when he rescued men from shattered trenches and attended to the wounded under a heavy shell and rifle fire" (Fig. 271b). Lance-Corporal Wm. Angus of the 6th Batt. Highland Light Infantry "left his trench voluntarily at Givenchy on June 12th, 1915 and in the teeth of terrible fire rescued a wounded officer from near enemy trenches. He was wounded about 40 times, some serious, during this gallant rescue" (Fig. 271c).

Fig. 271a. Drummer W. Kenny
(Cohen Weenen, Victoria Cross Heroes, 1916, No. 58)

Fig. 271b. Bandsman Thos. E. Rendle
(Gallaher, Victoria Cross Heroes 3rd Series, 1915, No. 51)

Fig. 271c. Lance-Corp. Wm. Angus
(Gallaher, Victoria Cross Heroes, 2nd Series, 1915, No. 45)

During the Gallipoli campaign a number of awards were given. On the day of the major landing on April 25 at Lancashire Landing and V Beaches, there were many V.C.s awarded for actions that morning. Six were won by the Lancashire Fusiliers and two by sailors. Others were also awarded this honor in different actions. Capt. Gerald Robert O'Sullivan of the 1st Batt. Royal Inniskilling Fusiliers volunteered, although in no way was he compelled to do so, to retake a vital lost portion of a trench (Fig. 272). He led a party to the attack. "During the action he was frequently exposed, and soon wounded, but so effectively bombed the enemy, that the trench was finally recaptured." Seaman Geo. McK. Samson of the *HMS Hussar* partook in a landing at V beach, Cape Helles, Gallipoli (Fig. 273a). "The landing was fraught with great danger and difficulty, but seaman Samson, with others, gallantly entered the water under a hail of bullets to place lighters in position. He also attended many wounded." On board the same vessel at the same landing, Midshipman George L. Drewry also won a V.C. (Fig. 273b). "Despite his wounds and a terrific fire, he very courageously lent a hand in getting lighters into position, working up to the waist in water."

Fig. 272. Capt. Gerald R. O'Sullivan
(Gallaher, Victoria Cross Heroes 3rd Series, 1915, No. 54)

Fig. 273a. Seaman George McK. Samson
(Gallaher, Victoria Cross Heroes 3rd Series, 1915, No. 59)

Fig. 273b. Midshipman George L. Drewry
(Gallaher, Victoria Cross Heroes 3rd Series, 1915, No. 67)

**Fig. 274a. Capt. Percy H. Hansen**
(Gallaher, Victoria Cross Heroes 3rd Series, 1915, No. 66)

**Fig. 274b. Corpl. William Cosgrove**
(Gallaher, Victoria Cross Heroes 3rd Series, 1915, No. 68)

**Fig. 274c. Corpl. Cyril R. G. Bassett**
(Gallaher, Victoria Cross Heroes 3rd Series, 1915, No. 69)

**Fig. 274d. 2nd Lieut. Hugo V. H. Throssell**
(Gallaher, Victoria Cross Heroes 3rd Series, 1915, No. 71)

**Fig. 275. Comm. Edward Unwin**
(Gallaher, Victoria Cross Heroes 5th Series, 1915, No. 107)

**Fig. 276a. Capt. Anketell M. Read**
(Gallaher, Victoria Cross Heroes 4th Series, 1915, No. 79)

**Fig. 276b. 2nd Lieut. Fredk. H. Johnson**
(Gallaher, Victoria Cross Heroes 4th Series, 1915, No. 96)

**Fig. 277. Capt. E. B. S. Bingham**
(Gallaher, Victoria Cross Heroes 6th Series, 1917, No. 139)

Some other awards given for the Gallipoli campaign were to Capt. Percy H. Hansen of the 6th Batt. Lincolnshire Regiment (Fig. 274a), Corpl. Wm. Cosgrove, 1st Batt. Royal Munster Fusiliers (Fig. 274b), Corporal Cyril R. G. Bassett of the N.Z. Division Signal Co. (Fig. 274c), and 2nd Lieut. Hugo V. H. Throssell of the 10th Light Horse Regt. (Fig. 274d). Commander Edward Unwin of the *HMS River Clyde* won this award during the memorable landing at Gallipoli, in April 1915. "Seeing the lighters connecting his ship with the shore breaking adrift, he entered the water under a hurricane of bullets on three occasions, and later rescued wounded men, only giving up when compelled by absolute exhaustion" (Fig. 275).

An example of true leadership during the heat of battle is provided by Captain Anketell M. Read of the 1st Northamptonshire Regt. This occurred during fighting near Hulluch (in the north of France) on the morning of September 25, 1915. "Although partially gassed, he gallantly rallied demoralized troops and moved about encouraging them under withering fire. He was mortally wounded during this courageous work" (Fig. 276a). Another such example is of 2nd Lieut. Fredk. H. Johnson of the Royal Engineers, who won this honor on Hill 70 (also in the north of France) on September 25, 1915. Although wounded in the leg, he remained on duty throughout the attack, and "at a critical juncture led many charges under heavy fire on a German redoubt. He repeatedly rallied the men near him and by his example saved the situation and firmly established his new position" (Fig. 276b).

During the Battle of Jutland Captain Edward Barry Steward Bingham of *HMS Nestor* (Fig. 277) "led his destroyer division in an attack. He sighted the enemy battle-fleet, and with dauntless courage closed to within 3000 yards to attain a favorable position for firing torpedoes. On making this attack, *Nestor* and *Nicator* were under concentrated fire."

As indicated in a few earlier examples, posthumous V.C. awards were also given. The Late Major Yate of the 22nd Batt. King's Own Yorks Light Infantry (Fig. 278a) received his award "in recognition of an act of desperate gallantry at Le Cateau on August 26th, 1914. He commanded one of the two companies that remained in the trenches until all the ammunition was exhausted, and then, at the head of all that remained of his company (twenty in all) charged the enemy." The Thomson and Porteous V.C. Heroes set provides a little more detail. He was picked up wounded by the enemy and died as a prisoner of war (Fig. 278b, 278c). Several other examples are described further on. In the Cohen Weenen Victoria Cross

Heroes set, a card describes how the Late Capt. T. Wright of the Royal Engineers won his award for gallantry at Mons (23/8/14) (Fig. 279). "He attempted twice, under heavy fire, to connect leads necessary to blow up a bridge. He was mortally wounded at Vailly." Captain A. J. Shout won the award "For most conspicuous bravery. With a small party, he charged down trenches strongly held by enemy and threw four bombs among them killing eight and routing the remainder. Later on, the same day, he captured a further length of trench under similar conditions and continued to bomb the enemy at close range, under heavy fire. He was severely wounded and eventually succumbed" (Fig. 280).

**Fig. 278a. The Late Maj. Yate** (Imperial Tobacco Co. [of Canada], Victoria Cross Heroes, 1915, No. 25)

**Fig. 278b. The Late Maj. Yate** (Thompson & Porteous, V.C. Heroes, 1916, No. 28)

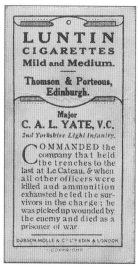

**Fig. 278c. The Late Maj. Yate, reverse side** (Thompson & Porteous, V.C. Heroes, 1916, No. 28)

**Fig. 279 The Late Capt. Theo. Wright** (Cohen Weenen, Victoria Cross Heroes, 1916, No. 56)

**Fig. 280 Capt. A. J. Shout** (Gallaher, Victoria Cross Heroes 8th Series, 1918, No. 188)

**Fig. 281. Lieut. G. A. Maling** (Gallaher, Victoria Cross Heroes 4th Series, 1915, No. 86)

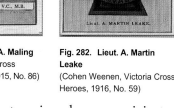

**Fig. 282. Lieut. A. Martin Leake** (Cohen Weenen, Victoria Cross Heroes, 1916, No. 59)

**Fig. 283a. Capt. Noel G. Chavasse** (Gallaher, Victoria Cross Heroes 7th Series, 1915, No. 159)

**Fig. 283b. Capt. Noel G. Chavasse, reverse side** (Gallaher, Victoria Cross Heroes 7th Series, 1915, No. 159)

The support services also were recipients of the Victoria Cross. Lieutenant Geo. A. Maling of the Royal Army Medical Corps was involved in the heavy fighting taking place near Fauquissart on September 25, 1915. "For 24 hours he continued to attend the wounded although he was once stunned and once covered with debris. Thus he attended with undaunted courage over 300 men, being under heavy fire a day and a night" (Fig. 281). Also from the R.A.M.C., Lieut. A. M. Leake (Fig. 282),

"already held a V.C. for bravery in South Africa during the Anglo-Boer War of 1899–1902. He has now been awarded a clasp (his second V.C.) for rescuing, under heavy fire, near Zonnebeke, wounded men that lay exposed near enemy trenches." Only one other person, Noel Chavasse, also of the Royal Army Medical Corps, won two V.C.s in the First World War (Figs. 283a, 283b).

A number of V.C. awards were given to the Colonial Forces fighting. One of the first of the overseas forces to be awarded the Victoria Cross was Havildar Ganga Singh of the Indian Army (Fig. 284). As described on the reverse of the card: "He is a fearless fighter at whom even the bravest enemy might quell, and was given the decoration for conspicuous valour. After killing a German officer, he seized the dead man's sword and slew ten other men with it. He was wounded five times in these encounters." Lance Naik Lala of the 41st Dogras, Indian Army "won this honour for conspicuous bravery in rescuing two wounded officers. He carried one officer to shelter and then crawled through a furious fire to rescue his adjutant. As returning with the latter was unwise under such heavy fire, Lala gave his clothing to keep the officer warm, and after dark he carried both into safety" (Fig. 285). 2nd Lieut. Arthur Seaforth Blackburn of the Australian Infantry "won the honour for dogged determination by which he captured an enemy trench, after personally leading four separate parties of bombers against it. He captured 250 yards of trench, then after crawling to reconnoitre, returned, attacked and seized another 120 yards of trench" (Fig. 286). Pte. W. F. Faulds of the South African Infantry won his honor "For most conspicuous bravery and devotion to duty. A bombing party under Lt. Craig attempted to rush across 40 yards of ground between British and enemy trenches. The majority of his party were killed or wounded. Unable to move, Lt. Craig lay midway between the two lines of trench. In full daylight, Faulds accompanied by two other men, climbed over the parapet, ran out, picked up the officer, and carried him back" (Fig. 287).

The clergy were also among recipients of the Victoria Cross. The Rev. Edward N. Mellish, who was a temporary Chaplain to the Forces, "won this honour for great devotion to duty in rescuing many men under heavy fire. Although his battalion had retired behind the fire, he preferred to stay and complete his rescue work, and for three days he repeatedly risked his life to help others" (Fig. 288). Rev. William Robert Fountaine Addison "won this honour for carrying a wounded man to the cover of a trench, and assisted several others to the same cover, after binding up their wounds under heavy rifle and machine gun fire. In addition, he encouraged the stretcher-bearers to go forward under heavy fire and collect the wounded" (Fig. 289).

**Fig. 284. Havildar Ganga Singh**
(Wills [Specialities], Victoria Cross Heroes, 1915, No.22)

**Fig. 285. Lance Naik Lala**
(Gallaher, Victoria Cross Heroes 5th Series, 1915, No. 106)

**Fig. 286. Lieut. Arthur Seaforth Blackburn**
(Gallaher, Victoria Cross Heroes 6th Series, 1917, No. 150)

**Fig. 287. Pte. William F. Faulds**
(Gallaher, Victoria Cross Heroes 8th Series, 1918, No. 177)

**Fig. 288. Rev. Edward N. Melish**
(Gallaher, Victoria Cross Heroes 5th Series, 1915, No. 114)

**Fig. 289. Rev. Wm. Robert Fountaine Addison**
(Gallaher, Victoria Cross Heroes 6th Series, 1917, No. 129)

A musician used his professional role in a way that won him this honor. Drummer Walter Ritchie of the Seaforth Highlanders, "on his own initiative stood on the parapet of an enemy trench, and under heavy machine gun fire and bomb attacks, repeatedly sounded the 'Charge' thereby rallying many men of various units, who, having lost their leaders, were wavering and beginning to retire. Throughout the day he carried messages over fire-swept ground" (Fig. 290). Drummer Spencer John Bent of the East Lancs. Regiment (Fig. 291) won his award as a result of action on the night of November 1, 1914. "This hero assumed command at the critical moment when his officer, Platoon Sergeant and Section Commander were all wounded, and he succeeded in holding a position near Le Gheer (in Belgium, near Ploegsteert), when a further stand against the enemy appeared hopeless."

Fig. 290. Drummer Walter Ritchie
(Gallaher, Victoria Cross Heroes 7th Series, 1917, No. 153)

Fig. 291. Drummer Spencer John Bent
(Wills [Specialities], Victoria Cross Heroes, 1915, No. 1)

Fig. 292a. Flight Lieut. R. A. J. Warneford
(Martins Ltd. V.C. Heroes, 1916, No. 24)

Fig. 292b. Flight Lieut. R. A. J. Warneford
(Gallaher, Victoria Cross Heroes 1st Series, 1915, No. 23)

Fig. 292c. Flight Lieut. R. A. J. Warneford
(Sinclair, Great War Leaders, 1915)

Fig. 293. Lance-Corpl. F. W. Holmes
(Thomson & Porteous, V.C. Heroes, 1916, No. 31)

An interesting set of twenty-five cards was issued by Martins Ltd. in 1916, titled V.C. Heroes. The front of the card illustrates a scene of action and below this is the same caption for each card, except that the name differs. It is "How ____ won the Victoria Cross." The reverse side of the card then provides the description. One card is of Flight Sub-Lieut. R. A. J. Warneford of the Royal Naval Air Service. "The intrepid airman flew over and destroyed a Zeppelin on June 7th, 1915 near Ghent. His machine capsized forcing him to descend upon enemy territory, but he arose again and flew back to his own lines in safety. He was accidentally killed 10 days later at Buc Aerodrome, France" (Fig. 292a). The Gallaher series of Victoria Cross awards (Fig. 292b) provides a little more detail of this event. It describes how he took his monoplane above a Zeppelin and dropped six bombs, causing the airship to explode. He is also illustrated on the 1915 issue Sinclair set of Great War Leaders (Fig. 292c). A somewhat similarly designed set is by Thomson and Porteous (V.C. Heroes, 1916), where the front of the card has a colored illustration of the actions occurring at the time of the awards. One card is of Lance-Corporal F. W. Holmes of the 2nd Battalion King's Own Yorkshire Light Infantry (Fig. 293). "At Le Cateau Lance Cpl. Holmes heroically carried a wounded comrade into safety under heavy fire, and later, by taking the place of a driver who had been wounded, succeeded in bringing a gun out of action."

Another set by Wills (New Zealand) of V.C.s from 1926 illustrates additional awards. Capt. J. McGregor, who was a soldier in the Canadian Army, won his award for "conspicuous bravery, leadership and self-sacrificing devotion to duty near Cambrai from 29th September to 3rd October, 1918 (Fig. 294). One of his bravest acts was, single handed and wounded, to engage the crews of enemy guns, putting them out of action and saving many casualties and enabling the advance to continue." This obviously is not referring to the Battle of Cambrai that was fought at the end of 1917. Amalgamated Press issued a set titled V.C.'s and their Glorious Deeds of Valour in 1930. It is an unnumbered set with no descriptive back. One chosen from this set, which does not provide much information historically, is labeled "Punjabi Saves Machine Gun." It shows a number of Indian troops in the midst of a battle (Fig. 295).

**Fig. 294. Capt. J. McGregor**
(Wills, [New Zealand], V.C.'s, 1926)

**Fig. 295. "Punjabi Saves Machine Gun"**
(Amalgamated Press, V.C.'s and Their Glorious Deeds of Valour, 1930)

**Fig. 296. Jos. Burton**
(Cope Bros., V.C. and D.S.O. Naval and Flying Heroes, 1916)

**Fig. 297. Capt. E. R. G. R. Evans**
(Cope Bros., V.C. and D.S.O. Naval and Flying Heroes, 1916)

**Fig. 298. Comm. Eric G. Robinson**
(Cope Bros., V.C. and D.S.O. Naval and Flying Heroes, 1916)

**Fig. 299. Comm. J. C. Wedgwood**
(Cope Bros., V.C. and D.S.O. Naval and Flying Heroes, 1916)

The one set that includes not only V.C. awards but also D.S.O. and D.S.C. awards is that by Cope Bros. titled V.C. and D.S.O. Naval and Flying Heroes (1916). The Distinguished Service Order, or D.S.O., according to the Robertson set of British Medals, was "Instituted for the purpose of recognizing distinguished services of Officers of the Naval and Military Services of the Empire, who have been specially recommended in Dispatches." J. Burton, Gunner, "Was Torpedo Boatswain of *HMS Lion* in the action off Dogger Bank 24th January 1915. For distinguished services rendered on that occasion he was mentioned in Admiral Beatty's Dispatch of January 27th, 1915, awarded D.S.C. March 3rd, 1915" (Fig. 296). Capt. E.R.G.R. Evans "Commanded *HMS Broke* when, on the night of April 20-21st, 1917 she and the *Swift* successfully engaged a flotilla of six German destroyers, of which two were sunk. 'In recognition of his splendid action' awarded the D.S.O. March 12th, 1917" (Fig. 297). Comm. E. G. Robinson

of the Royal Navy was awarded both the V.C. and the D.S.O. (Fig. 298). "On the 26th Feb. 1915, he advanced alone under heavy fire, into an enemy gun position and destroyed a 4-in. gun. He returned to obtain another charge and again went back to destroy a second gun. He would not allow members of his party to accompany him because of their conspicuous white uniforms." Com. J. C. Wedgwood won a D.S.O. "For conspicuous gallantry when in charge of a machine gun on board the *River Clyde* at the great Dardanelles landing (Fig. 299). For the part he played Commander Wedgwood was very highly recommended in dispatches by the Admiral in command. D.S.O. 24th April, 1915."

These examples cannot do justice to all the men who won this award. However, the ones included provide good insight into the actions of many individuals who went beyond the call of duty, and in a number of ways contributed to the ultimate Allied victory.

# CHAPTER 10

# ARMAMENTARIUM

## Land-Based Equipment

The First World War was the first truly industrialized and technologically-based war. This manifested itself in many ways, but mostly in weapons of destruction and mechanized war transportation. These were utilized on land, at sea and in the air. There are several card sets that clearly illustrate and explain these technological advances.

### MILITARY VEHICLES

Although the war began with the use of the horse, both in fighting and for transportation, in the case of the cavalry it rapidly became obsolete. However, despite the tremendous advances in motorized transportation to be described, the horse was still used extensively in the war. The wide variety of mechanized vehicles were more powerful and versatile, both for various types of transportation as well as in different capacities in battle. These vehicles are of three major categories: those used to transport soldiers and equipment, those used for support services, and those directly involved in the military actions. An important set produced by Wills in 1916 is titled Military Motors. However, because of the detail and sensitivity of the information contained in the set, the censors did not pass it for distribution. Subsequently some of these sets became available to collectors. Wills re-issued this set later the same year, presumably with enough modifications that permitted the censors to allow its distribution. In a set of fifty different cards a wide variety of mechanized vehicles and armor is illustrated and described. It is apparent from the description of these vehicles that a number of them were rapidly developed to address the unique challenges of trench warfare and an army bogged down in bad terrain. Some examples of these will be described according to the various categories. These vehicles were both manufactured and used by the Allies. British, French and Italian vehicles are illustrated in this set.

Pure mechanized transportation vehicles consisted of the motorcycle, motor busses, a motor raft, an officer's side car, motor transports, and a motor railway engine. This latter is of interest. The French must have developed these. As the reverse of the card of the motor railway engine describes (Fig. 300), "Owing to the enormous amount of traffic, the depth of the mud, and through being constantly subjected to heavy fire by the enemy, many of the roads in Northern France have

become almost useless. Welcome relief has been afforded by the construction of light railways. Motorcars, after being fitted with suitable wheels, are used as engines. Light trains are made up, and every satisfaction is given by the converted motor car in the new sphere of usefulness as a Railway Engine." Two varieties of cards are illustrated: the unpublished version that was censored, due to the sensitive military material it contained, and the later version that was passed for publication. Card No. 6 is of the British Motor Buses (Fig. 301). The description indicates that "These London Motor Buses which are now painted in a dull grey green to make them less conspicuous, are fulfilling a very important duty in transporting large bodies of troops and ammunition from the railhead to the back of the firing line. This form of mechanical transport enables a rapid concentration of troops at any given point, and adds greatly to the motility of our forces. The ever increasing work of our Army Transport Corps is greatly facilitated by the splendid service of these vehicles."

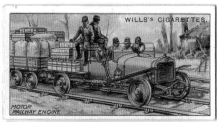

**Fig. 300. Motor Railway Engine**
(Wills, Military Motors [not passed by censors, and passed for publication], 1916, No. 38)

Fig. 301 **British Motor Bus**
(Wills, Military Motors [not passed by censors], 1916, No. 6)

**Fig. 302. Motor Baths**
(Wills, Military Motors [passed for publication, not passed by censors], 1916, No. 5)

Examples of support vehicles include "Motor Baths" (Fig. 302), a "Motor Horse Ambulance" (Fig. 303), a "Motor Restaurant and Soup Kitchen" (Figs. 304, 305), a "Motor Kitchen" (Fig. 306), a "Motor Operating Theatre" (operating room) (Figs. 307a, 307b), a "Motor Postal Car" (Fig. 308) and an "X-Ray Ambulance" (Fig. 309). These were built by different countries constituting the Allied forces. For example, the X-ray vehicle was Russian, the kitchen was Belgian-built, and various motor ambulances were produced by the New Zealanders, the Australians and the French. The description of the French ambulance states: "Our French Allies have devised a remarkably quick and effective method of transforming an ordinary Taxi-Cab into a most useful Ambulance Car. The body of the taxi is removed, and a strong wooden framework substituted…"

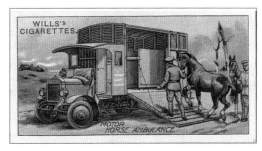

**Fig. 303. Motor Horse Ambulance**
(Wills, Military Motors [not passed by censors], 1916, No. 10)

**Fig. 304. Motor Restaurant**
(Wills, Military Motors [not passed by censors], 1916, No. 13)

Fig. 306 **Motor Kitchen**
(Wills, Military Motors [not passed by censors], 1916, No. 27)

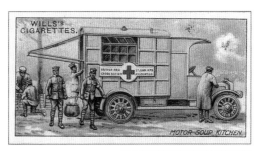

**Fig. 305. Motor Soup Kitchen**
(Wills, Military Motors [not passed by censors], 1916, No. 15)

**Fig. 307a. Motor Operating Theatre (Operating Room)**
(Wills, Military Motors [passed for publication, not passed by censors], 1916, No. 38)

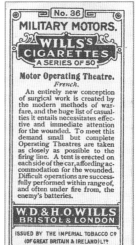

No. 36
**MILITARY MOTORS.**
**WILL'S CIGARETTES**
A SERIES OF 50

**Motor Operating Theatre.**
*French.*

An entirely new conception of surgical work is created by the modern methods of warfare, and the huge list of casualties it entails necessitates effective and immediate attention for the wounded. To meet this demand small but complete Operating Theatres are taken as closely as possible to the firing line. A tent is erected on each side of the car, affording accommodation for the wounded. Difficult operations are successfully performed within range of, and often under fire from, the enemy's batteries.

**W. D. & H. O. WILLS**
**BRISTOL & LONDON**

ISSUED BY THE IMPERIAL TOBACCO Cº
(OF GREAT BRITAIN & IRELAND) LTº

**Fig. 307b. Motor Operating Theatre, reverse side**
(Wills, Military Motors [not passed by censors], 1916, No. 38)

Fig. 308. Motor Postal Car (Wills, Military Motors [not passed by censors], 1916, No. 46)

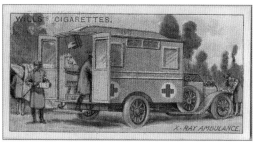

Fig. 309. X-Ray Ambulance (Wills, Military Motors [not passed by censors], 1916, No. 48)

Fig. 310. Anti-Aircraft Gun Motor (Wills, Military Motors [not passed by censors], 1916, No. 1)

Vehicles involved directly in the armed conflict included an "Anti-Aircraft Gun Motor" (Fig. 310), an "Armoured Tricycle" (Fig. 311) carrying a machine gun, and a "British Built Motor Fortress" (Figs. 312a, 312b) used for scouting as well as raids. It had the sleeve-valve engine that was almost noiseless. There were also various types of armored cars, including a British built one (Fig. 313a), a Belgian one (Fig. 313b) and a Serbian one (Fig. 313c). The "French Motor Auto-Gun" (Fig. 314) was an ingenious vehicle that according to its description had a recoiling gun, a driver, a gun crew and ammunition. It had an elaborate stabilizing mechanism for firing the gun.

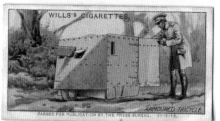

Fig. 311. Armoured Tricycle (Wills, Military Motors [not passed by censors, passed for publication], 1916, No. 3)

Fig. 313a. British Armoured Car Wills, Military Motors [not passed by censors], 1916, No. 2)

Fig. 312a. Motor Fortress (Wills, Military Motors [not passed by censors], 1916, No. 9)

Fig. 313b. Belgian Armoured Car (Wills, Military Motors [not passed by censors], 1916, No. 26)

Fig. 312b. Motor Fortress, reverse side (Wills, Military Motors [not passed by censors], 1916, No. 9)

Fig. 313c. Serbian Armoured Car (Wills, Military Motors [not passed by censors], 1916, No. 49)

Fig. 314 French Motor Auto-Gun (Wills, Military Motors [not passed by censors], 1916, No. 32)

The B.A.T. War Weapons set of 1914 illustrated a number of the above military vehicles. There are a number of cards with different "Armoured Cars." Unfortunately no further details of these are available. Vehicles not previously described and illustrated in this set are a "Wire Cutter" (Fig. 315), a "Trench Digger" (Fig. 316), an "Anti-Aircraft Gun" (Fig. 317) and a motorized "Searchlight" (Fig. 318). In the CWS Cigarettes set of War Series another vehicle illustrated is a "Field Bakery" (Fig. 319).

Fig. 315. Wire Cutter (B.A.T., War Weapons, 1914)

Fig. 316. Trench Digger (B.A.T., War Weapons, 1914)

Fig. 318. Motorized Search Light (B.A.T., War Weapons, 1914)

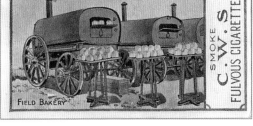

Fig. 319. Field Bakery (CWS Tobacco, War Series, 1914)

Fig. 317. Anti-Aircraft Gun (B.A.T., War Weapons, 1914)

## THE TANK

Without doubt, the singular most important military vehicle invented during the war, and one that had some impact on the outcome of this conflict, was the tank. On card No. 28 of the set Teofani (Past and Present), Weapons of War, there is an illustration of a tank (Figs. 320a, 320b). The description on the back indicates how "the Great War was responsible for many revolutionary developments in military methods, and perhaps the greatest of all was the introduction of the tank." It adds that "the earliest tanks were introduced at the Battle of the Somme in 1916 and they were clumsy and unreliable, but tremendous improvements then took place." The Pilot set of Britain's Defenders has an illustration of the tank with a rather dramatic description titling it "Land Battleships!" (Fig. 321). "Stark terror struck into the hearts of the German troops on the Somme in 1916 when out of the mists huge metal monsters, sending out a stream of death, appeared from the British side, lumbered on as though nothing could stop them, passed over trenches as though they did not exist. Tanks had arrived!"

Fig. 320a. The Tank (Teofani (Past & Present), Weapons of War, 1938, No. 28)

Fig. 320b. The Tank, reverse side (Teofani (Past & Present), Weapons of War, 1938, No. 28)

Fig. 321. "Land Battleships!" (Pilot, Britain's Defenders, 1950)

Fig. 322a. Mark IV Tank (Wills (Castella), The Story of the Tank, 1997, No.1)

At a more serious level the Wills (Castella) The Story of the Tank set of 1997 describes and illustrates various tanks. On one card there is an illustration of the first tank, a Mark IV (Figs. 322a, 322b). The rear of the card provides interesting information. It indicates that the development of the tank was a closely guarded secret, that the term tank referred to a water tank, and was used to avoid interest by spies. It describes this weapon as "rhomboid-shaped monsters that were awe-inspiring as they crawled remorselessly over the previously impassable barbed wire entanglements towards the German trenches in 1916." It then goes on to provide some technical aspects of this tank. It was powered by the 105 hp Daimler engine that was exposed to the crew and glowed red hot. It weighed twenty-eight tons. It was armed either with two six-pounder guns and three machine guns or six machine guns.

Fig. 322b. Mark IV Tank, reverse side (Wills (Castella), The Story of the Tank, 1997, No.1)

Another card of the same set illustrates and describes the French contemporary version of this tank. It was the Renault FT17 (Fig. 323). This tank, according to the description on the rear of the card, had a gun that was in a fully rotating turret.

**Fig. 323. Renault FT17 Tank**
(Wills (Castella), The Story of the Tank, 1997, No.2)

**Fig. 324. The Whippet Tank**
(Wills (Castella), The Story of the Tank, 1997, No.3)

**Fig. 325. A Tank**
(B.A.T., War Weapons, 1914)

Another World War I tank illustrated and described in this set (card No. 3) was the Whippet (Fig. 324). It had a top speed of eight mph, twice that of the Mark IV. It weighed only fourteen tons. One such vehicle was used by Lieutenant CH Sewell, who posthumously was awarded the V.C. for saving the crew of another Whippet tank in August 1918. The B.A.T. set illustrates a tank but provides no further details (Fig. 325).

**Fig. 326. Brigade of Howitzers**
(Imperial Tobacco Co., Modern War Weapons, 1916, No. 6)

## GUNS

Various forms of guns are illustrated well in card sets, especially the heavier equipment. Both Wills and the Imperial Tobacco Company issued the identical set in 1915 titled Modern War Weapons. This set included land, sea and air-based weapons. No. 6 illustrates a "Brigade of 5 in. Howitzers" (Fig. 326). John Player issued in 1917 a set of large cards of Artillery in Action. No. 1 is titled "A 15-inch Howitzer in Position" (Fig. 327a). It describes on the reverse side how it was built in response to the "monsters with which the Germans surprised us in 1914." "It is able to hurl a shell weighing two-thirds of a ton a distance of six miles." It also illustrates and describes 12-inch and 8-inch Howitzers (Figs. 327b, 327c, 327d).

**Fig. 327a. Howitzer in Position**
(John Player, Artillery In Action, 1917, No. 1)

**Fig. 327b. 12 inch Howitzer**
(John Player, Artillery In Action, 1917, No.3)

**Fig. 327c. 12 inch Howitzer, reverse side**
(John Player, Artillery In Action, 1917, No.3)

**Fig. 327d. 8 inch Howitzer**
(John Player, Artillery In Action, 1917, No.4)

An 18-pounder field gun (Fig. 328), an anti-aircraft gun (Fig. 329), and a Vickers Machine gun (Fig. 330) are also illustrated in these sets. The Stokes Trench Mortar is also illustrated and described (Fig. 331). According to the description "this was invented by Sir Wilfred Stokes, K.B.E., in the early days of the war as a reply to the German bomb-throwing machines."

A major Naval gun is illustrated and described in the Lychgate Press set of Images of the Great War. It is of the 6-inch long-range quick firer. It describes how it "has a range of 22,000 yards, but becomes really effective at 18,000 yards. It is also an excellent weapon, due to its ability to be very rapidly re-loaded" (Fig. 332).

**Fig. 328. 18 Pounder Field Gun**
(John Player, Artillery In Action, 1917, No. 7)

Anti-Aircraft Gun.

**Fig. 329. Anti-Aircraft Gun**
(John Player, Artillery In Action, 1917, No. 8)

Light Vickers Machine Gun.

**Fig. 330. Vickers Machine Gun**
(John Player, Artillery In Action, 1917, No. 11)

Stokes Trench Mortar.

**Fig. 331. Stokes Trench Mortar**
(John Player, Artillery In Action, 1917, No. 10)

**Fig. 332. Six-Inch Long-Range Firer**
(Lychgate Press, Images of the Great War, 2013, No. 8)

In the CWS Cigarettes set of War Series several guns are illustrated, including a modern Lee Enfield with Long Bayonet (Fig. 333) and a Maxim self-powered machine gun, invented by Sir Hiram Maxim in 1884 (Figs. 334a, 334b).

The process of the manufacture of munitions and shell-making is illustrated and described in Chapter 12: The Home Front, figures 482a, 482b, 504, 506a-506c, and 507a-507c.

Another card in the Lychgate Press set illustrates an ammunition dump behind British lines in France. The description indicates that "Factories in Britain are producing more shells in a fortnight, than they did in the whole of the first year of the war" (Fig. 335).

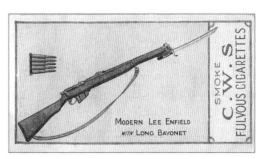

**Fig. 333. Lee Enfield**
(CWS, War Series, 1914)

127

**Fig. 334a. Maxim Machine Gun**
(CWS, War Series, 1914)

**Fig. 334b. Sir Hiram Maxim**
(Ogden's Guinea Gold,
General Interest 1-200,
c1901, No. 122)

**Fig. 335. Ammunition Dump**
(Lychgate Press, Images of
the Great War, 2013, No. 10)

In the Imperial Tobacco Co. set of Modern War Weapons several German weapons are also illustrated, for example, the "Latest German Howitzer" (Fig. 336). However, for a more extensive review of German weapons Adkin and Sons issued a set in 1917 titled War Trophies. It illustrates and describes a wide variety of captured German guns (Figs. 337a, 337b, 337c, 337d).

**Fig. 336. German Howitzer**
(Imperial Tobacco Co., Modern War
Weapons, 1916, No. 18)

**Fig. 337a. Krupp Gun**
(Adkin & Sons, War Trophies,
1917, No. 8)

**Fig. 337b. German Machine Gun**
(Adkin & Sons, War Trophies, 1917, No. 9)

**Fig. 337c. German Trench
Mortar**
(Adkin & Sons, War Trophies,
1917, No. 13)

**Fig. 337d. German Trench
Mortar, reverse side**
(Adkin & Sons, War Trophies,
1917, No. 13)

## CHEMICAL WEAPONS

The use of chemical weapons was a major and lethal aspect of land-based warfare introduced during the First World War. A variety of chemicals were used, such as tear gas, chlorine and phosgene. However, the most notorious one that is most remembered as integral to this war was mustard gas. It is a sulphur-based gas. The Germans first introduced this gas in July 1917 before the Third Battle of Ypres. Teofani issued a set in 1938 of Weapons of War, where one card is of "Mustard Gas" (Fig. 338). It describes "its most effective use in the Great War. All nations have made extensive preparations to defend themselves against it…"

Fig. 338. Mustard Gas
(Teofani (Past & Present), Weapons of War, 1938, No. 44)

Fig. 340a. German, Wesfalen
(Wills, The World's Dreadnoughts, 1910, No. 13)

Fig. 340b. German, Nassau
(Wills, The World's Dreadnoughts, 1910, No. 12)

Fig. 339a. HMS Dreadnought
(Wills, The World's Dreadnoughts, 1910, No. 5)

Fig. 339b. HMS Dreadnought, reverse side
(Wills, The World's Dreadnoughts, 1910, No. 5)

Fig. 341a. U.S., South Carolina
(Wills, The World's Dreadnoughts, 1910, No. 17)

Fig. 341b. Japan, Satsuma
(Wills, The World's Dreadnoughts, 1910, No. 18)

Fig. 341c. France, Voltaire
(Wills, The World's Dreadnoughts, 1910, No. 9)

## WARSHIPS AND NAVAL WEAPONS

In 1904 Admiral John Fisher was appointed First Sea Lord of the Admiralty. His immediate task was to reorganize and modernize the British Navy. He was the driving force behind the development of an all big gun battleship. This resulted in the launching in 1906 of the *HMS Dreadnought*, a battleship that revolutionized the Royal Navy. The name of this ship, "Dreadnought," was then taken to be associated with a whole generation of battleships. In 1910 Wills issued a set of The World's Dreadnoughts. Card No. 5 illustrates this original Dreadnought (Figs. 339a, 339b). The description on the reverse indicates that it had a displacement of 17,900 tons and lists the number of guns. It had a speed of 21 knots. Similarly, Churchman's Silhouettes of Warships illustrates this ship on card No. 4. This was soon followed by the German battleships of the same class, with the *Westfalen* and the *Nassau* both completed in 1909 and both illustrated on the Wills set (Figs. 340a, 340b). This same set illustrates similar ships from the United States, Japan, France and other major powers (Figs. 341a, 341b, 341c).

Fisher's committee also produced a new type of cruiser that was faster and became known as the battlecruiser class of ships. They were not very different from the dreadnoughts. The first of these was the *HMS Invincible* (Figs. 342a, 342b). This vessel and her sister ship the *Inflexible* (Fig. 343) are best known for the successful sinking of the German armored cruisers *Scharnhorst* and *Gneisenau* at the battle of the Falkland Islands in December 1914.

**Fig. 342a. HMS Invincible** (Mitchell, British Warships, Second Series, 1915, No. 43)

**Fig. 342b. HMS Invincible** (Sniders and Abrahams, Great War Leaders and Warships, 1915)

**Fig. 343. Inflexible** (Mitchell, British Warships, First Series, 1915, No. 11)

Fisher also was the force behind the introduction of submarines into the British Navy, three of which are shown in Cohen Weenen's War Series, Admirals and Warships, where the Submarines *E2, E4* and *D7* are illustrated (Figs. 344a, 344b, 344c). A Royal Navy submarine is illustrated in Will's Britain's Part in the War (Fig. 345). However, the submarine was used to a far greater extent by Germany and with significantly greater impact.

**Fig. 344a. E2 Submarine** (Cohen Weenen, War Series, Admirals and Warships, 1916, No. 8)

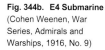

**Fig. 344b. E4 Submarine** (Cohen Weenen, War Series, Admirals and Warships, 1916, No. 9)

**Fig. 344c. D7 Submarine** (Cohen Weenen, War Series, Admirals and Warships, 1916, No. 24)

**Fig. 345. Royal Navy Submarine** (Will's, Britain's Part in the War, 1917, No. 9)

Fig. 346. **HMS Oak**
(Godfrey Phillips, British Warships, 1915, No. 5)

Fig. 347. **Light Cruiser**
(Phillips, War Pictures, 1915, No. 40)

Fig. 348. **Torpedo Boat Destroyer**
(Phillips, War Pictures, 1915, No. 41)

Fig. 349. **Minelayer**
(Phillips, War Pictures, 1915, No. 44)

Fig. 350. **Mine Trawler**
(Phillips, War Pictures, 1915, No. 45)

In the class of Destroyers, the *HMS Oak* (Fig. 346) was a "new type of ocean-going destroyer. Launched in 1912 *The Oak* was one of the swiftest vessels in the world. Utilizes oil fuel." Phillips issued a silk set in 1915 of War Pictures. It illustrates different types of vessels, including a light cruiser (Fig. 347), a torpedo boat destroyer (Fig. 348), a minelayer (Fig. 349) and a mine trawler (Fig. 350). Home and Colonial Stores set of War Pictures illustrates an armored cruiser (Fig. 351).

There are many card sets that illustrate and describe a large number of various warships. Only a few have been mentioned. In the naval section of Chapter 8: War Scenes, many vessels are described in the context of the various sea battles fought during the course of the war.

Fig. 351. **Armored Cruiser**
(Home and Colonial Stores, War Pictures, 1915, No. 61)

In the Ogdens 1915, the Wills 1916, and Imperial Tobacco Company 1916 identical sets of Modern War Weapons, a variety of torpedoes are illustrated, including the Whitehead Torpedo (Fig. 352), named after its inventor, British Engineer Robert Whitehead, who developed the first self-propelled torpedo. A number of naval guns are illustrated as well (Fig. 353).

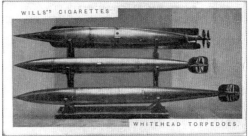

Fig. 352. **Whitehead Torpedo**
(Wills, Modern War Weapons, 1916, No. 20)

Fig. 353. **Naval Guns**
(Wills, Modern War Weapons, 1916, No. 5)

# Aviation

Aviation warfare took two forms in the First World War: there were mobile balloons and traditional aircraft.

## BALLOONS

Amalgamated Press issued a set of Famous Aircraft in 1927. One card illustrates a "Submarine Scout Ship" that according to the description "were commonly known as blimps and were very familiar round the coasts of Britain" (Fig. 354). Another card illustrates and describes the German Zeppelin Airship "which raided England during the war" (Fig. 355). Winston Churchill in his Naval Supplementary speech in the House of commons in 1914 indicated "A considerable new program of airship construction has been approved…A contract has been signed with Messrs. Armstrong for these large semi-rigid airships of an Italian design" (Fig. 356).

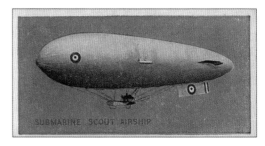

Fig. 354. Blimp (Amalgamated Press, Famous Aircraft, 1927, No. 2)

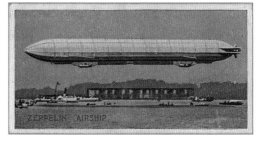

Fig. 355. Zeppelin Airship (Amalgamated Press, Famous Aircraft, 1927, No. 8)

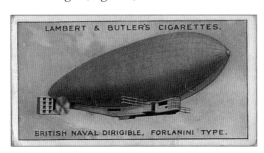

Fig. 356. British Naval Dirigible (Lambert and Butler, Aviation, 1915, No. 10)

Fig. 357. Wright Brothers First Flight (Trucards, History of Aircraft, 1970, No. 2.)

## AIRCRAFT

The first heavier-than-air mechanized powered flight in an aircraft had been undertaken only eleven years before the start of the war when the Wright brothers made the first flight (Fig. 357). In the decade that followed significant advances were made including trans-channel flights, first pioneered by the French designer Louis Bleriot who flew across the English Channel in 1909 (Figs. 358a, 358b).

At the start of the war, none of the great powers possessed any meaningful number of aircraft and those that were in operation were used mainly for reconnaissance purposes. Aircraft were also not very reliable and were somewhat fragile in 1914. However, over the course of the war significant advancement in the technology of airplanes occurred and airpower gained increasing importance in the execution of the war. By the end of the war there had been a tenfold increase in aerial forces. During this time there was not an established independent arm of the Allied forces devoted to the air. No air force arm had yet been established. Aircraft and squadrons were part of either the military or naval forces. Only later in the war did the British establish an independent air force.

The aircraft were initially developed and used mainly in support of the static war on land. They were involved significantly in battlefield reconnaissance, artillery observation, and communication with the infantry. As a result of these functions further development occurred with fighter aircraft to intercept and disrupt these activities. Thus in the latter half of the war the aerial campaign above the landlocked troops in the trenches increased in frequency and intensity. By the end of the war thousands of aircraft were deployed by all the air forces.

AVIATION SERIES
FIRST SERIES OF 25

("FLIGHT" Photograph)

3

BLERIOT MONOPLANE

Designed and built by M. Louis Bleriot this type of machine, fitted with a fan shaped three cylinder Anzani engine of only 25 h.p., flew the English Channel for the first time in 1909. Control was obtained by warping the wings.

ISSUED BY
R. & J. HILL, Ltd.
The Spinet House, London
Estd. 160 Years

Fig. 358a. Louis Bleriot (Hill, Aviation Series, 1934, No. 3)

Fig. 358b. Louis Bleriot, reverse side (Hill, Aviation Series, 1934, No. 3)

Fig. 360. **Dropping Bomb**
**From Airplane**
(Wills, Modern War Weapons,
1916, No. 3)

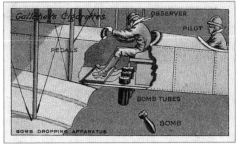

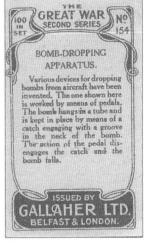

**Fig. 359. Royal Naval Air Service**
(Will's, Britain's Part in the War,
1917, No. 12)

**Fig. 361a. Bomb-Dropping Apparatus**
(Gallaher, Great War, Second Series, 1915, No. 154)

**Fig. 361b. Bomb-Dropping**
**Apparatus, reverse side**
(Gallaher, Great War, Second Series,
1915, No. 154)

In May 1912 the Royal Flying Corps was formed with military and naval wings. The Royal Naval Air Service was under the Admiralty (Fig. 359).

At first armed conflict from the airplane was very basic. In the Wills and the Imperial Tobacco Company sets of Modern War Weapons a card is titled "Dropping Bombs from Aeroplane" (Fig. 360). These bombs would be held over the side of the plane by the airmen and dropped onto the land below. Technology was rapidly developed to more effectively drop bombs. In the Gallaher Great War, Second Series, 1915 set, a card titled "Bomb-Dropping Apparatus" illustrates one of a variety of devices (Figs. 361a, 361b). The one in the illustration "is worked by pedals. The bomb hangs in a tube and is kept in place by means of a catch engaging with a groove in the neck of the bomb. The action of the pedal disengages the catch and the bomb falls." In the Kellogg Co. set of History of British Military Aircraft a card illustrates a Handley Page V/1500 bomber (Fig. 362). The reverse side description explains how "the Admiralty operated a bombing force and met with success early in the 1914-18 War. The bomber developed more quickly than the fighter...A further development, the H.P. 1500, was the largest aircraft flying during the Great War and ordered for the specific purpose of bombing Berlin."

**Fig. 362. Handley Page V/1500**
(Kellogg Co., History of British Military Aircraft, 1963, No. 2)

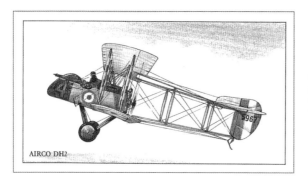

**Fig. 363. Airco DH2**
(Golden Era, Aircraft
of the First World War,
1994, No. 11)

**Fig. 364a. Sopwith Pup**
(Golden Era, Aircraft
of the First World War,
1994, No. 16)

**AIRCRAFT OF THE FIRST WORLD WAR**
*A Series of 24 Picture Cards*

**16. Sopwith Pup**
Described by pilots as 'the most delightful aircraft ever made', the Pup had almost perfect flying qualities - simple yet rugged, excellent manoeuverability and it made a stable gun platform. The Royal Naval Air Service were the first squadron to receive the new type in Autumn 1916. Initially equipped with a single Vickers, later armament progressed to Le Prieur Rockets or an upward firing Lewis, as on the night fighting version illustrated here. Pups were moved to home defence to combat German air raids, but proved inadequate in both range and altitude. The end of WWI saw many performing as trainers.
*Engine: 80hp Le Rhône*
*air cooled rotary*
*Span: 26'6" Maximum Speed: 111.5mph*

**GOLDEN ERA**
©Golden Era Tel: Billericay (0277) 632174

**Fig. 364b. Sopwith Pup, reverse side**
(Golden Era, Aircraft of the First World
War, 1994, No. 16)

In 1994 Golden Era issued a set titled Aircraft of the First World War. These cards illustrate and describe mostly Allied airplanes, but also some German ones. Among these are some famous British planes, such as the Airco DH2 (Fig. 363), three Sopwith models—Pup, 1½ Strutter and Tabloid (Figs. 364a, 364b, 364c, 364d)—and the R.A.F. (Royal Aircraft Factory) FE8 (Fig. 365). French aircraft included the SPAD XIII (Fig. 366), the Moraine Saulnier N (Fig. 367) and the Nieuport 17 (Fig. 368). There are several German aircraft included in this set, among them the Focker Dr1 (Fig. 369) and the Gotha GIV (Fig. 370).

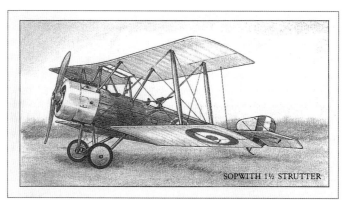

**Fig. 364c. Sopwith 1½ Strutter**
(Golden Era, Aircraft of the First World War, 1994, No. 13)

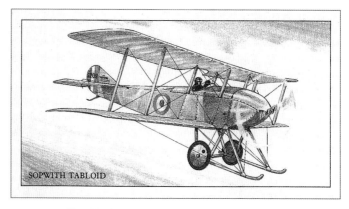

**Fig. 364d. Sopwith Tabloid**
(Golden Era, Aircraft of the First World War, 1994, No. 5)

**Fig. 365.  RAF FE8**
(Golden Era, Aircraft of the First World War,
1994, No. 12)

**Fig. 366.  SPAD XIII**
(Golden Era, Aircraft of the First World War,
1994, No. 17)

**Fig. 367.  Moraine Saulnier N**
(Golden Era, Aircraft of the First World War,
1994, No. 6)

**Fig. 368.  Nieuport 17**
(Golden Era, Aircraft of the First World War,
1994, No. 15)

**Fig. 369.  Focker Dr1**
(Golden Era, Aircraft of the First
World War, 1994, No. 10)

**Fig. 370.  Gotha GIV**
(Golden Era, Aircraft of the First World War,
1994, No. 20)

Even before the war efforts were made to develop machine-gun-carrying aircraft. At the outbreak of war the Royal Flying Corps, according to the reverse side description of a card in the Kellogg set, "persevered with biplanes...two-seat aircraft being used for reconnaissance. The fighter developed only slowly – the difficulty being to find an efficient way of firing a machine gun without hitting the propeller" (Fig. 371). However, the Vickers FB.5 aircraft was one such aircraft that found a way (Fig. 372). The description on the reverse side of the card indicates how it "holds the distinction of being the world's first aircraft specifically designed for aerial combat." Vickers had been working under Admiralty contracts since November 1912 to develop a machine-gun firing attack aircraft that did not interfere with the propeller. In February 1913 they showed such a plane at the Aero show in London. It was called the EFB-1 (Experimental Fighting Biplane). The gun was nose-heavy and crashed on the first test flight. They went on to develop five such experimental planes until there was the successful FB. 5. The Airco DH1 was a similar type of plane. In July 1915 the Fokker E (Eindekker) I became operational. This plane gave the Germans air superiority until 1916. Card No. 10 describes how "Fokker engineers quickly developed arguably the most important advancement in aerial combat, the first single-seat fighter with a synchronized machine gun" Fig. 373).

Fig. 371. Biplane (Kellogg Co., History of British Military Aircraft, 1963, No. 4)

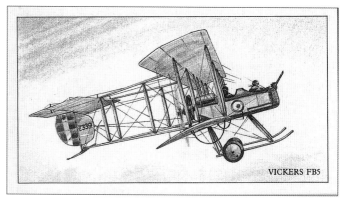

Fig. 372. Vickers FB.5 (Golden Era, Aircraft of the First World War, 1994, No. 7)

Fig. 373. Focker Eindekker EIII (Golden Era, Aircraft of the First World War, 1994, No. 10)

Fig. 374. Nieuport 27 (Rockwell, Early Allied Planes, 2000, No. 7)

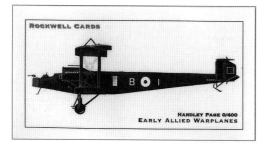

Fig. 375. Handley Page 0/400 (Rockwell, Early Allied Planes, 2000, No. 10)

Rockwell issued a set in 2000 titled Early Allied Warplanes. It indicates in the description of the Nieuport 27 (Fig. 374) that it was an extremely sophisticated plane, but no sooner had it been introduced in 1917 than it was superseded by another French plane, the Spad XIII (See Fig. 366). Although this plane was of French design, it is best known for its services with the American Expeditionary Force. Another card illustrates the famous Handley Page 0/400 that was the standard British bomber in 1917 (Fig. 375). Player's Doncella Golden Age of Flying set illustrates on a card the Royal Aircraft Factory SE5a, a plane that proved to be a very effective fighter (Figs. 376a, 376b).

**Fig. 376a. RAF SE5a**
(John Player (Doncella), The Golden Age of
Flying, 1977, No. 5)

THE
DONCELLA
GOLDEN AGE OF
FLYING

Series of 24                                                  No. 5

ROYAL AIRCRAFT FACTORY
SE.5A   F904 (G-EBIA)

Designed at Farnborough, the SE.5A entered
service with the Royal Flying Corps in 1917
and in the hands of such pilots as Ball,
Mannock and McCudden soon proved to be
an outstanding fighter. Over 5,000 were built
and after the War a number were converted
for civil use and used for sky-writing.
F904, now the only airworthy SE.5A, was one
of the aircraft used for civil purposes. It was
found hanging from the roof of the Armstrong
Whitworth factory at Baginton and acquired
by the Shuttleworth Collection. Apprentices
at the Royal Aircraft Establishment restored
the aircraft to its original condition and it is
displayed statically at Farnborough apart
from infrequent flights on special occasions.

Engine – 200 h.p. Hispano Suiza

Collect the series in the special Golden Age of Flying
Folder (opens out to a wall chart). Send a 25p postal
order (crossed and made payable to John Player and
Sons) plus your name and address to Doncella Album,
P.O. Box 55, John Player and Sons, Nottingham.

Issued by John Player and Sons, Imperial Tobacco Limited,
in conjunction with
The British Aircraft Preservation Council, Manchester.

**Fig. 376b. RAF SE5a, reverse side**
(John Player (Doncella), The Golden
Age of Flying, 1977, No. 5)

**Fig. 377. Short
Seaplane Type 184**
(Kellogg Co.,
History of British
Military Aircraft,
1963, No. 3)

SHORT SEAPLANE TYPE 184

In the Kellogg History of British Military Aircraft set, there is a card of a Short Seaplane Type 184 (Fig. 377). The reverse side description states "By 1912 the Admiralty seaplanes were mostly of Short Bros. manufacture. Before 1914, at Mr. Winston Churchill's instigation, Short's produced the first successful torpedo planes." Another important plane of the First World War was the Avro 504 (Fig. 378). It was first flown in 1913. It was used both as a bomber and a fighter. However, as the card description indicates, "it was as the world's finest trainer that it became universally known. Over eight thousand were built during the war."

At the onset of the Battle of Verdun on February 21, 1916, the Germans had air superiority and were blocking the French squadrons. However, by April the French had provided their specialist fighter squadrons with the new Nieuport 11 plane and they then rapidly gained air superiority. As for the Royal Flying Corps (RFC), they had their planes replaced with the new Sopwith 1 ½ Strutter, that had initially been earmarked for the Royal Naval Air Service (RNAS). This allowed them to

counteract the German Fokker Eindecker. With these modern planes the Allies maintained air superiority throughout the Battle of Verdun, ending in December, and of the Somme between July and November 1916. In the first half of 1917 the Germans raised specialist fighter squadrons called Jagdstaffeln that were equipped with their new Albatross D.III (Fig. 379). These became the best fighter on the field at that time. This culminated in devastating losses to the RFC, which was using the BE.2e, a slight improvement of the old BE.2c. However, in the latter half of 1917 the British Sopwith Camel (Figs. 380a, 380b) and S.E.5a and the French SPAD S.XIII were the major airplanes used, and by year end the Allies once again held air superiority. In 1918 increasing shortages of supplies to the Central Powers led to a further superiority of the Allies.

The overall impact of air power in the First World War was mainly tactical rather than strategic. However, by performing aerial photography and aerial spotting, it provided significant support to the artillery, which did play a critical role in the war.

**Fig. 378. Avro 504**
(John Player (Doncella), The Golden
Age of Flying, 1977, No. 4)

**Fig. 379. Albatross D.III**
(Golden Era, Aircraft of the First
World War, 1994, No. 19)

Fig.380a. Sopwith Camel
(Golden Era, Aircraft of the First
World War, 1994, No. 21)

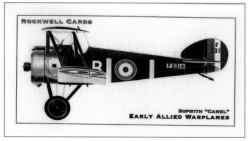

**Fig. 380b. Sopwith Camel**
(Rockwell, Early Allied Planes, 2000, No. 5)

# CHAPTER 11

# UNIFORMS, ARMY LIFE and MILITARIA

## Uniforms

There are many general military card sets that depict all forms of uniforms throughout the ages, including those that happened to be in use during the early part of the twentieth century. Most of these regiments participated in the War. However, to describe and illustrate these uniforms in general is a separate study in its own right. This section will deal predominantly with those sets that were produced during the war, related to the war era and also depicting war uniforms. Examples of uniforms of regiments that participated in the war and are mentioned in this book will also be illustrated.

The classical image of the World War I soldier is of the private in his battle uniform, including his World War One helmet, and either marching or in the trenches. However, there were also the formal, ceremonial uniforms of the soldiers, officers and other military and naval leaders. These were worn often during the war, particularly when away from the battlefield. This obviously applies more to the officers than to the privates and non-commissioned rank.

The Sunday Stories silk set The King and His Soldiers, 1916, has a varied collection of uniforms of the soldiers both in their battle and ceremonial dress. The first card is of H.M. King George V in his khaki uniform. The colonies are well represented in this set, with soldiers in battle uniform from Australia, Canada, India, and South Africa (Fig. 381).

**Fig. 381. The King and Colonies**
Sunday Stories, The King and His Soldiers, 1916)

Those attired in formal uniform are from various regiments in the My Weekly, Our Soldier Boys set of 1915. There are soldiers from the Argyll and Sutherland Highlanders (Fig. 382), the 15th (King's) Hussars (Fig. 383), the Royal Army Medical Corps (Fig. 384), the Royal West Kents (Fig. 385), Royal Irish Rifles (Fig. 386), Royal Marines (Fig. 387), and the 17th (Duke of Cambridge's Own) Lancers (Fig. 388). The reverse sides of these cards have a poem about the Allied soldier or the regiments. Two examples are shown: one of the Canadians and the other of the Royal Army Medical Corps (Figs. 389a, 389b).

**Fig. 382. Argyll and Sutherland Highlanders** (My Weekly, Our Soldiers Boys, 1915)

**Fig. 383. The 15th (King's) Hussars** (My Weekly, Our Soldiers Boys, 1915)

**Fig. 384. Royal Army Medical Corps** (My Weekly, Our Soldiers Boys, 1915)

**Fig. 385. Royal West Kents** (My Weekly, Our Soldiers Boys, 1915)

**Fig. 386. Royal Irish Rifles** (My Weekly, Our Soldiers Boys, 1915)

**Fig. 387. Royal Marines** (My Weekly, Our Soldiers Boys, 1915)

**Fig. 388. 17th (Duke of Cambridge's Own) Lancers** (My Weekly, Our Soldiers Boys, 1915)

**Fig. 389a. Canadians, reverse side**
(My Weekly, Our Soldiers Boys, 1915)

**Fig. 389b. RAMC, reverse side**
(My Weekly, Our Soldiers Boys, 1915)

Wilbur and Sons issued a set of large cards in 1915 titled Soldiers of the Allies. This set shows soldiers in their full battle dress complete with their equipment. Soldiers of England (Fig. 390), Scotland (Fig. 391), France (Fig. 392) and Italy (Fig. 393) are illustrated. The reverse of each card has a poem describing the soldier. For example, the Scottish soldier is described as follows (Fig. 394):

In cap and kilt of gayest plaids,
This "Highland Laddie" joins the fray,
He marches on with fearless stride
To fight for life and liberty.

**Fig. 390. England**
(Wilbur and Sons, Soldiers of the Allies, 1915)

**Fig. 391. Scotland**
(Wilbur and Sons, Soldiers of the Allies, 1915)

**Fig. 392. France**
(Wilbur and Sons, Soldiers of the Allies, 1915)

**Fig. 393. Italy**
(Wilbur and Sons, Soldiers of the Allies, 1915)

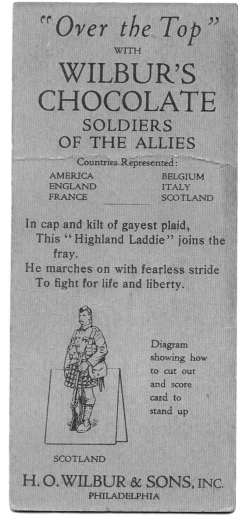

"Over the Top"
WITH
WILBUR'S
CHOCOLATE
SOLDIERS
OF THE ALLIES

Countries Represented:

AMERICA — BELGIUM
ENGLAND — ITALY
FRANCE — SCOTLAND

In cap and kilt of gayest plaid,
This "Highland Laddie" joins the fray.
He marches on with fearless stride
To fight for life and liberty.

Diagram showing how to cut out and score card to stand up

SCOTLAND

H. O. WILBUR & SONS, INC.
PHILADELPHIA

**Fig. 394. Scotland, reverse side**
(Wilbur and Sons, Soldiers of the Allies, 1915)

Ray and Co. issued a set titled War Series in 1915 that illustrates soldiers in their ceremonial uniforms. One card is of the 1st Life Guards (Fig. 395). Some other regiments illustrated are the Grenadier Guards (Lieutenant) (Fig. 396), the 13th Hussars (Fig. 397), the 1st (Royal) Dragoons (Fig. 398) and the London Scottish (Fig. 399). The reverse of each card provides a brief description of that regiment. Also illustrated are soldiers of the Allies.

**Fig. 395. 1st Life Guards**
(Ray and Co., War Series, 1915, No. 31)

**Fig. 396. Lieut. Grenadier Guards**
(Ray and Co., War Series, 1915, No. 42)

**Fig. 397. 13th Hussars**
(Ray and Co., War Series, 1915,
No. 46)

**Fig. 398. 1st (Royal) Dragoons**
(Ray and Co., War Series, 1915,
No. 51)

**Fig. 399. London Scottish**
(Ray and Co., War Series, 1915,
No. 63)

Phillips issued a set in 1915 titled War Pictures. It contains a large number of silk illustrations of soldiers, mainly in dress uniforms from a large variety of regiments that fought in the war, including British and Colonial, as well as Allied soldiers. A few examples include a Trooper of the Life Guards (Fig. 400), a Colour Sergeant from the Irish Guards (Fig. 401), a British officer in service dress (Fig. 402), the 14th King George's Own Ferozepure Sikhs (Fig. 403), a French Dragoon (Fig. 404), and a Belgian Grenadier (Fig. 405).

**Fig. 400. Trooper Life Guards**
(Phillips, War Pictures, 1915. No. 9)

**Fig. 401. Colour Sergeant, Irish Guards**
(Phillips, War Pictures, 1915. No. 15)

**Fig. 402. British Officer**
(Phillips, War Pictures, 1915. No. 25)

**Fig. 403. 14th KG Own Ferozepure Sikhs**
(Phillips, War Pictures, 1915. No. 28)

**Fig. 404. French Dragoon**
(Phillips, War Pictures, 1915. No. 55)

**Fig. 405. Belgian Grenadier**
(Phillips, War Pictures, 1915. No. 50)

Other examples of the uniforms of just a few regiments that participated in the War are also illustrated. When Churchill was at the front in 1916 he first joined the Grenadier Guards, as illustrated in the My Weekly series (Fig. 406). Subsequently, he commanded a brigade of the Royal Scots Fusiliers. An officer of this regiment is illustrated in Ogden's Soldiers of the King issued in 1909 (Fig. 407a). Another example of an officer is from Wills' 1912 issue of Types of the British Army (Fig. 407b). The Royal Scots Fusiliers is also illustrated in the 4th Series John Brindley set, History and Traditions of the British Army, 1990 (Fig. 407c). Shepherds Dairies issued a set in 1915 of War Pictures. One card shows a driver of the Royal Horse Artillery in his ceremonial uniform on a horse (Fig. 408).

**Fig. 406.  Grenadier Guards**
(My Weekly, Soldiers of the King, 1915)

**Fig. 407a.  Royal Scots Fusiliers**
(Ogden's Soldiers of the King, 1909, No. 38)

**Fig. 407b.  Royal Scots Fusiliers**
(Wills, Types of the British Army 1912, Reprint 1995)

**Fig. 407c.  Royal Scots Fusiliers**
(John Brindley, History and Traditions of the British Army, 4th Series, No. 107)

107. The Royal Scots Fusiliars.

**Fig. 409.  2nd Life Guards Officer**
(Laurens, British Cavalry Uniforms, 1975)

**Fig. 408.  Royal Horse Artillery**
(Shepherds Dairies, War Pictures, 1915, No. 13)

**Fig. 410.  1st Life Guards Officer**
(My Weekly, Soldiers of the King, 1915)

The Household Division served illustriously in many of the battles of the War. Laurens issued a set of playing cards in 1975 titled British Cavalry Uniforms. One illustrates a 2nd Life Guards Officer in Full Dress in the uniform of 1900 that was the same uniform as the one during the War (Fig. 409). My Weekly issued a set of Soldiers of the King in 1915. One is of a 1st Life Guards Officer (Fig. 410). Others have also been illustrated (Figs. 395, 396, 400, 401, 406, 418).

**Fig. 411. The Royal Engineers**
(Morning Foods Ltd, British
Uniforms, 1954, No. 4)

12. The Royal Welsh Fusiliers.

**Fig. 412. Royal Welsh
Fusiliers**
(John Brindley, History and
Traditions of the British Army,
1st Series, 1990, No. 12)

**Fig. 413. Lancashire Fusiliers**
(Ewebanks Ltd, British Uniforms,
1956, No. 16)

**Fig. 414. Middlesex Battalion or
London Scottish**
(Morning Foods Ltd, British
Uniforms, No. 3)

**Fig. 415. Royal Inniskilling
Fusiliers**
(Law, Types of British Soldiers,
1914)

**Fig. 416a. The Kings Royal Rifles**
(Phillips, Types of British Soldiers,
1900, M665)

**Fig. 416b. The Kings Royal Rifle
Regiment**
(John Brindley, Victorian and
Edwardian Soldiers in Full Dress,
1988, No. 19)

A few other examples of regiments that participated in various aspects of the war, most of which are mentioned in this book and which can be illustrated include the Royal Engineers (Fig. 411), the Royal Welsh Fusiliers (Fig. 412), Lancashire Fusiliers (Fig. 413), 7th Middlesex Battalion or London Scottish (Fig. 414), Royal Inniskilling Fusiliers (Fig. 415), the Kings Royal Rifle Regiment (Figs. 416a, 416b), Royal Horse Artillery (Fig. 417), Irish Guards (Fig. 418), Highland Light Infantry (Fig. 419), Gordon Highlanders (Fig. 420), Royal Army Medical Corps (Fig. 421), and the Royal Flying Corps (Figs. 422a, 422b). In the Butterworth & Son set on the History of the Suffolk Regiment, the front of the card illustrates a private in his uniform (Fig. 422c) and the reverse side of the card gives a history of the involvement of the regiment throughout the war (Fig. 422d).

**Fig. 417. Royal Horse Artillery**
(Chix Confectionary, Military Uniforms, 1970,
No. 20)

**Fig. 418. Irish Guards**
(Chix Confectionary, Military Uniforms, 1970, No. 39)

**Fig. 419. Highland Light Infantry**
(John Brindley, History and Traditions of the British Army, 1st Series, 1990, No. 25)

**Fig. 420. Gordon Highlanders**
(Chix Confectionary, Military Uniforms, 1970, No. 17)

**Fig. 421. Royal Army Medical Corps**
(Chix Confectionary, Military Uniforms, 1970, No. 49)

**Fig. 422a. Royal Flying Corps**
(Ewebanks Ltd, British Uniforms, 1956, No. 22)

**Fig. 422b. Royal Flying Corps**
(Brindley, History and Traditions of the British Army, 3rd Series, 1990, No. 88)

**Fig. 422c. British Private, 1917**
(Butterworth & Son, History of the Suffolk Regiment, No. 13, 1999)

**Fig. 422d. British Private, reverse side**
(Butterworth & Son, History of the Suffolk Regiment, No. 13, 1999)

The British American Tobacco Co. (BAT) set of Britain's Defenders, 1914, illustrates several of the military leaders resplendent in their uniforms. These illustrations are mainly of the headdress and upper chest. Examples of these leaders' headdress include those of General Edmund H. H. Allenby (Fig. 423), Ad. Hon. Sir H. Meux (Fig. 424), General Sir Douglas Haig (Fig. 425) and Lieut.-Gen. Sir H. C. O. Plumer (Fig. 426). The Wills Specialities set of the same title from 1914 also illustrates other leaders' headdress. These include the headdress of Admiral of the Fleet Sir A. D. Fanshawe (Fig. 427), Gen. Hon. Sir A. H. F. Paget (Fig. 428), and Gen. Sir Leslie Rundle (Fig. 429).

**Fig. 423. Partial Uniform of Allenby**
(B.A.T., Britain's Defenders, 1914, No. 13)

**Fig. 424. Partial Uniform of Meux**
(B.A.T., Britain's Defenders, 1914, No. 14)

**Fig. 425. Headdress of Haig**
(B.A.T., Britain's Defenders, 1914, No. 17)

**Fig. 426. Headdress of Plumer**
(B.A.T., Britain's Defenders, 1914, No. 25)

**Fig. 427. Headdress and Uniform of Fanshawe**
(Wills Specialities, Britain's Defenders, 1914, No. 5)

**Fig. 428. Headdress of Paget**
(Wills Specialities, Britain's Defenders, 1914, No. 10)

**Fig. 429. Headdress of Rundle**
(Wills Specialities, Britain's Defenders, 1914, No. 19)

**Fig. 430a. Headdress and Uniform of Colville**
(Wills Scissors, Britain's Defenders, 1914, No. 4)

**Fig. 430b. Headdress and Uniform of Jellicoe**
(Wills Scissors, Britain's Defenders, 1914, No. 6)

**Fig. 430c. Headdress and Uniform of Goodenough**
(Wills Scissors, Britain's Defenders, 1914, No. 8)

The Wills Scissors set, with the same title and year of issue, in addition illustrates the headdresses of Vice-Ad. Hon. Sir S. C. Colville (Fig. 430a), Admiral Sir John R. Jellicoe (Fig. 430b) and Commodore W. E. Goodenough (Fig. 430c). Vice-Ad. Sir David Beatty (Fig. 431) and Admiral Sir P. Scott (Fig. 432) are also illustrated. Headdresses of army leaders include General Sir F. R. Wingate (Fig. 433a) and General Sir Ian S. M. Hamilton (Fig. 433b).

Sinclair issued a set in 1926 titled British Sea Dogs. It illustrated the uniforms and outfits of various naval service men. One illustrates an Officer of the Royal Navy (Figs. 434a, 434b). Another card illustrates and describes the outfit of a diver (Figs. 435a, 435b), while a third illustrates and describes a Flying Officer of the R.N.A.S. (Figs. 436a, 436b).

**Fig. 431. Headdress of Beatty**
(Wills Scissors, Britain's Defenders, 1914, No. 41)

**Fig. 432. Upper Uniform of Scott**
(Wills Scissors, Britain's Defenders, 1914, No. 47)

**Fig. 433a. Upper Uniform of Wingate**
(Wills Scissors, Britain's Defenders, 1914, No. 31)

**Fig. 433b. Upper Uniform of Hamilton**
(Wills Scissors, Britain's Defenders, 1914, No. 46)

**Fig. 434a. Officer of the Royal Navy**
(John Sinclair, British Sea Dogs, 1926, No. 5)

**Fig. 434b. Officer of the Royal Navy, reverse side**
(John Sinclair, British Sea Dogs, 1926, No. 5)

Fig. 435a.  Outfit of a Diver
(John Sinclair, British Sea Dogs, 1926, No. 22)

Fig. 435b.  Outfit of a Diver, reverse side
(John Sinclair, British Sea Dogs, 1926, No. 22)

Fig. 436a.  Flying Officer R.N.A.S.
(John Sinclair, British Sea Dogs, 1926, No. 46)

Fig. 436b.  Flying Officer R.N.A.S., reverse side
(John Sinclair, British Sea Dogs, 1926, No. 46)

# Army Life

In 1915 Clarke issued a set titled *Army Life*. These illustrations were essentially of life away from the battlefield, many of them showing soldiers undergoing various aspects of their training. One is of "War Kite Drilling" (Fig. 437a). The reverse side indicates who invented this kite and to what effective purpose it was used in scouting (Fig. 437b). Another illustrates the method used in "Filtering Water" (Fig. 438). The reverse side describes the necessity to obtain water for troops when on active service. Attached to various units are up-to-date filtering carts. The description provides an important statistic. For an army of one hundred sixty thousand men and seventy thousand horses, one million, five hundred thousand gallons of water are required per day. A further card is titled "Unpacking Wagons" (Fig. 439). It describes how most military wagons can be packed into a very small space. An ordinary pattern four-wheeled Army Service Corps wagon can be completely built up in sixty seconds.

Fig. 437a.  War Kite Drilling
(Clarke, Army Life, 1915, No. 3)

Fig. 437b.  War Kite Drilling, reverse side
(Clarke, Army Life, 1915, No. 3)

Fig. 438.  Filtering Water
(Clarke, Army Life, 1915, No. 8)

Fig.439.  Unpacking Wagons
(Clarke, Army Life, 1915, No. 16)

One card illustrates and describes the process of "Making Gas for War Balloons" (Fig. 440a), while others show the filling of the balloons with this gas (Fig. 440b) and then a "Balloon Drill" (Fig. 440c). Other titles of cards are "Firing from a Gun Pit" (Fig. 441), "Lamp Signalling" (Fig. 442), "Picking up Wounded" (Fig. 443), and the last card in the set is "Flag Signalling" (Fig. 444). The reverse side of this last card describes how it is one of the first methods of signaling ever adopted, and is still used extensively in the soldier's training.

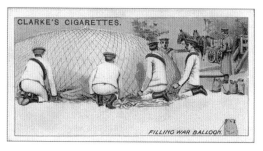

Fig. 440a. Making Gas for War Balloons (Clarke, Army Life, 1915, No. 19)

Fig. 440b. Filling the Balloon (Clarke, Army Life, 1915, No. 20)

Fig. 441. Firing from a Gun Pit (Clarke, Army Life, 1915, No. 5)

Fig. 440c. Balloon Drill (Clarke, Army Life, 1915, No. 22)

Fig. 442. Lamp Signalling (Clarke, Army Life, 1915, No. 12)

Fig. 443. Picking Up Wounded (Clarke, Army Life, 1915, No. 14)

Fig. 444. Flag Signalling (Clarke, Army Life, 1915, No. 25)

Ogden's set of Infantry Training from 1915 consists of fifty cards showing soldiers performing all different commands, usually when on parade. Examples include "Stand at Ease" (Figs. 445a, 445b), "The Present from the Slope" (Figs. 446a, 446b), "Saluting with and without Arms" (Fig. 447a, 447b), "Right and Left Parry" (Fig. 448), and various field signals (Fig. 449). These cards also illustrate the soldiers' uniform during the period of the war.

**Fig. 445a. Stand at Ease**
(Ogdens, Infantry Training,
1915, No. 1)

**Fig. 445b. Stand at Ease**
(Ogdens, Infantry Training,
1915, No. 2)

**Fig. 446a. Present from the Slope**
(Ogdens, Infantry Training, 1915,
No. 12)

**Fig. 446b. Present from the Slope**
(Ogdens, Infantry Training, 1915,
No. 14)

**Fig. 447a. Saluting with Arms**
(Ogdens, Infantry Training, 1915,
No. 29)

**Fig. 447b. Saluting without Arms**
(Ogdens, Infantry Training, 1915,
No. 32)

**Fig. 448. Right and Left Parry**
(Ogdens, Infantry Training, 1915, Nos. 39, 40)

**Fig. 449. Field
Signals**
(Ogdens, Infantry
Training, 1915,
Nos. 46-50)

# Militaria

Militaria may be defined as military objects or articles of historical interest.

Player issued in 1924 two sets (1st and 2nd Series) of one hundred fifty cards titled Army Corps and Divisional Signs 1914-1918. This set illustrates and describes a wide variety that were used during the war. A sample of these and that are illustrated include the 11th Corps (Fig. 450), the 36th Division (Fig. 451), the Cavalry Corps (Figs. 452a, 452b), the Guards Division (Fig. 453) and the Fourth Army (Figs. 454a, 454b).

The reverse of the Cavalry Corps card indicates that Saint George is regarded as the patron saint of the mounted soldier, hence the adoption of this sign by the Cavalry Corps to replace their original sign—a lady's head. For the Guards Division, the reverse description indicates how the officer who designed it wanted a clear and easily recognized sign, and thought of a human eye. The red and blue border represents the colors of the Guards Brigade.

**Fig. 450. 11th Corps**
(John Player, Army Corps and Divisional Signs 1914-1918, 1924, No. 3)

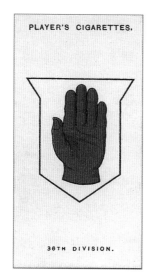

**Fig. 451. 36th Division**
(John Player, Army Corps and Divisional Signs 1914-1918, 1924, No. 8)

**Fig. 452a. Cavalry Corps**
(John Player, Army Corps and Divisional Signs 1914-1918, 1924, No. 12)

**Fig. 452b. Cavalry Corps, reverse side**
(John Player, Army Corps and Divisional Signs 1914-1918, 1924, No. 12)

**Fig. 453. Guards Division**
(John Player, Army Corps and Divisional Signs 1914-1918, 1924, No. 13)

**Fig. 454a. Fourth Army**
(John Player, Army Corps and Divisional Signs 1914-1918, 1924, No. 81)

**Fig. 454b. Fourth Army, reverse side**
(John Player, Army Corps and Divisional Signs 1914-1918, 1924, No. 81)

Morris issued a set of fifty cards in 1928 titled Victory Signs Series. They were distinguishing marks of the British Army. Several examples include those of the 5th Army (Fig. 455), the Cavalry Corps (Fig. 456), the 36th Division (Fig. 457), the No. 2 Water Tank Co. (Fig. 458), and the 22nd Motor Ambulance Column (Figs. 459a, 459b).

The reverse side of the 5th Army card describes how Sir Hugh Gough, a keen hunting man, introduced the sign of the racing red fox with a white splash in its tail as a sign for the 5th Army when he took command.

**Fig. 455. 5th Army**
(Morris, Victory Signs Series, 1928, No. 2)

**Fig. 456. Cavalry Corps**
(Morris, Victory Signs Series, 1928, No. 9)

**Fig. 457. 36th Division**
(Morris, Victory Signs Series, 1928, No. 26)

**Fig. 458. No. 2 Water Tank Company**
(Morris, Victory Signs Series, 1928, No. 46)

**Fig. 459a. Motor Ambulance Column**
(Morris, Victory Signs Series, 1928, No. 45)

**Fig. 459b. Motor Ambulance, reverse side**
(Morris, Victory Signs Series, 1928, No. 45)

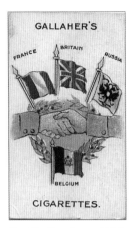

**Fig. 460. Flags France, Britain, Russia, Belgium**
(Gallaher, Flags of the Allies, 1914, No. 7)

**Fig. 461. Ireland**
(Gallaher, Flags of the Allies, 1914, No. 12)

**Fig. 462. Australia**
(Gallaher, Flags of the Allies, 1914, No. 16)

**Fig. 463a. Russia**
(Gallaher, Flags of the Allies, 1914, No. 21)

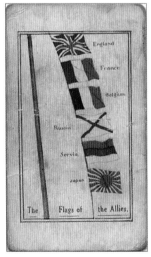

**Fig. 463b. The Flags of the Allies**
(S.H. Dawes, Army Pictures, Cartoons etc., 1916)

Gallaher in 1914 and Wills in 1915 each issued different types of sets of the Flags of the Allies. The Gallaher set illustrated the flag on the front of the card. The Wills set was made of silk and had the flag embroidered on the front with a description on the supporting board on the back. An interesting flag from the Gallaher set shows the flags of France, Britain, Russia and Belgium with two hands clasping each other (Fig. 460). Ireland is illustrated on card No. 12 (Fig. 461), Australia on No. 16 (Fig. 462), and Russia on No. 21 (Fig. 463a). In the Wills set examples include Australia, the Union of South Africa, Canada, India, Servia and France. Gallaher issued a more extensive set in 1914 titled The Allies Flags. Additional examples are New Zealand, Belgium, Ireland, and Scotland. Another illustrated card of the flags of the Allies is by Dawes in the set Army Pictures, Cartoons, etc. (Fig. 463b).

# CHAPTER 12

# The HOME FRONT

Although the majority of card sets of the War deal with the personalities, the actions at the battlefront, and of the individual battles, there are a number of sets that illustrate and describe the critical work that was done in the United Kingdom, far away from the fields of battle.

These fall under several categories. The first relates to the critical work of recruitment for what was initially an entirely volunteer-based armed service. Conscription was only introduced later in the war. Another category of card sets is that illustrating the many propaganda and morale-boosting posters that were widely and effectively used during the war. A third category deals with the labor force at home. With so many men off fighting the war, a large pool of workers was required to fill this void. These cards describe how that void was filled. Still another category is that of the news media and how they employed the power of cartoons to transmit a variety of messages to the public. This last category is dealt with separately in Chapter 13.

Fig. 464a. "Your Country Needs You"
(Wills, Recruiting Posters, 1915)

Fig. 464b. "Fall In"
(Wills, Recruiting Posters, 1915)

Fig. 464c. "Come Along Boys"
(Wills, Recruiting Posters, 1915)

Fig. 464d. "Line Up Boys!"
(Wills, Recruiting Posters, 1915)

## Recruiting Posters

When Britain entered the war, it had only a volunteer army. Therefore, until conscription was introduced in 1916, recruiting soldiers was a major priority of the government. A variety of techniques were employed. The use of advertisements with posters in public places was an important component. These posters fell under several categories. The most important category has been titled as creating an army from volunteers.

This required an aggressive propaganda campaign. This campaign was also directed at recruiting Irish citizens. Recruitment of the self-governing colonial countries of Canada, South Africa, Australia and New Zealand was also a focus of this campaign. It took the form of helping the mother country or the "Old Lion." Some of these posters show the women as symbols of patriotism and the national conscience.

Fig. 465a. "Remember Belgium"
(Wills, Recruiting Posters, 1915)

Fig. 465b. "He did his duty"
(Wills, Recruiting Posters, 1915)

Fig. 465c. "He did his duty,"
reverse side
(Wills, Recruiting Posters, 1915)

Fig. 465d. "Think, Are You Content"
(Wills, Recruiting Posters, 1915)

There are several card sets that illustrate most of these aspects of recruitment through the use of posters. There was only one set produced during the early years of the war. In 1915 Wills issued a set of twelve cards titled Recruiting Posters. Most of the other card sets are copies of the recruiting posters. These other sets were issued towards the end of the twentieth century. The posters were a combination of highly patriotic ones, and those that psychologically were aimed at producing a sense of guilt for those not yet enlisted, therefore encouraging the men to enlist. This goal was achieved by the combination of the image on the poster and the words on it. The more patriotic ones were of the nature of "Your Country Needs You, Follow Me" (Fig. 464a); "Fall In, Answer Now in Your Country's Hour of Need" (Fig. 464b); "Come Along Boys!, Enlist Today" (Fig. 464c); and "Line Up Boys!, Enlist Today" (Fig. 464d). The ones that produced more of a sense of guilt if one were not to enlist were, for example: "Remember Belgium, Enlist Today" (Fig. 465a); "He Did His Duty, Will You Do Yours?" (Figs. 465b, 465c); and "Think, Are You Content for Him to Fight for You?" (Fig. 465d).

Phillip Lewis Agencies issued an interesting set of fifty-four large playing cards in 2003. It was titled First World War 1914-1918, International Historic Posters from the Imperial War Museum, London. It contains what has to be without doubt the iconic and most enduring recruiting poster of all time. It is the one of Lord Kitchener in his army uniform and magnificent moustache pointing a finger. The slogan states "Britons wants you. Join your country's Army! God Save the King" (Fig. 466). Two recruiting posters from this large set were addressed to the Irish citizen. One of these was titled "Irishmen. Avenge the *Lusitania*. Join an Irish Regiment today." (Fig. 467a). Another one was of the guilt form, "For the glory of Ireland will you go or must I?" (Fig. 467b). This latter showed a housewife urging a man to enlist. Another one was to encourage people to invest in war bonds. It stated "Buy War

Fig. 466. "Britons Wants You"
(Phillip Lewis Agencies, First World War, 1914-1918, International Historic Posters from the Imperial War Museum, London, 2003)

Bonds" (Fig. 468). Still another posed a question: "Will you answer the call? Now is the time. And the place is the nearest recruiting office" (Fig. 469). One was for the Marines: "If you want to fight, join the Marines" (Fig. 470). An American recruiting poster similar to the Kitchener one has a man with a top-hat and the Stars on it pointing a finger saying "I want you for the U.S. Army. Nearest recruiting station" (Fig. 471). This set also has other posters that will be reviewed later.

**Fig. 467a. "Irishmen. Avenge the Lusitania"**
(Phillip Lewis Agencies, First World War, 1914-1918,
International Historic Posters from the Imperial War
Museum, London, 2003)

**Fig. 467b. "For the Glory of Ireland"**
(Phillip Lewis Agencies, First World War, 1914-1918,
International Historic Posters from the Imperial War
Museum, London, 2003)

**Fig. 468. "Buy War Bonds"**
(Phillip Lewis Agencies, First World War, 1914-1918,
International Historic Posters from the Imperial War
Museum, London, 2003)

**Fig. 469. "Will You Answer the Call?"**
(Phillip Lewis Agencies, First World War, 1914-1918,
International Historic Posters from the Imperial War
Museum, London, 2003)

Other sets included some recruiting posters. In Rockwell's World War One Posters issued in 2001, one card is aimed at the British Empire. It shows a male lion standing on a rock (England). The card has written on it "The Empire needs men. The overseas states all answer the call. Helped by the young lions the old lion defies his foe. Enlist now" (Figs. 472a, 472b). Another card is of soldiers climbing on board a train with the statement "There's room for you. Enlist today" Fig. 473). Yet another recruiting poster again shows a top-hatted man with a British flag on his waistcoat asking the question "Who's Absent? Is it you?" (Fig. 474).

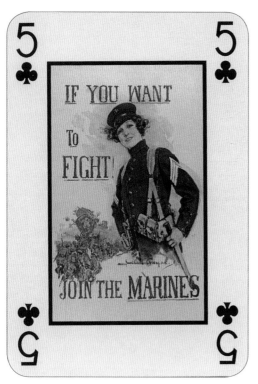

**Fig. 470. "…Join the Marines"**
(Phillip Lewis Agencies, First World War, 1914-1918, International Historic Posters from the Imperial War Museum, London, 2003)

**Fig. 472a. "The Empire Needs Men"**
(Rockwell, World War One Posters, 2001, No. 2)

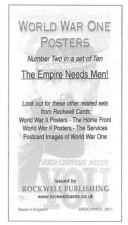

**Fig. 472b. "The Empire Needs Men," reverse side**
(Rockwell, World War One Posters, 2001, No. 2)

**Fig. 471. "I Want You for the U.S. Army"**
(Phillip Lewis Agencies, First World War, 1914-1918, International Historic Posters from the Imperial War Museum, London, 2003)

**Fig. 473. "There's Room for You"**
(Rockwell, World War One Posters, 2001, No. 6)

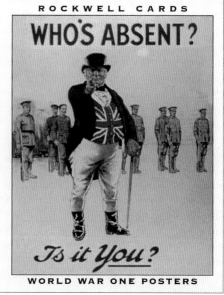

**Fig. 474 "Who's Absent?"**
(Rockwell, World War One Posters, 2001, No. 10)

Although not a recruiting poster, there is a card from the set Types of London, issued by the firm Carreras. This set will be discussed in more detail further on. Card No. 8 is of a Recruiting Sergeant (Fig. 475). On the reverse of the card he is described "with his jaunty air and bright ribbon (he) is a reminder of the days of our 'contemptible little Army' as the Kaiser foolishly called it to his cost. The Recruiting Sergeant used to haunt Trafalgar Square on the lookout for likely recruits. Conscription, of course, put an end to his activities."

Fig. 475. **Recruiting Sergeant**
(Carreras, Types of London, 1919, No. 8)

## Morale-Boosting Cards

Rockwell also issued a set of ten cards in 1999 titled Postcard Images of World War One. Most of these are comical images from both the home front and the battlefront. Card No.1 is an illustration by J. L. Biggar. It shows a British soldier holding the flag. On the front is inscribed a quotation from Lord Kitchener: "We are Proud of You." At the bottom of the card is "British to the Backbone" (Fig. 476). Another card is taken from the popular Scottish football cry, which was taken up enthusiastically by Tommy from the first landing of the BEF in August 1914. The front illustrates a soldier with his mouth

wide open screaming "No-o-o!" (Fig. 477). On the bottom of the card is an explanation of this. "Although From Friends and home sweet home I'm sad at being parted, this view will tell what I will yell if asked 'Are you downhearted?'" A series of four postcards was printed that was designated the "Take me back to dear old Blighty" series. Each of these cards depicts a verse from the popular song. During the War, many series illustrated songs and hymns that were both patriotic and sentimental. Two examples are provided from the Rockwell set (Fig. 478a, 478b).

Fig. 476. "**British to the Backbone**"
(Rockwell, Postcard Images of World War One, 1999, No. 1)

Fig. 477 "**No-o-o!**"
(Rockwell, Postcard Images of World War One, 1999, No. 8)

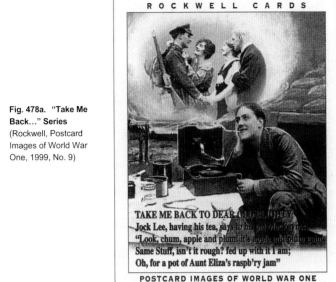

Fig. 478a. "Take Me Back..." Series (Rockwell, Postcard Images of World War One, 1999, No. 9)

Fig. 478b. "Take Me Back..." Series (Rockwell, Postcard Images of World War One, 1999, No. 10)

## Women and the Home Front

One of the most dramatic social changes that occurred in British society, beginning with the War, was the permanent incorporation of large numbers of women into the workforce. This came about as a result of the depletion of the male workforce, first due to voluntary enlistment and then later by conscription. This work involved two major aspects. The first was running the general domestic economy, and the second was devoted to producing the ammunition and equipment required in the execution of the war. Women comprised the overwhelming majority of this replacement workforce. Women were recruited to the workforce also by the use of propaganda posters. In 1914 there were nearly six million paid women in the workforce. By July 1918 there were over seven million three hundred thousand.

In 1916 Carreras issued a set of fifty cards titled Women on War Work. Carreras appears to have been the only tobacco company that addressed this aspect of the war in detail. The war was an important factor in Carreras deciding to start issuing cigarette cards. Their subjects and descriptions were also of a highly patriotic nature. This series perfectly illustrates and describes the vast array of occupations that these women held. A sample of these cards illustrating and describing the positions are: "Motor Driving" (Fig. 479), "Driving Goods Delivery Van" (Fig. 480), "Dentists" (Fig. 481), "Making Shells" (Figs. 482a, 482b), "Ambulance Service" (Fig. 483), "Harrowing Wheat" (Fig. 484), "Grocer's Assistant" (Fig. 485), "Tram Conductor" (Fig. 486), "Glass Manufacture" (Figs. 487a, 487b), "Sheet Iron Worker" (Fig. 488), and "Shipyard Worker" (Fig. 489). Each one of these cards has an accompanying description on the reverse side. For example, the description on the Goods Delivery Van states, "Since War started, the able-bodied young men who used to drive delivery wagons have been called up and their places have been taken by women. They make just as good and careful drivers as the men, and it is quite a common sight to see women driving the Royal Mail Vans, as well as delivery vans for private firms." The Tram Conductor states, "The lady tram conductor is now quite a familiar sight in all the big towns. There seems no reason why they need give up this work after the war, although it is quite likely they may do so."

Fig. 479. Motor Driving (Carreras, Women on War Work, 1916, No. 1)

Fig. 480. Driving Goods Delivery Van (Carreras, Women on War Work, 1916, No. 7)

**Fig. 481  Dentists**
(Carreras, Women on War Work, 1916, No. 10)

**Fig. 482a.  Making Shells**
(Carreras, Women on War Work, 1916, No. 11)

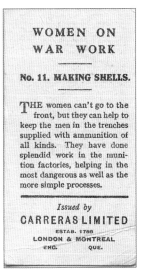

**Fig. 482b.  Making Shells, reverse side**
(Carreras, Women on War Work, 1916, No. 11)

**Fig. 483.  Ambulance Service**
(Carreras, Women on War Work, 1916, No. 13)

**Fig. 484.  Harrowing Wheat**
(Carreras, Women on War Work, 1916, No. 15)

**Fig. 485.  Grocer's Assistant**
(Carreras, Women on War Work, 1916, No. 22)

**Fig. 486.  Tram Conductor**
(Carreras, Women on War Work, 1916, No. 28)

**Fig. 487a.  Glass Manufacture**
(Carreras, Women on War Work, 1916, No. 36)

**Fig. 487b.  Glass Manufacture, reverse side**
(Carreras, Women on War Work, 1916, No. 36)

**Fig. 488.  Sheet Iron Worker**
(Carreras, Women on War Work, 1916, No. 46)

**Fig. 489.  Shipyard Worker**
(Carreras, Women on War Work, 1916, No. 50)

The descriptions on a few of these cards explain this phenomenon further. Card No. 19 is titled "Mechanics, Electrical Engineering" (Fig. 490). The description states, "Since so many men have been called up, while at the same time a tremendous amount of extra work has been thrown onto the engineering trades, it has been found that women make very satisfactory substitutes, particularly where a light and delicate touch is required for precision work." As an indication of the dawning recognition of the dramatic social changes, card No. 42 of a woman "Barrowing Coke" (Fig. 491) states "Nearly all the Gas Companies now employ women to perform many of the tasks upon which only men were engaged before the war. Barrowing coke is one of the things they can manage very capably." However, on one of the cards there is also an indirect reference to the ambivalence to the idea of women doing such labor permanently. Card No. 39 illustrates a "Steam Roller Driver" (Fig. 492) and the description on the reverse side refers to this ambivalence: "Even in this heavy work, women have done wonderfully well, showing both nerve and capacity which has surprised many people. Still, it is one of the war-time occupations which they will no doubt be glad to relinquish when they are no longer needed."

Fig. 490. Mechanics, Electrical Engineering (Carreras, Women on War Work, 1916, No. 19)

Fig. 491. Barrowing Coke (Carreras, Women on War Work, 1916, No. 42)

Fig. 492. Steam Roller Driver (Carreras, Women on War Work, 1916, No. 39)

Fig. 493. Female Window Cleaner (Carreras, Types of London, 1919, No. 67)

Fig. 494. Flag Seller (Carreras, Types of London, 1919, No. 88)

Fig. 495. Telephone Girl (Carreras, Types of London, 1919, No. 19)

In 1919 Carreras issued the set Types of London. The illustrations on this set were by the war artist and correspondent for the *Illustrated London News*, Julius M. Price. A number of the subjects are related specifically to the war and from their descriptions, most likely he began work on this series during the war. Some of the subjects were in the same genre as the Women on War Work set; card No. 67 is of a "Female Window Cleaner" (Fig. 493). The description of this card brings out this social change. "The Female Window Cleaner…is one of the curious developments resulting from the Great War. The success with which she carries out her dangerous duties speaks volumes for her pluck and adaptability." Card No. 88 was specific war-related work.

It is of the "Flag Seller" (Fig. 494). "Flag days in London during the Great War will be long remembered. The bevy of charming ladies in their dainty frocks always imparted a touch of vivacity to the grey old London streets – and the charity for which they gave their services always benefited largely." Although the Zeppelin was the major flying machine used by the Germans in bombing English cities, by 1916 they had developed an effective airplane, the Gotha G.V. bomber, and this created initial panic among the British public. Thus in describing and illustrating card No. 19, the "Telephone Girl" (Fig. 495), the point is brought out how "many of the girls have displayed extra-ordinary pluck during air raids, remaining at their work with the greatest coolness."

There are several cards from this set that illustrate and describe direct war-related work carried out mainly on the home front, but also sometimes at the battlefront. Card No. 78 is of a "Wren" (Fig. 496). These were women who in their "smart uniform of the Royal Naval Service – known popularly as the 'Wrens' – is only occasionally seen in London as of course their work is mainly near the Fleet." The "W.A.A.C." is shown on card No. 80 (Fig. 497) "as the Women's Army Auxiliary Corps is familiarly known to have done splendid work, not only in England, but in the actual War Zone. The fact that Queen Mary in accepting the command of the corps undoubtedly enormously enhanced its popularity." The "V.A.D.," as shown on card No. 75 (Fig. 498), is described as follows: "Voluntary Aid Detachment is one of the organizations that women have taken up with extraordinary enthusiasm. And in the actual war zone its work was carried on with a devotion that will never be forgotten." The "Salvation Army Lass" illustration (Fig. 499) has a description of this service. "The Salvation Army has indeed done splendid work during the War, and its women have done an enormous amount of good by visiting and comforting the wives and children of our heroes."

Fig. 496. Wren
(Carreras, Types of London, 1919, No. 78)

Fig. 497. W.A.A.C.
(Carreras, Types of London, 1919, No. 80)

Fig. 498. V.A.D.
(Carreras, Types of London, 1919, No. 75)

Fig. 499. Salvation Army Lass
(Carreras, Types of London, 1919, No. 46)

Fig. 500. The Wounded Tommy
(Carreras, Types of London, 1919, No. 70)

Fig. 501. National Guard Volunteer
(Carreras, Types of London, 1919, No. 70)

There are a few cards in the Types of London set that address military personal who are either part-time or permanently on the home front. One card illustrates the Wounded Tommy (Fig. 500). The esteem in which they were held by the public and the compassion felt for them is clear from the description: "The wounded men have a great claim upon our consideration and it is always a pathetic spectacle to see some fine young fellow maimed for life. The blue hospital uniform is in itself a badge of honour, which ensures respect everywhere. The men are encouraged to be out as much as possible." There was also a different type of volunteer to the armed services. Card No. 70 illustrates a "Private in the National Guard (Volunteer)" (Fig. 501). The description highlights how all age groups were involved. "It was once asserted that a man was too old at forty. But this was before the war. Now one sees grey-haired veterans in khaki as alert as youngsters. For instance the National Guard which at all hours is on duty at the different termini directing soldiers on their way."

Fig. 502a. The Tram Conductor
(The Happy Home, Women on War Work,
1915)

Fig. 502b. The Tram Conductor,
reverse side
(The Happy Home, Women on War
Work, 1915)

Another set by *The Happy Home*—a news publication—issued in 1915, titled Women on War Work, is thematically a similar issue. Thus examples of card titles are "The Postwoman," "The Lift Girl," "The Fire Woman," "The Window Cleaner" and "The Baker." The reverse descriptions are in the form of rhymes.

The Tram Conductor (Figs. 502a, 502b) is described as follows:

> Queen of the Tramcar! So trim and so neat;
> Radiant your smile every day as we meet.
> "Fare" is your welcome, in tones sweet and low.
> And we repeat "Fair? Yes, decidedly so!"

For the Lamplighter (Fig. 503) it is:

> At dusk you light me on my way
> Lest my unwary feet shall falter.
> Perhaps – who knows? – some other day
> I'll lead you blushing, to the altar.

For the Munitions Worker (Fig. 504) the rhyme is:

> Maidens fair in cap and apron
> Making shells by day and night.
> Yours is an heroic labour
> In the cause of truth and right.

Fig. 503. The Lamplighter
(The Happy Home, Women on War Work,
1915)

Fig. 504. Munitions Worker
(The Happy Home, Women on War Work,
1915)

Fig. 505. British Red Cross
(Phillips, War Photos, 1916, No. 20)

Other sets are not dedicated to this subject, but individual cards are of this subject matter. Two examples are Godfrey Phillips, War Photos, 1916, card No. 20 titled "British Red Cross (Women Section)" (Fig. 505). The illustration shows women carrying a long pole-like structure that could be a stretcher. They appear to be in training. The second example is from the set by Gallaher titled The Great War, Second Series. In a series of four cards titled "Munitions Shell Making 1, 2, 3, 4" respectively, three of the four illustrate women making the shells in a factory (Figs. 506a, 506b, 506c, 506d, 506e). Card Nos. 126 and 141, both titled "Munitions," are thematically similar, with women working in the factory showing further steps in the shell-making process (Figs. 507a, 507b, 507c).

**Fig. 506a. Munitions Shell Making**
(Gallaher, The Great War, Second Series, 1915, No. 111)

**Fig. 506b. Munitions Shell Making**
(Gallaher, The Great War, Second Series, 1915, No. 115)

**Fig. 506c. Munitions Shell Making**
(Gallaher, The Great War, Second
Series, 1915, No. 120)

**Fig. 506d. Munitions Shell Making**
(Gallaher, The Great War, Second
Series, 1915, No. 119)

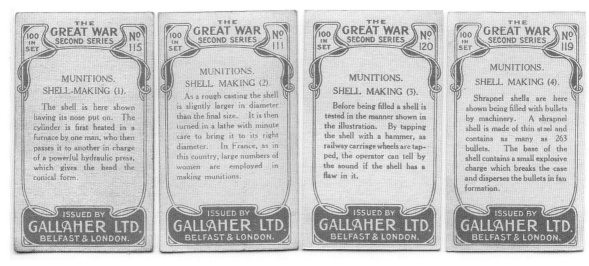

**Fig. 506e. Munitions Shell Making, reverse sides**
(Gallaher, The Great War, Second Series, 1915, Nos.
111, 115, 119, 120)

**Fig. 507a. Munitions**
(Gallaher, The Great War, Second
Series, 1915, No. 141)

**Fig. 507b. Munitions**
(Gallaher, The Great War, Second Series,
1915, No. 126)

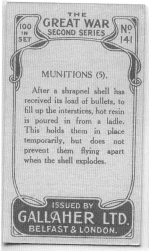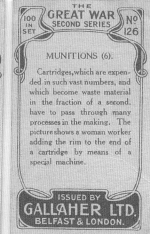

**Fig. 507c. Munitions,
reverse sides**
(Gallaher, The Great
War, Second Series,
1915, Nos. 141, 126)

At home there was also the effort to boost the morale of the soldiers on the battlefront. One of these was to send gift packages to the soldiers. In 1916 Abdulla issued a set of Great War Gift Packing Cards. One of these illustrates women preparing such packages (Fig. 508) with a comment below the illustration:

Dear Boys, who gallantly
Fight with the Colours, -
We send our hearts to you
With these Abdullas.

Another card is a naval one, titled "Ready" (Fig. 509). Below that is the comment "With the Thanks and Best Wishes of Abdulla & Co., Ltd."

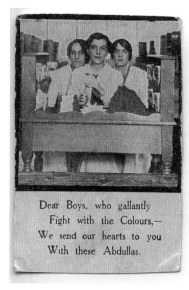

**Fig. 508. Gift Package**
(Abdulla, Great War Gift Packing Cards, 1916)

**Fig. 509. Ready**
(Abdulla, Great War Gift Packing Cards, 1916)

# Other Civilians

Lea issued a set in 1914–1915 titled Civilians of Countries Fighting with the Allies. The titles of individual cards include "A French Barrister" (Fig. 510), "A Peasant of Auvergne" (Fig. 511), "A Belgian Fisherman" (Fig. 512), "A Boer Farmer of the Transvaal" (Fig. 513), "A Japanese Gentleman" (Fig. 514), and "A Montenegrin" (Fig. 515). As an example, the description of card No. 14 of the "Brahmin with red clay hubble bubble pipe" (Fig. 516) is as follows: "The Brahmins are members of a sacred caste of Hindus who claim direct descent from, or immediate relationship with Brahina. They are considered as custodians and mediators of religion and are therefore, of high priestly rank. Brahmanism has been modernized, and made great strides during the nineteenth century, and has been aided by the spread of education."

**Fig. 510. French Barrister**
(Lea, Civilians of Countries Fighting with the Allies, 1914-15, No. 1)

**Fig. 511. Peasant of Auvergne**
(Lea, Civilians of Countries Fighting with the Allies, 1914-15, No. 3)

**Fig. 512. Belgian Fisherman**
(Lea, Civilians of Countries Fighting with the Allies, 1914-15, No. 6)

**Fig. 513. Boer Farmer**
(Lea, Civilians of Countries Fighting with the Allies, 1914-15, No. 13)

**Fig. 514. Japanese Gentleman**
(Lea, Civilians of Countries Fighting with the Allies, 1914-15, No. 17)

**Fig. 515. Montenegrin**
(Lea, Civilians of Countries Fighting with the Allies, 1914-15, No. 21)

**Fig. 516. Brahmin**
(Lea, Civilians of Countries Fighting with the Allies, 1914-15, No. 14)

# CHAPTER 13

# WAR HUMOR and LITERARY ASPECTS

Humor has been and remains an integral part of war. Humor has a role in the culture of the times. With a cartoon, the individual viewer either immediately appreciates and understands it, or does not. Particularly with political cartoons, there is much that goes into it. There is both the historical background as well as the caricature. Humor has then a role in both shaping and reflecting cultural aspects. War and patriotism particularly have lent themselves to humor. World War One was no exception. Much humor came out of this war in many ways, at the political, military and civilian levels. At the literary level at the time of the war, serious war poetry was possibly the highest form of literary output, but no card sets were issued with these. The literary aspects that found their way into card sets were mainly in the news media, either magazines or newspapers that illustrated these political cartoons with their in-depth descriptions. Cigarette and trade card issuers provided

a number of sets that gave the reader and viewer a good sense of the war from this perspective. This information is valuable in providing a greater understanding on this particular aspect of the war. Some examples will be described. A major aspect of these cartoons was demonizing the enemy. The "Hun" and particularly Kaiser Wilhelm II were depicted as cruel and monstrous creatures who flauted all norms of society. The "personification of a state" was a part of the European political culture. In a number of these cartoons, therefore, the monarch or the political leader reflected the larger society. Most of these cartoons appeared either in the regular press or in specific magazines. Furthermore, there has always been the debate as to how much the press was an indicator of pubic opinion versus playing a strong role in formulating public opinion. A number of these cartoons can certainly be considered in this context.

**Fig. 517a. English-French Dictionary, front exterior cover**
(Carreras, The Handy Black Cat English-French Dictionary, 1915)

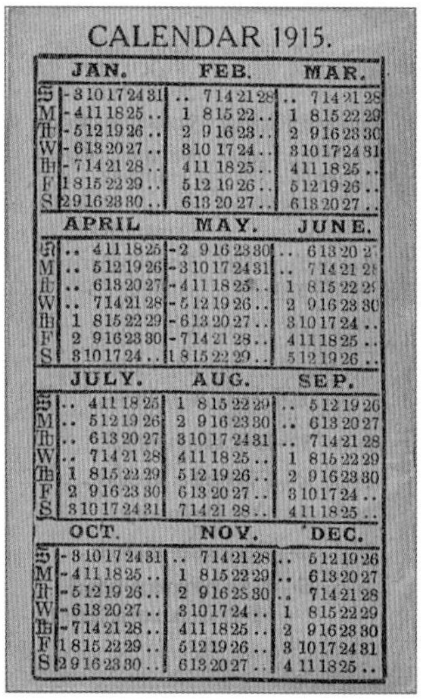

**Fig. 517b. English-French Dictionary, rear exterior cover**
(Carreras, The Handy Black Cat English-French Dictionary, 1915)

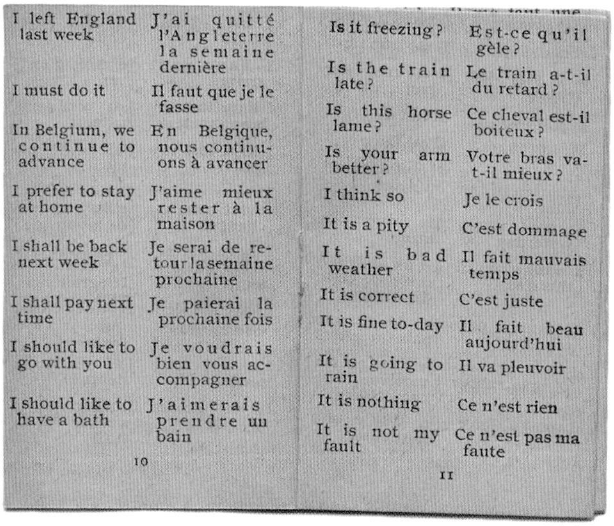

**Fig. 517c. English-French Dictionary, interior pages**
(Carreras, The Handy Black Cat English-French Dictionary, 1915)

There was one card company that stood out in how it embraced both the true literary as well as the war humor aspects of the war in its card sets. That company was Carreras Limited. From the literary perspective, Carreras produced a set of five booklets in 1915 titled "The Handy Black Cat

English-French Dictionary." These booklets were made to look like cards and were the size of standard cigarette cards. A booklet consisted of either a dictionary with direct English-French translations or booklets with phrases in English and the equivalent in French. The company included these in millions of their cigarette packs that were sent to the Western front. The company viewed this as a patriotic contribution to the war effort in that it would allow the British soldier to be able to communicate better with his French ally. Today these booklets are extremely rare. The exterior covers and an interior page are illustrated (Figs. 517a, 517b, 517c). There is a poignancy to these booklets, since it is not difficult to conjure in the mind that these few relics that still exist today, were at one time in the trenches with the soldiers.

Without doubt the most famous cartoonist from the War was Louis Raemaekers. He was a Dutch painter and cartoonist who worked for the Amsterdam Telegraaf during World War I. He was noted for his strong anti-German attitude. His cartoons showed the German military in Belgium, the Germans as barbarians, and the Kaiser as Satan. The Germans not only placed a reward for his capture, but also forced the neutral Dutch government to put him on trial for endangering Dutch neutrality. He was acquitted by a jury. He subsequently left for England because of the bounty on his head. In England he worked for *The Times*. After the war Raemaekers' *Cartoon History of the War* was published.

In 1916 Carreras published a set of one hundred forty cards titled Raemaekers War Cartoons. Card No. 1 is a photographic portrait of Louis Raemaekers (Fig. 518) with a brief

Fig. 518. Louis Raemaekers (Carreras, Raemaekers War Cartoons, 1916, No. 1)

Fig. 519a. Christendom after Twenty Centuries (Carreras, Raemaekers War Cartoons, 1916, No. 2)

Fig. 519b. We Wage War on Divine Principles (Carreras, Raemaekers War Cartoons, 1916, No. 3)

description of the genre of his work on the reverse side of the card: "Louis Raemaekers, who will possibly be known to Fame as the greatest of all Cartoonists, is a young Dutch artist. So bitterly true are his wonderful cartoons that the Germans have set a price on his head. There could be no more realistic history of the war than Raemaekers cartoons."

The set begins with a religious subject matter; the first card is titled "Christendom after Twenty Centuries," and the second is "We Wage War on Divine Principles" (Figs. 519a, 519b). In the former there is the bowed figure of the whole civilized world, and the fate the German has brought upon it is represented by the whip and sword. The figure demonstrates suffering and the cartoon characterizes the ruin that Germany's war has wrought on the finer side of civilization. The latter card description is "The Kaiser as maker of this war has broken every ideal of the Christian Faith. In this fine cartoon he is afraid to look upon the face of Christ who stands for Justice, Mercy and Goodwill towards men."

A Belgian theme card is titled "Spoils for the Victors, Belgium" (Fig. 520). It illustrates German soldiers looting and describes on the reverse side: "In express violation of the rules of war, the conquered areas of Belgium and France were given over to pillage by the German troops, in which even the Crown Prince took part. The enormous fines extracted from occupied towns are also violations of the Rules of War." Another Belgian theme card is titled "Mon Fils, Belgium, 1914" (Fig. 521). It shows a German soldier standing over a mother on her knees looking for her son among a number of corpses. On the reverse it has the soldier addressing the woman "Ah, was your boy among the twelve this morning? Then you will find him among this lot." The description states that "…since the beginning of the war in most cases these murders have been indiscriminate, and unconnected with any act of hostility toward the invaders. Murder is part of the German system of terrorism." After the fall of Antwerp Raemaekers published a cartoon titled "A Pitiful Exodus" (Fig. 522). It shows the citizens leaving the city and the description states that "The flight of refugees from Antwerp formed one of the tragedies of the war, reducing prosperous citizens to absolute poverty.…" Two other cards address the sad state of the women of Belgium. Titled "The Mothers of Belgium" and "The Widows of Belgium" (Figs. 523a, 523b), they illustrate women in a sad state. The description on the latter card provides the rationale for so many widows: "This procession of sorrow, which is a part of the suffering of Belgium, is one result of King Albert's heroic decision to resist the violation of his country, and of Germany's treachery to her pledged word. No German excuses can explain away such suffering as is shown in this cartoon."

In its attempt to get Holland to enter the war on Germany's side, Raemaekers depicted that pressure in a cartoon

Fig. 520. Spoils for the Victors, Belgium
(Carreras, Raemaekers War Cartoons, 1916, No. 16)

Fig. 521. Mon Fils, Belgium
(Carreras, Raemaekers War Cartoons, 1916, No. 20)

Fig. 522 A Pitiful Exodus
(Carreras, Raemaekers War Cartoons, 1916, No. 21)

Fig. 523a. The Mothers of Belgium
(Carreras, Raemaekers War Cartoons, 1916, No.33)

Fig. 523b. The Widows of Belgium
(Carreras, Raemaekers War Cartoons, 1916, No. 34)

titled "Better a Living Dog than a Dead Lion" (Fig. 524). The cartoon illustrates a German soldier on a wagon being pulled by a man on his knees with a chain around his neck held by the soldier. The Driver says, "You are a worthy Dutchman. He who lies in that grave was a foolish idealist." The description elaborates: "One of the great levers that Germany has used in attempting to induce Holland to come into the war on the German side is the fate that followed Belgium's resistance. The grave of the 'idealist' is that of Belgium." In a similar coercive vein, Germany tried to keep Italy out of the war by bribing it with an offer of Trentino that belonged to Austria. Titled "Have Another Piece" (Fig. 525a), it illustrates the Kaiser offering the Austrian Emperor's foot (Trentino) to Italy. Since 1882 the Triple Alliance consisting of Germany, Austria and Italy prevented Italy from claiming Trentino, which by nationality is Italian. Another related card, titled "The Broken Alliance & Italy" (Fig. 525b), shows an Italian holding a chain in the face of the Kaiser and Emperor of Austria and saying "Twenty years and more you've forced me to wear this chain." Meanwhile, another card indicates the growing allegiance between Italy and France (Fig. 526). Titled "The Latin Sisters," the description indicates "The feeling of Italy toward France has undergone a great change since the Franco-German War of 1870, and the two nations are now in full sympathy with each other. This has been shown by their close co-operation in the various phases of the Great War."

Fig. 524. Better a Living Dog…
(Carreras, Raemaekers War Cartoons, 1916, No. 58)

Fig. 525a. Have Another Piece
(Carreras, Raemaekers War Cartoons, 1916, No. 68)

Fig. 525b. The Broken Alliance and Italy
(Carreras, Raemaekers War Cartoons, 1916, No. 70)

Fig. 526. The Latin Sisters
(Carreras, Raemaekers War Cartoons, 1916, No. 69)

May 1915 brought the sinking in the Atlantic Ocean of the British passenger liner *Lusitania*. To this day, controversy exists as to the exact circumstances of its sinking. At the time of her sinking she was carrying many passengers. There is a series of four cards in the Raemaekers set (Figs. 527a, 527b, 527c, 527d, 527e) illustrating and describing this episode. These are based on religious, ethical, political and criminal reasons. The first is titled "Easter 1915" and shows Germany and her allies mocking Christianity. The second one is titled "*Lusitania* Amok" and illustrates an insane creature representing the state of mind

of the German people when the sinking of the *Lusitania* was greeted with an outburst of rejoicing. The next one is titled "Murder on the High Seas." At that time America was still neutral and therefore, according to the card description, it prohibited them from taking action over the *Lusitania* crime, but nevertheless it stirred the whole of America against Germany. The last one is titled "The 'Lusitania,' Herod's Nightmare." The description states that there is no parallel in history for the murder of innocents since the days of Herod (Fig. 527e).

**Fig. 527a.  Easter 1915**
(Carreras, Raemaekers War Cartoons, 1916, No. 83)

**Fig. 527b.  Lusitania Amok**
(Carreras, Raemaekers War Cartoons, 1916, No. 84)

**Fig. 527c.  Murder on the High Seas**
(Carreras, Raemaekers War Cartoons, 1916, No. 85)

**Fig. 527d.  The "Lusitania,"
Herod's Nightmare**
(Carreras, Raemaekers War Cartoons, 1916, No. 86)

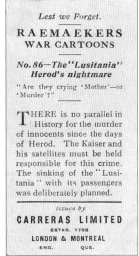

**Fig. 527e.  The "Lusitania",
Herod's Nightmare, reverse side**
(Carreras, Raemaekers War Cartoons, 1916, No. 86)

In terms of mocking the Turks for being deluded into joining the war on the side of the Germans, there are two cards that address this issue. The first is titled the "Holy War" (Figs. 528a, 528b) and has a quotation by the Turk: "But he is so great." To which Kaiser William responds "No one so great save Allah, and I am his prophet." The second one is titled "The Order of Merit" (Fig. 529) and there is a quotation by Turkey: "And is this all the compensation I get?" This refers to Turkey receiving the Iron Cross as small compensation for the loss of Erzeroum, Trebizon, and the fertile areas in Asia Minor that have fallen into Russian hands.

Fig. 528a. Holy War
(Carreras, Raemaekers War Cartoons, 1916, No. 109)

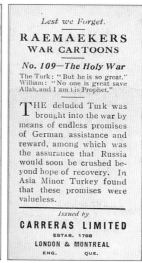

Fig. 528b. Holy War, reverse side
(Carreras, Raemaekers War Cartoons, 1916, No. 109)

Fig. 529. The Order of Merit
(Carreras, Raemaekers War Cartoons, 1916, No. 110)

Fig. 530. Europe 1916
(Carreras, Raemaekers War Cartoons, 1916, No. 127)

Fig. 531a. Braggart
(Carreras, Raemaekers War Cartoons, 1916, No. 128)

Fig. 531b. Braggart, reverse side
(Carreras, Raemaekers War Cartoons, 1916, No. 128)

The devastating effects of the War by 1916 are epitomized in what is considered one of Raemaekers' finer cartoons. This one, titled "Europe 1916," asks the question, "Am I not yet sufficiently civilized?" (Fig. 530). It illustrates Europe in 1916, tortured and suffering as a drooping figure roped to the heavy wheel. He still mocks Germany in another card titled the "Braggart" (Figs. 531a, 531b), quoting "It was I who opened fire on Rheims." It illustrates the fat bully typical of German "Kultur" rejoicing in its crimes, listing the *Lusitania* sinking, sinking of hospital ships, and the ruins of Rheims Cathedral.

Finally, looking towards the end of the War and Germany's ultimate defeat, Raemaekers has two prophetic cartoons. The first is titled and illustrates "The Wandering Jew" (Fig. 532). The description states that like the wandering Jew of old the Kaiser is doomed to wander from place to place, defeated in all his attempts at world conquest. Wherever he goes he can find no peace. The second is titled "Retribution" (Fig. 533). It shows the Kaiser surrounded by all the war dead. The description says that "Surely, when the reckoning for all the horrors that Germany has wrought has been made, the spectres of the dead without number that have been slain in the war will haunt the author of that war, as shown here."

Fig. 532. The Wandering Jew
(Carreras, Raemaekers War
Cartoons, 1916, No. 136)

Fig. 533. Retribution
(Carreras, Raemaekers War
Cartoons, 1916, No. 137)

Fig. 534a. The Teutonizing
of Turkey
(Wills, Punch Cartoons,
series 1, 1916, No. 4)

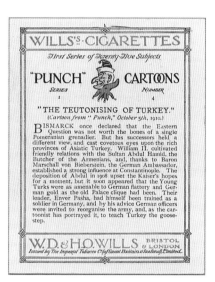

Fig. 534b. The Teutonizing
of Turkey, reverse side
(Wills, Punch Cartoons,
Series 1, 1916, No. 4)

*Punch Magazine* was a weekly magazine of humor and satire that originated in the mid-nineteenth century. It survived through to the mid-twentieth century. It originated the term "cartoon" for a comic drawing. In 1916 Wills issued two series of large card sets, each of twenty-five cards, titled *Punch Cartoons*. These were all related to Germany, beginning in the late nineteenth century and then mostly war-related. One of the early cards (Figs. 534a, 534b) is titled "The Teutonizing of Turkey." In a clever illustration it has the German Emperor and a Turkey doing a dance around each other with the Kaiser saying "Good Bird." The reverse description indicates how Bismarck once declared that "The Eastern Question was not worth the bones of a single Pomeranian grenadier." William II held a different view and cultivated friendly relations with Sultan Abdul Hamid. The Young Turks after 1908 were as amenable to German flattery and German gold as the old Palace clique had been.

In a tribute to Belgium's brave stance against the German invasion *Punch* issued a cartoon on August 12, 1914, titled "Bravo, Belgium!" (Fig. 535). The description on the reverse provides information on how Belgium's heroic stand against the German invasion, with General Lemans' magnificent stand at Liege for two weeks, not only resulted in significant German losses but that they lost something more valuable—time.

It goes on to state that "But for the Belgians, the Germans would have been well on to the road to Paris before the British Expeditionary Force had landed in France." A later cartoon of October 21, 1914, titled "Unconquerable" (Figs. 536a, 536b), illustrates a mocking Kaiser resting on his sword in front of him, saying to the King of the Belgians "So you see—you've lost everything." A proud King Albert retorts back, "Not my soul."

**Fig. 535. Bravo Belgium**
(Wills, Punch Cartoons, Series 1, 1916, No. 7)

**Fig. 536a. Unconquerable**
(Wills, Punch Cartoons, Series 1, 1916, No. 18)

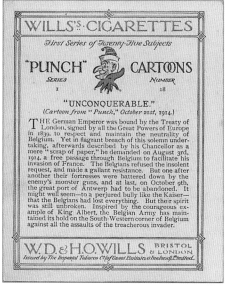

**Fig. 536b. Unconquerable, reverse side**
(Wills, Punch Cartoons, Series 1, 1916, No. 18)

**Fig. 537. Good Hunting**
(Wills, Punch Cartoons, Series 1, 1916, No. 23)

A card of the November 19, 1914, issue of *Punch* shows two male lions, one holding a carcass and titled "Good Hunting" (Fig. 537). The reverse description is of the feats of the German fast light cruiser *Emden*. It describes how between September and November 1914 it destroyed seven British destroyers in the Bay of Bengal, then bombarded Madras, passing on into the Gulf of Arabia where it captured several more vessels, and then in November it arrived at the Keeling Cocos Islands in the Indian Ocean where it tried to cut a cable. A wireless message was received by the Australian cruiser *Sydney* and after a short sharp fight the *Emden* was run ashore. It provides further information of what was still old-fashioned military professionalism. The commander, "Captain von Muller was captured unwounded, and in consideration of his humane treatment of the crews that had fallen into his hands – a great contrast to the behavior of German officers in general – he was allowed to retain his sword."

*Punch* also illustrated the visit of King George V to the front (Fig. 538). The first card in the second series, of December 9, 1914, titled "The King at the Front," illustrates him standing on a mound and saluting the soldiers, saying "'Tommy' (having learned the language). 'VIVE LE ROI!'" The reverse of the card brings up an interesting military point. "Not since George II commanded the British Army at Dettingen in 1743, had an English sovereign seen his troops on active service, until George V arrived at British headquarters on November 30th, 1914."

**Fig. 538. The King at the Front**
(Wills, Punch Cartoons, Series 2, 1916, No. 1)

In recognition of Canada's heroic role in the Second Battle of Ypres *Punch* produced a cartoon on May 5, 1915, titled "Canada!, Ypres: April 22-24, 1915" (Fig. 539a). It illustrates a soldier holding the Canadian flag in his left hand and in his right hand an elevated rifle with his cap on the bayonet. The reverse of the card describes the role the Canadians had played on the Western Front (Fig. 539b).

**Fig. 539a. Canada!, Ypres**
(Wills, Punch Cartoons, Series 2, 1916, No. 11)

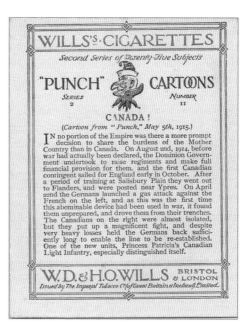

**Fig. 539b. Canada!, Ypres, reverse side**
(Wills, Punch Cartoons, Series 2, 1916, No. 11)

**Fig. 540. The Old Man of the Sea**
(Wills, Punch Cartoons, Series 2, 1916, No. 17)

A card published on July 21, 1915, titled "The Old Man of the Sea" (Fig. 540) shows the Kaiser, whom the cartoon names Sinbad the Kaiser, bent over carrying the old man and saying "This submarine business is going to get me into trouble with America; but what can an All-powerful do with a thing like this on his back?" The description on the back of the card indicates that everyone who has read The Arabian Nights remembers the adventure of Sinbad the Sailor with the horrible old man whom he took on his back and could not dislodge. The description goes on to to indicate that this cartoon is based on the Kaiser probably having second thoughts about "the submarine blockade inaugurated by Admiral von Tirpitz in February, 1915" and the Kaiser effusively supporting this. He had "joined in the German rejoicing of the sinking of the *Lusitania*." But, a month or two later he was beginning to wonder whether this new "frightfulness" was not after all a mistake. Not only had President Wilson issued a rebuke, but the blockade was infringing on international standards, as well as outraging humanity. Also a good many of the German submarines had been destroyed by nets and other devices adopted by the British navy. Not long after this cartoon appeared, Admiral von Tirpitz was given a long holiday.

*Punch* addressed the problems with the Russian army in a cartoon of September 15, 1915, titled "The Call of the Tsar" (Fig. 541). He asks the question "Who will follow me for Holy Russia's Sake?" The illustration is of him standing in the field among his army in disarray. He wears his crown, lifts his sword and holds a flag in his left hand. The reverse description on the card states, "Things had been going badly for Russia in the summer of 1915. Both in Galicia and Poland the Russian armies had been driven back, and one by one all the great Polish fortresses from Warsaw to Brest-Litowsk had been evacuated. Then it was that the Tsar, who had hitherto entrusted the disposition of his forces to his cousin the Grand Duke Nicholas, startled the world by the announcement that he himself had taken supreme command. 'With firm faith in the clemency of God,' ran the Imperial rescript, 'with unshaken assurance in final victory, we shall fulfill our sacred duty to defend our country to the last.'"

**Fig. 541. The Call of the Tsar**
(Wills, Punch Cartoons, series 2, 1916, No. 20)

As the War approached the end of its second year, *Punch* published a cartoon created by Bernard Partridge on December 29, 1915. It was titled "Dead Sea Fruit" and illustrated a paunchy Kaiser William II seated and dejected (Fig. 542). The description on the reverse side praises the artist in so skillfully penetrating the heart of his subject. It further describes how "One feels that the Kaiser must have looked just like that if at the close of the year he dared think over the past and forecast the future. Everywhere his armies had apparently been successful. They had overrun Belgium and Poland, Serbia and Montenegro, and still held nearly all their conquests. And yet, what good were these barren gains of territory? He had not broken the spirit of one of his foes; peace was as far off as ever; and Germany was slowly but surely bleeding and starving to death. What a contrast between the Prussian Eagle flapping its wings over the chair and the dejected figure seated within it!"

Due to rationing Wills did not publish any further *Punch* cartoons covering the remainder of the War.

**Fig. 542. Dead Sea Fruit**
(Wills, Punch Cartoons, Series 2, 1916, No. 25)

One set of cards that is rare and difficult to obtain is titled Army Pictures, Cartoons, Etc. Several issuers published the set between 1915 and 1916. Wakeford (Umbrellas), Prudhoe and Dewhurst Tobacco were among the issuers. One card from the Prudhoe set illustrates a young boy in his scouts uniform waving his hat saying "Good-bye! I'm Just Off to the War!" (Fig. 543a). Another card from this set brings out where the future of Britain lies, presumably both during the war and after, by illustrating mythological Britannia guiding a young Boy Scout (Fig. 543b). Pure humor, but with a message, is illustrated in the card titled "Comrades in Arms" (Fig. 543c). In typical anti-German propaganda, there is an illustration of a dog biting the rear end of an overweight German soldier (Fig. 543d). Dawes also produced a set of Army Pictures and Cartoons. One of the cartoons is titled "A German Surprise," and shows Germans popping out of a beer mug (Fig. 543e). Two food-related cards from the Prudhoe set shows a mother and young chicken (Fig. 544a). The caption captures the daily economic hardship of war. The youngster asks the mother "Please Ma, Can't I have a Little Brother?" To which she replies "What? With eggs at 3d each! No, certainly not!" The other card is directed at softening the blow of the high price of food by the illustration accompanied by the caption "Don't be Alarmed—Grub's Going Down" (Fig. 544b).

**Fig. 543a. Good-bye! I'm Just Off to the War!**
(Wakeford, Army Pictures, Cartoons, 1915)

**Fig. 543b. Britannia's Hope**
(Prudhoe, Army Pictures, Cartoons etc., 1916)

**Fig. 543c. Comrades in Arms**
(Prudhoe, Army Pictures, Cartoons etc., 1916)

**Fig. 543d. Got Him—Good Dog**
(Prudhoe, Army Pictures, Cartoons etc., 1916)

**Fig. 543e. A German Surprise**
(S.H. Dawes, Army Pictures, Cartoons etc., 1916)

**Fig. 544a. Mother and Chick**
(Prudhoe, Army Pictures, Cartoons, 1915)

**Fig. 544b. Grub's Going Down**
(Prudhoe, Army Pictures, Cartoons etc., 1916)

Martins issued a famous single card set in 1916. It is titled "Arf A Mo Kaiser!" (Fig. 545). This card has an illustration of a British soldier lighting a pipe with a helmeted German crouching in the background. The card was issued with the permission of the "Weekly Dispatch" Tobacco Fund. The reverse description, both informative and advertising, states: "The spirit of humour for which 'Tommy' is renowned has been caught by the artist, Mr. Bert Thomas, in a moment of happy inspiration. It is the most popular cartoon of the War, just as Arf a Mo cigarettes are the most popular 'fags' with the men in the trenches. Many millions are being sent every week through the patriotic Funds from all over the world, supplied by Martins."

Several companies, tobacco and trade (Thomson and Porteous, Wm McKinnell, Maynards, Dobson and Co. and others), issued a set titled European War Series. They were all in the form of cartoon drawings, either with a message or just descriptive of some military aspect. In the Thomson and Porteous set, No. 2 illustrates a young child with a helmet, a sword in the right hand and British flag in the left titled "Waiting for Daddy, Must Take Care of Mummy Now" (Fig. 546). The reverse description in verse states:

My daddy's at the War, you know.
I'm not quite big enough to go,
So I'm in charge at home, you see!
It's lucky mummy still has me!

Another card shows a woman in colorful dress pinning something on a soldier's jacket. It is titled "Take This Back to Tipperary" (Fig. 547). The reverse side description is in verse:

Not on the battlefield alone
Are Tommy Atkins' victories won,
Big-hearted and without care,
He's making "conquests" everywhere.

Hill's issued a famous set in different formats titled Fragments From France. The cartoons and the title of the set were based on the drawings of one of the most famous British World War One cartoonists, Captain Bruce Bairnsfather. In an article commemorating the fiftieth anniversary of his death in 2009, the World War One Historical Association's magazine described his work in the following way: "His cartoons of the soldiers and their life in the trenches made them and the nation laugh." However, the article continues, "because he showed the men and the battlefields as they really were—dirty, generally fed-up and surrounded by the destruction caused by shelling—the Establishment disapproved of his work and he was never formally recognized." An introductory description from his recently published biography provides more insight into his cartoons. "When war broke out he re-enlisted in the Royal Warwickshires. He served in the mud and misery of the trenches of the infamous Plugstreet (Ploegsteert) Wood

Fig. 545. Arf a Mo Kaiser!
(Martins, Arf a Mo Kaiser, 1916)

where he started drawing cartoons which realistically and yet humorously depicted the appalling conditions of the trenches. They were soon published as the series that came to be known as *Fragments from France* and they became an immediate roaring success. Soon his principal character, a phlegmatic, mustachioed soldier known as 'Old Bill,' was immortalized in the famous situation of 'The Better 'Ole' and reproduced on pottery, on postcards, playing cards, in books, plays, films...." In fact, on the bottom half of the reverse side of each card in the set, there is this statement: "There could be no better reflection of the bright spirit of the Empire's gallant sons than is depicted in these sketches, drawn by one who himself has endured the grim reality of war."

Fig. 546. Waiting for Daddy
(Thomson and Porteous, European War Series, 1915, No. 2)

Fig. 547. Take This Back to Tipperary
(Thomson and Porteous, European War Series, 1915, No. 6)

One card, titled "They've Evidently Seen Me," depicts a soldier with his head and shoulders sticking out of a chimney (Fig. 548). A bomb has just passed the house, blowing out half of the bottom of the chimney. Another one is titled "The Same Old Moon" (Fig. 549). The front of the card is split with two drawings. The top one illustrates a woman (obviously the wife of a soldier) peering out the window of her country cottage, looking on the peaceful moon. The lower drawing is of a soldier crawling through a field, torn up by constant shelling, with the moon shining on him. The reverse side comment is:

Her: "And to think that it's the same dear old moon that's looking down on him!"

Him: "This blinkin' moon will be the death of us."

Another card, titled "The Professional Instinct Again," shows a soldier in the trench juggling five hand grenades (Fig. 550). The reverse side has a heading "Keeping His Hand In." Private Smith, the company bomber (formerly Shinio the popular juggler), frequently causes considerable anxiety to his platoon. A card titled "Coiffure in the Trenches" illustrates one soldier cutting the hair of another while a bomb flies past (Fig. 551a). He says "Keep you 'ead still, or I'll have yer blinkin ear off!" A delightful card shows a disgruntled soldier eating his plum and apple pudding out of a can (Fig. 551b). It is titled "The Eternal Question." On the reverse side he asks "When the 'ell is it goin' to be strawberry?" An Anonymous Tobacco Card set based on the Hills Fragments From France series has a card titled "The Late Comer." It illustrates a soldier returning at night to the trench (Fig. 552).

Thus, the humor of the war can be seen to be cynical, patriotic, depicting the German as losing at all stages and depressed, while also clearly depicting the ravages of the war. Others showed what life was like at the battlefront and in the trenches. Some were purely funny, but all had a definite underlying stark message.

**Fig. 548. They've Evidently Seen Me**
(Hill, Fragments From France, 1916)

**Fig. 549. The Same Old Moon**
(Hill, Fragments From France, 1916)

**Fig. 550. The Professional Instinct Again**
(Hill, Fragments From France, 1916)

**Fig. 551a. Coiffure in the Trenches**
(Hill, Fragments From France, 1916)

**Fig. 551b. The Eternal Question**
(Hill, Fragments From France, 1916)

**Fig. 552. The Late Comer**
(Anonymous Tobacco UK, Fragments From France, 1916)

# CHAPTER 14

# GERMAN ISSUED CARD SETS

Germany was also a prolific issuer of cigarette and trade cards. To non-German speaking collectors their main value lies in the illustrations on the cards, since the descriptions are all in German. The firm of Eckstein Halpaus in Dresden is a particularly important issuer of that period.

One set issued by this company is titled Die Reichswehr. It consists of nearly three hundred cards. Like many of the British equivalent cards, this extensive set, beautifully illustrated, covers all aspects of army life. Without understanding the descriptions, the illustrations provide significant information. These begin with illustrating groups of soldiers in different uniforms, both formal and in battle dress (Nos. 1–15) (Figs. 553a, 553b, 553c).

Fig. 553b. Uniforms (Eckstein Halpaus, Die Reichswehr, No. 10)

Fig. 553a. Uniforms (Eckstein Halpaus, Die Reichswehr, No. 1)

Fig. 553c. Uniforms (Eckstein Halpaus, Die Reichswehr, No. 15)

Another large series of cards shows soldiers in various aspects of their training (example Nos. 17–33, 66–68) (Figs. 554a, 554b, 554c, 554d) and under different conditions (Nos. 34–42) (Fig. 555). Card No. 69 (Fig. 556) shows a number of officers in the field studying a large document spread out on a table, presumably planning an exercise or battle attack.

Fig. 554a. Training (Eckstein Halpaus, Die Reichswehr, No. 20)

**Fig. 554b. Training**
(Eckstein Halpaus, Die Reichswehr, No. 30)

**Fig. 554c. Training**
(Eckstein Halpaus, Die Reichswehr, No. 68)

**Fig. 555. Using a Horse**
(Eckstein Halpaus, Die Reichswehr, No. 40)

**Fig. 556. Studying a Document**
(Eckstein Halpaus, Die Reichswehr, No. 69)

A number of cards show soldiers with warhorses under different conditions (Nos. 1, 40, 43, 44, 46, 54, 57, 83, 84, 87) (Fig. 557). Various military vehicles and motorcycles are illustrated (Nos. 89, 90, 92, 94, 95, 96 and many others) (Fig. 558a, 558b). A field ambulance is also shown (Fig. 559). Soldiers at leisure playing various sports cover a number of cards. There is the vaulting athlete (Fig. 560a), the ball players, the boxers, those engaged in various equestrian sports (Nos. 123, 127 and 128) (Fig. 560b), and swimmers (No. 122). Army musicians are illustrated on Nos. 152 and 182 (Fig. 561). What is obviously the equivalent of the Royal Army Medical Corps (Fig. 562) shows medical workers carrying a wounded soldier on a stretcher. Card No. 224 is another example of them at work. As an indication of their preparedness for the war's poisonous gas use, card No. 218 illustrates a soldier wearing his gas mask. Card Nos. 246 and forward illustrate various aspects of the navy. These include a number of different warships (Nos. 246–260) (Fig. 563) and sailors in various activities (Nos. 261–269) (Fig. 564).

**Fig. 557. Warhorse**
(Eckstein Halpaus, Die Reichswehr, No. 84)

**Fig. 558a.  Armored Vehicle**
(Eckstein Halpaus, Die Reichswehr, No. 92)

**Fig. 558b.  Motorcycle**
(Eckstein Halpaus, Die Reichswehr, No. 94)

**Fig. 559.  Field Ambulance**
(Eckstein Halpaus, Die Reichswehr, No. 98)

**Fig. 560a.  Vaulting**
(Eckstein Halpaus, Die Reichswehr, No. 126)

**Fig. 560b.  Equestrian Sports**
(Eckstein Halpaus, Die Reichswehr, No. 128)

**Fig. 561.  Army Musicians**
(Eckstein Halpaus, Die Reichswehr, No. 152)

**Fig. 562.  Medical Corps**
(Eckstein Halpaus, Die Reichswehr, No. 186)

**Fig. 563.  The Navy**
(Eckstein Halpaus, Die Reichswehr, No. 256)

**Fig. 564.  Sailors**
(Eckstein Halpaus, Die Reichswehr, No. 262)

Another large and important set by this firm is titled Der Weltkrieg 1914–1918. It consists of two hundred seventy cards and covers all aspects of the war. The initial cards show both military and civilian figures at gatherings, probably at the beginning of the war. A card shows British troops waiting to get onto buses to go to the front (Fig. 565). Card No. 19 is of Belgians carrying their possessions on a horse-drawn cart. Card No. 63 meanwhile shows Serbian refugees in flight in November 1915. No. 26 from August 23, 1914, shows Hindenburg and Ludendorff peering through a periscope in the field. No. 31 shows a critical, but not a direct military aspect of the war: it is of a field bakery with many large ovens. No. 36 illustrates Turkish infantry on the move adjacent to a river. Just as in the British card sets, there are a number of cards showing German troops in the trenches and using various types of military equipment (Card Nos. 54, 70, 77, 91, 109) (Fig. 566).

**Fig. 565. London Transport Buses** (Eckstein Halpaus, Die Weltkrieg, No. 14)

**Fig. 566. Artillery** (Eckstein Halpaus, Die Weltkrieg, No. 77)

**Fig. 567. British POWs** (Eckstein Halpaus, Die Weltkrieg, No. 102)

**Fig. 568 New York Document Signing** (Eckstein Halpaus, Die Weltkrieg, No. 126)

There is a card that shows British prisoners of war marching (Fig. 567). One card is of a photograph taken in late 1916 or early 1917 (Fig. 568). It is of a meeting in New York where a document is being signed and there is a large American flag as a backdrop. President Wilson is mentioned in the description on the reverse side. There are many cards showing the destruction and devastation of war, both in the field and in the city. Card No. 128 from 1917 illustrates the destroyed Cathedral of St. Quentin in France. The Germans actually occupied this city at the beginning of the war and it remained in their hands throughout the war. Interestingly, the famous British poet Wilfred Owen, who was tragically killed a week before armistice, fought there. Card No. 162 shows British troops marching through the desert in the Palestinian campaign.

There are a number of aviation cards. A card shows arms being given to one of the flyers, presumably before takeoff (Fig. 569). Another example is from 1918 (No. 177); it illustrates a German bomber being loaded with its bombs under the wings. Several cards illustrate colonial troops. One is of the Askari in German East Africa (Fig. 570). Two Sudanese soldiers (Zuaves) are pictured on another card (Fig. 571).

The British American Tobacco Co. issued a German set in the German language in 1933. Titled Der Weltkrieg (The World War), it advertises their Gold Dollar brand of cigarettes. It is essentially the same as the Eckstein Halpaus set of the same name. There were also other German companies that issued the same set.

**Fig. 569. Before Takeoff**
(Eckstein Halpaus, Die Weltkrieg, No. 138)

**Fig. 570. Askari**
(Eckstein Halpaus, Die Weltkrieg,. No. 249)

**Fig. 571. Sudanese Zuaves**
(Eckstein Halpaus, Die Weltkrieg, No. 267)

# FULL TITLES of CIGARETTE and TRADE CARDS CITED

A. and B.C., Winston Churchill, 1965

Abbey Grange Hotel, Fighting Vessels, 1986

Abdulla & Co. Ltd, Great War Gift Packing Cards, 1916

Adkin and Sons, Notabilities, 1915

Adkin and Sons, A Royal Favourite, 1900

Adkin and Sons, War Trophies, 1917

Alex. Jones & Co. Portrait of Queen Victoria, 1897

Amalgamated Press Ltd, The Great War 1914–1918, 1928

Amalgamated Press Ltd, Great War Deeds (M16), 1927

Amalgamated Press Ltd, Great War Deeds (M32), 1927

Amalgamated Press Ltd, Heroic Deeds of the Great War, 1927

Amalgamated Press Ltd, Thrilling Scenes From the Great War, 1927

Amalgamated Press Ltd, Exploits of the Great War, 1929

Amalgamated Press Ltd, V.C.'s and Their Glorious Deeds of Valour, 1930

The American Tobacco Co., Famous Queens, 1910

The American Tobacco Co., World War I Scenes, 1917-18

Anonymous Tobacco Co., Great War Incidents, 1916

Anonymous Tobacco UK, Fragments From France, 1916

E. & W. Anstie, King George V (small), c. 1915

Ardath Tobacco Co. Ltd, Empire Personalities 1937

Ardath Tobacco Co. Ltd, Great War Series, first, 1916

Ardath Tobacco Co. Ltd, Silver Jubilee, 1935


Barratt & Co. Ltd, History of Air, 1960,

Bewlay and Co. Ltd, War Series, 1915

Bouchere's Firm, War Portraits, 1916

Brasella, German Heroes & Leaders of the World War

J.M. Brindley, History and Traditions of the British Army, 1st Series, 1990

J.M. Brindley, History and Traditions of the British Army, 2nd Series, 1990

J.M. Brindley, History and Traditions of the British Army, 4th Series, 1990

J.M. Brindley, Victorian and Edwardian Soldiers in Full Dress, 1988

British American Tobacco Co. Ltd, Britain's Defenders, 1914

British American Tobacco Co. Ltd, Historical Figures, 1st Series, 1961

British American Tobacco Co. Ltd, Military Portraits, 1917

British American Tobacco Co. Ltd, Naval Portraits, 1917

British American Tobacco Co. Ltd, Notabilities, 1917

British American Tobacco Co. Ltd, War Weapons, 1914

Brooke Bond & Co. Ltd, History of Aviation, 1972

Butterworth & Son, History of the Suffolk Regiment, 1999


The Canterbury Electric Theatre, War Portraits, 1916

Carlton Picture House, War Portraits, c. 1916

Carreras Ltd, British Prime Ministers, 1928

Carreras Ltd, The Handy Black Cat English-French Dictionary (booklet), 1915

Carreras Ltd, Raemaekers War Cartoons, 1916

Carreras Ltd, Types of London, 1919

Cereal Food, Famous People and Places, 1949

Chix Confectionary Co. Ltd, Military Uniforms, 1970

W.A. and A.C. Churchman, Silhouettes of Warships, 1915

W.A. and A.C. Churchman, Boer War Generals (CLAM), (black front), c. 1901

Wm. Clarke and Son, Army Life, 1915

Cohen Weenen & Co. Ltd, Celebrities [Sweet Crop over 250' back, coloured], 1900

Cohen Weenen & Co. Ltd, War Series - Leaders of the War, 1916

Cohen Weenen & Co. Ltd, Silhouettes of Celebrities, 1905

Cohen Weenen & Co. Ltd, Victoria Cross Heroes, 1916

Cohen Weenen & Co. Ltd, War Series. Admirals and Warships, 1916

F. Colton, War Portraits, 1916

Cope Bros. & Co. Ltd, British Admirals, 1915

Cope Bros. & Co. Ltd, V.C. and D.S.O. Naval and Flying Heroes, 1916

Cope Bros. & Co. Ltd, War Pictures, 1916

CWS (Co-operative Wholesale Society) Tobacco, War Series, 1914)

S. H. Dawes. Army Pictures, Cartoons etc., 1916

J. W. Dewhurst, Army Pictures, Cartoons etc., 1916

Major Drapkin & Co., Celebrities of the Great War, 1916 (printed back)

J. Edmondson & Co. Ltd, War Series, 1916

Edwards, Ringer and Bigg Ltd., Portraits of His Majesty in Uniforms of British & Foreign Nations, 1902.

Edwards, Ringer and Bigg Ltd., War Map of the Western Front, 1916

Ewbanks Ltd, British Uniforms, 1956

Gallaher Ltd, The Allies Flags, 1914

Gallaher Ltd, British Naval Series, 1914

Gallaher Ltd, Great War Series, 1915

Gallaher Ltd, The Great War, Second Series, 1915

Gallaher Ltd, The Great War Victoria Cross Heroes
  1st Series (1-25), 1915
  2nd Series (26-50), 1915
  3rd Series (51-75), 1915
  4th Series (76-100), 1915
  5th Series (101-125), 1916
  6th Series (126-150), 1917
  7th Series (151-175), 1917
  8th Series (176-200), 1918

Gallaher Ltd, Royalty Series, 1902

Gallaher Ltd, The South African Series, 1901

Golden Era, Aircraft of the First World War, 1994

T.P.&R. Goodbody, Boer War Celebrities [CAG], 1900

Goodies Limited, Wicked Monarchs, 1973

The Happy Home, Women on War Work, 1915

Hignett Bros. and Co., Military Portraits, 1914

R & J Hill Ltd, Aviation Series, 1970

R & J Hill Ltd, Fragments From France, 1916

R & J Hill Ltd, Great War Leaders [canvases], 1919

Home and Colonial Stores Ltd, War Pictures, 1915

Ideas, Great War Leaders, Unknown publication date

Imperial Tobacco Company of Canada Ltd, Modern War Weapons, 1916

Imperial Tobacco Company of Canada Ltd, Victoria Cross Heroes, 1915

International Tobacco Ltd, "Gentleman, The King!", 1937

Kellogg Company of Great Britain Ltd, History of British Military Aircraft, 1963

Kinnear Ltd, Liverpool, Royalty, 1897

Lambert & Butler, Aviation, 1915

Lambert & Butler, History of Aviation (green front), 1932

Lambert & Butler, Naval Portraits, 1914

Lambert & Butler, Royalty, Notabilities & Events, 1902

Laurens, British Cavalry Uniforms, 1975

C. & J. Law, Types of British Soldiers, 1914

R. J. Lea Ltd., Chairman's War Portraits, 1915

R. J. Lea Ltd, Civilians of Countries Fighting with the Allies, 1914-15

R. J. Lea Ltd., War Pictures, Series 1, 1915

Liebig, The Dardanelles, 1911

Liebig, King Albert of Belgium, F1336, 1937

Lever Bros., Celebrities, 1905

Lever Bros., Celebrities [Black Border], 1905

Lychgate Press, Images of the Great War, 2013

Lychgate Press, Images of the Great War, 3rd series, 2013

Lychgate Press, Images of the Great War, 4th series, 2013

Richard Lloyd & Sons, Boer War Celebrities, 1901

J. Lyons, HM Ships 1902-1962, 1962

Martins Ltd., V.C. Heroes 1916

Martins Ltd., 'Arf a Mo Kaiser,' 1915

Maypole, War Series, 1915

Meadow Dairy Co., War Series, 1915

J Milhoff & Co. Ltd., Men of Genius, 1924

Stephen Mitchell & Son, British Warships, First Series, 1915

Stephen Mitchell & Son, British Warships, Second Series, 1915

Stephen Mitchell & Son, A Gallery of 1935, 1936

B. Morris and Sons Ltd., London, Victory Signs Series, 1928

Morning Foods Ltd, British Uniforms, 1954

B. Muratti, Sons & Co. Ltd, Crowned Heads, 1912

B. Muratti, Sons & Co. Ltd, Great War leaders, Series P, 1916

B. Muratti, Sons & Co. Ltd, War Series II, 1917

Murray, Sons & Co. Ltd, War Series, series K, 1915

My Weekly, Battle Series, 1916

My Weekly, Soldiers of the King, 1915

Nugget Polish Co., Allied Series, 1910

Ogden's Ltd, Set 71-S, c. 1902

Ogden's Ltd, Infantry Training, 1915

Ogden's Ltd, Modern War Weapons, 1915

Ogden's Ltd, Soldiers of the King, 1909

Ogden's Guinea Golds, General Interest, 1-200, c 1901

Ogdens Guinea Golds Numbered, Set 71-S

A. Parodi, War Portraits, 1916

James Pascall Ltd, War Portraits, 1920

J.A. Pattreiouex, Builders of the Empire, 1929

Periodical, Great War Pictures, 1917

Phillip Lewis Agencies, First World War 1914-1918, International Historic Posters from the Imperial War Museum, London, 2003.

Godfrey Phillips Ltd, British Admirals [anonymous issue, silk], 1915

Godfrey Phillips Ltd, British, Warships [green], 1915

Godfrey Phillips Ltd, Great War Leaders and Celebrities IV, Extra Large Size, Anonymous, 1916

Godfrey Phillips Ltd, Great War Leaders II (anonymous), 1915

Godfrey Phillip Ltd, Great War Leaders and Celebrities, B.D.V. Extra-Large Size, 1916

Godfrey Phillips Ltd, In the Public Eye, 1935

Godfrey Phillips Ltd, Personalities of Today, 1927

Godfrey Phillips Ltd, Real Photo Series – Admirals and Generals of the Great War, 1916

Godfrey Phillips Ltd, Russo-Japanese War Series, 1904, 2001 Reprint

Godfrey Phillips Ltd, Types of British Soldiers, 1900

Godfrey Phillips Ltd, War Pictures, 1915

Godfrey Phillips, Ltd War Photos, 1916

The Picture House, Harrogate, War Series, 1916,

The Picture House Harrogate, War Portraits, 1916

The Pilot, Britain's Defenders, 1950

John Player & Sons, Army Corps and Divisional Signs 1914-1918, 1st Series, 1924

John Player & Sons, Army Corps and Divisional Signs 1914-1918, 2nd Series, 1924

John Player & Sons, Artillery in Action, 1917

John Player & Sons, England's Military Heroes (narrow card), 1898

John Player & Sons, The Golden Age of Flying, 1977

John Player & Sons, Regimental Uniforms, 1914

John Player & Sons, Straight Line Caricatures, 1926

Pritchard and Burton, Royalty Series, 1902

Prudhow, Pictures, Cartoons etc., 1916

The Queen's Theatre, War Portraits, 1916

Ray and Co. Ltd, War Series, 1915

Ringtons Ltd, Ships of the Royal Navy, 1961

Robertson, British Medals, 1914

Rockwell, Early Allied Warplanes, 2000

Rockwell, Postcard Images of World War One, 1999

Rockwell, World War Posters (Normal and Large Cards), 2001

Salmon and Gluckstein Ltd, Heroes of the Transvaal War, 1901

Salmon and Gluckstein Ltd, Her Most Gracious Majesty Queen Victoria, 1897

John Scerri (Malta), Prominent People, c. 1930

Schuh Tobacco Co., Official War Photographs, 1918

Shepherds Dairies, War Pictures (Series), 1915

John Sinclair Ltd. British Sea Dogs, 1926

Robert Sinclair Tobacco Co. Ltd, Great War Leaders, 1915

Singleton & Cole Ltd, Famous Officers, 1915

F. & J. Smith, War Incidents (1st Series), 1914

F. & J. Smith, War Incidents (2nd Series), 1915

Sniders and Abrahams Pty Ltd, Crests of British Warships, 1915

Sniders and Abrahams Pty Ltd, European War Series, 1916

Sniders and Abrahams Pty Ltd, Great War Leaders and Warships, 1915

J.F. Sporting Collectibles, Boer War Officers, 2008

Starline (USA), Americana (American History), 1992

Sunday Stories, The King and His Soldiers, 1916

Sunny Boy Cigarettes, British Naval Series, 1960

Sweetule Products, Naval Battles, 1959

Taddy & Co., Admirals and Generals – The War, c. 1915

Taddy & Co., Autographs, 1910

Taddy & Co., Boer War Leaders, 1901

Taddy & Co., British Medals and Ribbons, 1912

Taddy & Co., Russo-Japanese War (1-25), 1904

Taddy & Co., Russo-Japanese War (26-50), 1904

Taddy & Co., Victoria Cross Heroes - Boer War, 1902

W. & M. Taylor, War Series, 1915

Teofani and Co. Ltd., (Past and Present), Weapons of War, 1938

Thomson and Porteous, European War Series, 1916

Thomson and Porteous, V.C. Heroes, 1916

Trucards, History of Aircraft, 1970

Trucards, World War I, 1970

W. E. Turner, War Pictures, 1916

Wakeford, Army Pictures, Cartoons etc., 1915

Henry Welfare & Co., Prominent Politicians, c. 1911

Westminster Tobacco Co. Ltd, The Great War Celebrities, 1914

Wilbur and Sons, Soldiers of the Allies, 1915

W.D. & H.O. Wills, Allied Army Leaders, 1917

W.D. & H.O. Wills, Allied Army Leaders 1917, 2000 Reprint

W.D. & H.O. Wills, (Scissors), Britain's Defenders, 1914

W.D. & H.O. Wills, (Specialities), Britain's Defenders, 1914

W.D. & H.O. Wills, Britain's Part in the War, 1917

W.D. & H.O. Wills, Builders of the Empire, 1898

W.D. & H.O. Wills, Coronation Series, 1902

W.D. & H.O. Wills, Flags of the Allies, 1915

W.D. & H.O. Wills, (Scissors), Military Portraits, 1917

W.D. & H.O. Wills, Military Motors (not passed by censor), 1916

W.D. & H.O. Wills, Military Motors (passed for publication), 1916

W.D. & H.O. Wills, Military Portraits, 1917

W.D. & H.O. Wills, Modern War Weapons, 1916

W.D. & H.O. Wills, Punch Cartoons (Series 1), 1916

W.D. & H.O. Wills, Punch Cartoons (Series 2), 1916

W.D. & H.O. Wills, Recruiting Posters, 1915

W.D. & H.O. Wills (Overseas), Royalty, Notabilities and Events in Russia, China and South Africa, 1900-1902

W.D. & H.O. Wills, Ships, 1895

W.D. & H.O. Wills, (Castella), The Story of the Tank, 1997

W.D. & H.O. Wills, The World's Dreadnoughts, 1910

W.D. & H.O. Wills, Types of the British Army 1912, Reprint 1995

W.D. & H.O. Wills, (New Zealand), V.C.'s, 1926

W.D. & H.O. Wills, (Specialities), Victoria Cross Heroes, 1915

W.D. & H.O. Wills, War Incidents, (1st Series), 1916

W.D. & H.O. Wills, War Incidents, (2nd Series), 1917

W.D. & H.O. Wills, Warships, 1926

W.D. & H.O. Wills, Warships, 1926

J. Wix & Sons Ltd, Builders of the Empire, 1937

# SELECTED REFERENCES

Bagnell, Dorothy. *Collecting Cigarette Cards and Other Trade Issues.* London: The London Cigarette Card Co., Ltd., 1978.

Brown, Malcolm. *The Imperial War Museum Book of The First World War.* London: Sidgwick & Jackson, 1991.

Clark, Christopher. *The Sleepwalkers: How Europe Went to War in 1914.* New York: HarperCollins, 2013.

Doggett, Frank. *Cigarette Cards and Novelties.* London: Michael Joseph Ltd., 1981.

Fitzsimmons, Bernard, ed. *Warships of the First World War.* SPC Publishing, 1973.

Gilbert, Martin. *First World War.* London: Weidenfeld and Nicolson, 1994.

Gilbert, Martin. *The Routledge Atlas of the First World War, Third Edition.* London: Routledge, 2008.

Holt, Tonie, and Valmai Holt. *Battlefields of the First World War.* Pavilion Books Ltd, 1993.

Hoover Institute of Stanford University. Library Exhibit, *British Images of the First World War.* Stanford, CA, January–March 2008.

Howsden, Gordon. *Collecting Cigarette and Trade Cards.* London: New Cavendish Books, 1995.

Keegan, John. *The First World War.* New York: Alfred A. Knopf, 1999.

Murray, Martin. *The Story of Cigarette Cards.* Hendon, London: Murray Card (International) Ltd., 1987.

Neiberg, Michael S. *Journal of the World War One Historical Association.* World War One Historical Association, 2012.

Tucker, Spencer C. *The Great War 1914–18.* UCL Press Ltd, 1998.

Walter, George, ed. *The Penguin Book of First World War Poetry.* London: Penguin Books, 2006.

Winter, J. M. *The Experience of World War One.* New York: Oxford University Press, 1995.